THE GAY STATE

THE GAY STATE

The Quest for an Independent Gay Nation-State
and What it Means to Conservatives
and the World's Religions.

Garrett Graham

iUniverse, Inc.
New York   Bloomington

New York * London * Amsterdam * Washington, DC

The Gay State is a Division of GSGS Corp.
The Gay State Government Services Corporation
Printing and Services Distribution Dept..
Old Chelsea Station, Suite 2
New York, New York, USA, 10113
www.TheGayState.EU
E-Mail: TheGayState@GMail.com

This 2010 edition is published by iUniverse and may be ordered through booksellers
or by contacting: iUniverse
1663 Liberty Drive
Bloomington, IN 47403
Visit www.iuniverse.com or call toll-free 1-800-Authors (1-800-288-4677)

Because of the dynamic nature of the Internet, any Web addresses or links contained in
this book may have changed since publication and may no longer be valid. The views
expressed in this work are solely those of the author and do not necessarily reflect the
views of the publisher, and the publisher hereby disclaims any responsibility for them.

Library of Congress Cataloging-in-Publications Data
p.; cm
Graham, Garrett, 1959-
Library of Congress Control Number: 2010927573

THE GAY STATE The Quest for an Independent Gay Nation-State and What It
Means to Conservatives and the World's Religions.

photo credit; Kiri Bermack

Hardcover ISBN: 978-1-4502-0994-6
Soft cover ISBN: 978-1-4502-0992-2
E-Book ISBN: 978-1-4502-0993-9

Book also available on CD-Rom by contacting www.TheGayState.EU

1. The Gay State.
1. International Politics. 2. Gay and Lesbian Studies.
3. Current Events. 4. Social Studies. 5. Non-Fiction.
6. Political Science 7. Gay Nationalism
I. Graham, Garrett. II Title.

12 11 10 09 08   10 9 8 7 6 5 4 3 2 1

To people everywhere,
who dream a dream of freedom.
Here's to you, that we may never give up, and may we one day
meet in our own independent Gay State.

With love, to Sue, Tom, and Theresa,
family members of choice.

And to Taylor and Bridget;
and Brian, Maureen, and Katie;
though I've been an "eccentric uncle"
often from afar, know that I love you and
thank you for keeping me young.

"*I am not interested in picking up crumbs of compassion thrown from the table of someone who considers himself my master. I want the full menu of rights.*"

~ Bishop Desmond Tutu
South African Cleric and Activist.

"A nation that continues year after year to spend more money on military defense than on programs of social uplift is approaching spiritual doom."

~ Rev. Martin Luther King, Jr.

Contents

"We are a people – one people, who for thousands of years have had to hide ourselves from history. No more."

~ *Theodore Becker*

Acknowledgment.

I am but one man out of hundreds of millions over the span of modern history who has pondered the notion of how spectacular we could be as a people if we were to have our own Gay homeland. Like many reading these words, I have witnessed our Gay oppression and have been the victim of it. I have been afflicted by the pain and loss in a world that exposed the underbelly of hatred and prejudice only because of who and what we are. There are places on this Earth where I came close to dying only because of my Homosexuality and my belief in equality. The local populace viewed Gays such as myself with contempt. They would like nothing more than to exterminate us from their presence because of their collective inhumanity, the hatred toward Gays, the intolerance to diversity and generally xenophobic responses to life. Yet these places and people have played a role in shaping me. I am humbled yet impassioned at all of the suffering in the world. But as it has been said, a journey of a thousand miles begins with the first step. That first step was in seeking out like minds, being in one another's presence and formulating a concept to advance our freedom.

There are several people who provided the genesis for the concepts behind this booklet. I wish to thank them for nurturing my inspiration. **Harvey Milk**, assassinated while serving the community in San Francisco – I think of him often and hope he would be pleased with the words contained on these pages. Mr. Milk was a common man with uncommon passion, and sometimes that alone can make a difference. **Pim Fortuyn**, the inspiring and openly Gay Dutch leader who was assassinated in the service to his country. His courage and his story need to enlighten many dark corners in this world. If I ever live to see a Gay State, there should surely be a monument to Pim Fortuyn. For those of you familiar with earlier editions, you already know this: I also hold an enormous debt to the thinking of **Theodor Herzl**, a brilliant man who died more than 100 years ago in 1904. His writings on Zionism and the concept of a Jewish State have transcended time, and I borrowed heavily from his words and views. Feeling a spiritual affinity of sorts, I may have channeled "my Teddy" from a great beyond. Of course I wish that he were a member of our "club," and although he was a liberal, drawn to "the arts" as an author and as a playwright, I cannot confirm or deny his Homosexuality or if he was in fact, a Heterosexual. I also wish to thank my mother **Lillian** – a modest woman who knew the value of living life by the golden rule. She died in the spring of 2009 while I prepared this edition of *The Gay State*. Her kindness and gentleness and compassion I pray stay with me forever. Any nation will do well to have citizens with her kind and thoughtful demeanor.

As I don't live merely among the dearly departed, there are still more of those I wish to thank who still have a pulse. I owe so much to my partner **Mike**, who still makes my blood race, who has stood by my side, in good times and bad, in sickness and health and in rich times and poor times for more than fourteen years now. May we grow old together, and I will consider myself to be the luckiest man alive. He often gave me great advice, alas, not always heeded. I also want to thank **Dr. Howard Dean**, the former Governor of Vermont and a non-Gay Heterosexual, who had the courage to stand up to America's broken if not corrupt political machine and speak his mind. This special brand of courage is becoming increasingly rare in American politics. Through his example, I found my voice and Gov. Dean continues to inspire countless Americans. Now, his country needs him more than ever. **Stephen Amoroso** is one of the finest people I have ever known. He has been my counsel and my rock. I have relied on his wisdom in some of my darkest days and always found joy in his presence. Any state, Gay or otherwise, would be fortunate to have the likes of him on a leadership panel. His wisdom and intellect have played a significant role in the shaping of this booklet. Finally, I need to extend my gratitude to so many in the **LGBT movement** who have provided mountains of data and statistics. The **ilga.org** (the International Lesbian and Gay Association) does amazing work in reporting the global condition of our Gay community. **Louis Crompton**, thank you for your incredible guidance through our complex Gay history; your insight is invaluable to anyone who seeks out the uncomfortable truth and the "kaleidoscope of horrors" we as a people have been forced to endure for millennia. In the end, may we all march together and receive our Promised Land.

There are still other people who participated in the production of this booklet. Thank you to **Nancy Kellogg**, my assistant in putting all of the early pieces in place. My days would have been much more stressful without **Jack Flannigan**, the Gay State Press Secretary and **Messrs. Steve and Adam Markowitz**, my Production Assistants who did their best to keep me on task. My agent and friend **Dottie Shapiro**, a special thank you for having saved me on a number of occasions. **Ethan Goolsbee**, my editor who along with his staff helped mash together my words into something that might inspire a movement. Thank you to **Jeni Senter**, my friend and colleague from afar, a supremely talented academic and acclaimed writer of distinction who is as sharp as they come and makes me look better than I am. **Toby Wertheim** and the headquarters for **CBS**, both in New York, who helped pave the way with their endless contacts and to **CBS**, for making so much of its video production expertise available to our growing staff. Thank you to **Bill Harer** who lent his insight to this production, though I suspect we were not always of the same mind. It is no small miracle that this manuscript ever found its way out of my office and onto the bookshelves that span the globe. To our translators and distribution teams who made it possible for a farmer in the Philippines, a bartender in New Delhi, a truck driver in Suriname, and a lawyer in Angola to realize there is a reason to hope for a better life; to you all, our movement would be much less without your commitment. And to **Pharfel**, who motivated me to keep working into the wee, very late hours and sometimes, around the clock, to get this work done. And even now as I have learned that it is never really done, he still remains by my side.

A very special, unique and heartfelt thank you must be offered to **"Dr. X,"** a top secret and confidential source (you know who you are and I thank you) who guided my work and made this booklet possible, in recognition of his important and continuing classified contribution without jeopardizing any vital national secrets of nations that will be friendly to the Gay State. The world is slowly acknowledging that our centuries of torture and abuse are shameful and reprehensible and men and womyn of courage are standing with us.

A book launch is a part of the book process that introverted writers usually prefer not to think about. I for one am guilty of this charge. It stands to reason that the book launch is only one of the steps that lead to a successful distribution of a literary work.

We are quite fortunate to have so many supporters in introducing this third edition. Let me thank just a few of them publicly. **The Leslie/Lohman Gay Art Foundation** is one of the most amazing art galleries in all of the United States. It graciously offered up some incredibly inspiring space within its arts compound for hosting a reception. For decades, they have had the courage to exhibit Gay art that had been shunned from the mainstream art houses. We are grateful and proud to support their courageous and worthwhile mission. We have also received very gracious and generous offers from The **National Press Club** in Washington, DC; the **Yale Club**; **The National Arts Club**; and the **Overseas Press Club** (all in Manhattan) as well as **The Metropolitan Clubs** and **The University Clubs.** One thing is certain; that is all of these facilities are first rate and we are grateful for their support.

In the last several months, activities surrounding *The Gay State* have occurred at a dizzying pace. Our offices adjacent to the **United Nations** have proved to be too small and lacking in proper security as we move forward. We are grateful for the generosity of **The Regus Group** for securing additional office facilities for the back office and administrative requirements necessary to advance our cause. Our facilities within the iconic **Chrysler Building** (New York) are Class A in every way. It is one of the world's preeminent commercial office firms with a truly international presence. The support of their very professional staff must be acknowledged, and we are very thankful.

The book cover has received so much praise and for the final result, I need to thank **Kiri Bermack**, an exceptionally talented Graphic Artist who lent us her time and talent for this ongoing project. Skilled, dependable and a visionary, she has made my life much easier in the production of this booklet. She is a New York based designer with an international portfolio. Check out her work at **www.KiriBermack.com**.

Before we go any further, I must issue an advisory to readers of several stylistic aspects to this pamphlet that have caused some consternation. I have decided that Gay deserves to be capitalized, just as being Irish or German or American is capitalized. We are a people, - one people and Gay is our self identification. I have also chosen to capitalize Homosexual as well as Heterosexual when used in this work. Homosexual is not merely a "condition" or a "symptom." It defines the sexual nature of our innate being, without which, far fewer of us would stand on the mantle of our Gayness. That's my story and I'm sticking with it. Also, out of respect for the female gender of our species, our cohabitants on this planet, our loves, our mentors, our comrades and collaborators, I have chosen to identify them as "womyn." They surely can stand alone without "man" in their name, and to all the womyn who read this, I hope I have not done any of you a disservice by this way of thinking.

Also, at the risk of sounding Trumanesque, the buck stops with me. I want to say that I alone am responsible for the content of this booklet. Any errors or omissions are my responsibility, and I regret any discomfort any of these mistakes may cause you.

Before we get in too deep together, this is probably the best time to inform readers of an ongoing effort related to the book and the movement. Having the ability to amass a readership of this size is humbling, and I am compelled to do my part in erasing the hardship that exists for many of our people. Toward that end, I want to mention that we are initiating the **Garrett Graham Peace Foundation**. It is an international non-profit organization that provides educational assistance to young, aspiring Gay leaders from around the world. The objective of the Foundation is to bring successful LGBT applicants to the U.S. for one semester for an intensive internship that will enrich them with the skills necessary to provide a voice and the necessary leadership to their fellow Gay compatriots in their land of birth. After the semester internship in Gay media relations, social justice activism, and a broad based Gay equality experience, they will enroll in one of the universities in the United States that specializes in Gay Studies and Gay History. I firmly believe that in launching this program we will immeasurably improve the lives of all participants. And over time, we may well bear fruit throughout the world by virtue of educating our people and bringing hope to lands where before there was none. This process is just one more way we are working to build a global network of Gay leaders. We ask you to remember us and lend your support in this endeavor.

Lastly, I want to thank you, the readers, who have purchased this work and devoted the time to study it. There will be no movement unless we all come together and rise up. Those of you who purchased the 2007 or 2008 editions of this book will, I trust, be pleasantly surprised with all of the new data and expansion on some very key concepts. Your opinions, your thoughts on this booklet and all suggestions are welcome in e-mail form at GarrettGrahamAndTheGayState@GMail. com. For more information on the topic, you may wish to go to **www. TheGayState.EU**. Also, please check in for updates on the movement and see our progress at **TheGayStateBlog.** There will be some of you sufficiently inspired to join and become a FIGS member. **FIGS** – supporters of a Free, Independent Gay State is an international body that works to promote our cause. By contacting Garrett Graham, you too, can become a "Figgie." As this manuscript moves on in the editorial and production process, we are securing more representatives in nations all around the world to advance our cause and bring the good news to our people.

So, to all parties who have devoted such efforts to emancipate our people around the world, I thank you, and indeed, the global Gay community thanks you. We have all played our part in the history of our Gay culture, and we all are examples of a world coming to support our destiny! Gay independence and a free Gay nation-state! Now rally around us men and womyn and you may find that the answers to basic questions are far beyond what you may have imagined.

"If we do not hang together, we shall surely hang separately."

Thomas Paine

"We may have all come on different ships, but we're in the same boat now."
~ Martin Luther King, Jr.

The Preface.

So you are starting your own country, are you? It is a question often asked, but usually to young boys with fanciful notions of creating a domain of their own. The general consensus is that the silliness of creating a new land and appointing a new government is reserved for youthful fantasies that are typically outgrown in the adolescent years. Such feelings of otherness, of a separateness dissipate as humankind immerses itself into the daily grind of routine.

The desire of forming a country however, need not be solely the domain of childhood fantasies. Nations have been formed to represent places, peoples and ideals. As many readers know, two English speaking nations that sprang from nothing more than an idea are the United States of America and of course, Australia. And they are but among dozens of other new nations in recent decades. It took an enormous amount of will, perseverance and bloodshed to raise these self determined interests to the point of true sovereignty, but they were created through the compilation of simple human endeavours. The nations began on distant and foreign lands and were formed almost entirely by non-indigenous people, who through the fate of time, circumstances and mobility, acquired land to form a country.

In the lifetime of the readers of this booklet, many other countries have also formed, as the rise in the number of nations now belonging to The United Nations organization would attest. Many are tied to a particular place, some as shared ideals and as a particular people. The forming of the state of Israel was a concept that was decades and centuries in the making. The desire among the Jewish people who were spread out all over the globe, was to form a nation and they considered lands in all corners of the world. Only after World War II did the impetus exist for the Jewish people to create their state in the original lands of their forefathers. In the late 1800's and early 1900's movements existed to create a Jewish State and they considered locations ranging from Argentina, then considered wildly desolate and remote to most Europeans, to locations in what was then often referred to as the Orient. More important than "where" was the fact of getting a land on which to create their nation.

In modern history, I don't know of a text more capable of lifting up so many oppressed minorities as *The Jewish State*, by Theodor Herzl. I mentioned Herzl earlier and can not overplay the value of his message. Those of you who read the 2007 edition of **The Gay State** know it was an homage to Herzl. I want the readers of these pages to soak up the glorious phrasing and thinking of Herzl. Whether you are an oppressed group in the hills of Africa, on the plains of Asia for instance, or a Gay youth enduring life in America's Bible Belt, *The Jewish State* is both at once consoling in ones plight and inspirational in finding a way to a brighter future.

Having served my time as a publisher, I know well the intricacies of Copyright law. Herzl's work, like very few writers in history, continues to be relevant more than a century since his death. As the copyright protections have expired on his literary masterpiece, his work in *The Jewish State* is widely available on the internet. A favorite website for many such literary classics is www.Gutenberg.org. I encourage the readers of **The Gay State** to visit the site to read *The Jewish State*, free of charge on the Gutenberg site, along with many other literary masterpieces. You too, will come to see his work as one that speaks to oppressed peoples everywhere.

You will see that Herzl's words, messages and concepts live on in this third edition of **The Gay State**. We have tried to remain true to the promoting of his thinking and the inclusions of his passages. I think Herzl would be pleased to see his work has had such an enormous impact on society many decades after the release of *The Jewish State*. Furthermore, Herzl I believe, would have fully approved of Israel and the states current tolerance (although in our current age of modernity, "tolerance" is by no means good enough for our people) and wide acceptance of its Gay community, placing it in the top ten percent of enlightened nations on Earth, with regard to its inclusion and treatment of Gays.

The world of publishing has undergone enormous changes in just the first decade of the 21st century. Compared to the time of Herzl's writing of *The Jewish State*, virtually no aspect of publishing is the same. As the writer of **The Gay State,** I hold no illusions that this booklet will endure with the same staying power. If these words matter to anyone one hundred years from now, have at it! My wildest expectation is only that it will inspire some of my Gay brothers and sisters with hope and a validation for a future filled with possibilities, much the way Herzl's work encouraged the world's Jewish community. Unlike in Herzl's time, the internet allows for the coalescing of the disgruntled and the haters. In almost every way, the most hostile receptors of **The Gay State** are Muslim fundamentalists, self-righteous Christian practitioners and political conservatives. These are the demographic groups where anti-Gayism festers and spreads and in the comfort of their large assemblies, members find validation in their bigotry, self-righteousness and intolerance.

Surprisingly, we even find hostile receptors within our own Gay community. A thorough psychological assessment of these individuals is required; objectives we will not serve in this project. Suffice it to say jaded and self-loathing Gays fear our global emancipation. It's human nature to be fearful of the unknown and like old men who do not easily leave their cells, many Gays refuse to believe the best about themselves. Life-long oppression does this to the human spirit. Granted, being negative and a naysayer is the safe and easy way and those Gays living in relative luxury are most quick to scoff at concepts of Gay nationalism. The most pretentious and arrogant of our people, I now speak directly to you: what have you done to alleviate the suffering of our Gay brothers and sisters everywhere? It need not be the size and scale of ones efforts to improve our community, but merely that you tried. Perched in your luxury condo or country home, deriding others who aspire to improve the lives of those most marginalized is an insult of the worst kind to your global Gay community. I often wonder if Herzl, living in an age of limited communication means, faced such similar degrees of hatred from those within and outside his community. In these moments I remember the words of Dag Hammarskjöld: "Never 'for the sake of peace and quiet,' deny your own experience or convictions."

Far beyond Herzl and his work on behalf of Jewish people everywhere, a reader of *The Gay State* would do a disservice to himself if he presumed Herzl and Graham were both activists promoting Zionism solely. On the contrary, what Herzl and Graham share in their respective booklets is the desire for liberty, freedom and a national identity and a national homeland for their respective peoples. Toward that end, Thomas Paine's writings scream of the yearning for independence. *Common Sense* was Paine's call to arms for all Americans and has been studied by American schoolchildren everywhere. His other works, *The Crisis*, *The Rights of Man* and *The Age of Reason* only solidify the natural and inherent drive for people to be free of tyranny. Therefore, the argument in this booklet is not a new one – the establishment of a Gay State. The world speaks of outrage, disgust, intolerance and hatred against the Gay culture, and this is what awakens this dormant desire and earnest concept.

I know I am not inventing anything original with *The Gay State*, as the reader should be constantly aware when reading my explanations. I have borrowed heavily to express how we find ourselves in this situation at this point in time. The most comfortable amongst us, the financially well to do, are often blinded to the realities and will not understand the desperate circumstances that exist around the world.

As our struggle has endured for thousands of years and in every corner of the globe, I am inventing neither the condition of the Gay community as it developed through history, nor the means to remedy it. The material components of the structure which I lay out are present in reality and within easy reach – anyone can convince himself of that. Thus, if anyone wants to characterize this attempt to solve the Gay question with one word, then it should not be called a "fantasy," but at most a "hypothesis."

At the outset I must guard this paper from being treated as a childish dream. In doing so I am only preventing superficial observers from possibly committing a silly and naive blunder. To those who refer to the notion of an independent Gay nation-state as a fanciful utopia, I must strongly disagree. They do our people a grave disservice. The alternative to our independence, of course, would be to remain in one's nation of birth, to live and die as an outsider, never fully acknowledged for who you are, nor appreciated for your innate goodness – a goodness made in the eyes of God. Had I chosen instead to simply produce a work of fiction on life in a Gay nation, I could have spared myself from the constant criticisms from our detractors, which let me assure you, the fanatics who wish to exterminate us get themselves all riled up at the prospects of our advancement. So yes, a simple novel of science fiction might well have proved entertaining, but our movement is not about being entertained. For that genre, countless works have been produced, if idle pleasure and armchair reading is the desired outcome. Frankly, our global conditions are far too dire to not take our circumstances seriously. And I think the situation of the Gay community throughout the world is sufficiently dire to render all fanciful notions of utopian wishful thinking as unfitting for the times.

The plan before you, however, contains the utilization of a driving force that exists in reality. In all modesty, I am only indicating what generations of amiable thinkers have pondered, and that includes many of the various components that would be considered in the building of a modern state. There are, in our ranks, talented and gifted architects more competent than I to assemble all the necessary aspects needed to complete the actual construction of our newly created political entity. Readers will discover in the pages before them that we possess all that we need to create a free and beautiful new land, and we can do so without squandering bountiful resources and opportunities as so many other "new" countries have that have come before us.

What matters is the driving force to a new Gay State. That driving force is the distress of the global Gay community. Who dares to deny that this force exists? We shall deal with it in the chapter on the causes of anti-Gay forces.

Think for a moment of the steam power that is generated by boiling water in a tea kettle and which then lifts the kettle lid. This tea kettle phenomenon exists in the pro-Gay rights movement and the many other organized efforts to combat anti-Gay hysteria.

This force, if properly used, is powerful enough to run powerful machines and transport extraordinary equipment and legions of men. The machine, or the global Gay rights organizations that will ally with us, will muster the strength and power to do magnificent work.

I am profoundly convinced that I am right; I do not know whether I shall be proved right in my lifetime. The men and womyn who inaugurate this movement will not likely live to see its glorious conclusion. Nation building can take generations. But the very inauguration will bring these committed patriots honor for generations of Gay citizens to come and the happiness of inner freedom into their lives.

To protect my plan from the suspicion that it is a utopian fantasy, I shall use picturesque details in my description, but will keep such descriptions to a minimum. As it is, I suspect that unthinking scoffers will attempt to invalidate the whole idea by distorting my outline. Political opponents boasting of their moral superiority, some refer to it as "The Sarah Palin Effect," will demean and disparage every nugget of detail that they can twist to their advantage. A generally intelligent

Gay man to whom I presented the matter said that details of the future presented as reality were the hallmark of utopia. This is a fallacy. I concede that arbitrary implementation of my concepts could just as likely lead to a "Mosquito Coast" of the new millennium.

Every minister of finance uses future figures in his budgetary estimates – not just figures derived from the averages of previous years and the past revenues of other states, but also figures for which there is no precedent, for example, when a new tax is instituted. Economists, financiers and all readers familiar with profit and loss statements will understand this. Certain assumptions to future performance can be made when considering that the Gay demographic is more educated than the general population, which raises the Gay states potential to a new, never-before-seen potential. Will this cause anyone to regard a draft of fiscal law as Utopian, even if he knows that it will never be possible to stick to the estimate very closely? Again, it is a certainty that opponents will pick at any scab until there is blood, and only then will they scoff in indignation and herald our people inept.

Frankly, I expect even more of my readers. I ask the educated readers whom I am addressing to rethink and revise many old notions. And I am particularly imposing upon the existing Gay leadership throughout the world, those who have actively striven to fill a leadership role within their local Gay community, to the extent of asking them to look upon their previous efforts as misguided and ineffectual. This will not come easily as in all dark corners of the world; we have had brave leaders in the Gay community who have given much of themselves to make their world a bit better. Yet, we as a people, scattered about in over 195 nations, must begin to think of ourselves as "one." Our mission is greater than can be responsibly accommodated by a local city Gay task force, whether it be in Los Angeles, Auckland, Alexandria, or Buenos Aires. We must change our thinking to that of a global force and claim our rightful place in the world.

In presenting my idea I face a danger. If I describe all those things of the future with restraint, it will seem as though even I do not believe that they are possible. If, on the other hand, I predict their realization unreservedly, everything may look like a figment of my imagination, and the opponents will diminish our vision as a Polly-Anna form of wishful thinking. In fact, I have in every way employed a tempered restraint in every assessment to nation building.

Therefore I say clearly and emphatically: I do believe that my vision can be put into practice, even though I do not presume to know for certain the final form every aspect of the idea will take. The Gay State is something the world needs and consequently will come into being.

If this idea were only to be pursued by one person, it would be a rather narcissistic and perhaps delusional task; but if many Gays agree to work on it simultaneously, it is entirely reasonable and carrying it out will present no major obstacles. People when working as a unified mass, have been known to move mountains or build Pyramids. The idea depends only on the number of its adherents. Perhaps our ambitious young people will provide the energy to harness the power in masses, will stand on the shoulders of those of us who have come before them, and all of us, united as one movement, will see to it that this idea is disseminated.

With the third publication of this pamphlet I consider my task as completed. I have come to expect a uproar in some quarters – where there are those who find the notion of our rising to be their peers on the international stage preposterous. Reasoned criticisms usually quickly give way to veiled anti-Gayism. Their minds will not be changed in the pages of this pamphlet, and I, therefore, do not waste the time to engage them. If attacks from estimable opponents force me to do so, or if it becomes necessary to refute unforeseen objections and eliminate errors, I will then speak freely on the topic. This booklet is a collaboration and compilation of sources and ideas. Our freedom will also be earned as a hard fought collaboration. We are a people – one people.

In the culture of my immediate communities where I divide most of my personal time, perhaps I am not seeing these issues as most others do. Am I ahead of my time? Are the sufferings of the Gay community still not great enough? Do millions more need to be put to death, subjected to public beatings and floggings or forced into financial ruin, lost careers, ruined families and lives destroyed? How many more Gay bashings must occur, and how many more parents will murder their own Gay children in order to save the honor of their good family name? At present, there are more than 80 nations that have made Gay sex illegal. Men loving men, and to a slightly lesser degree, womyn loving womyn, can face five, ten, or even fifteen years in prison for making love in the privacy of their own homes. Time will tell if we as a people are thirsty enough for freedom, and the response to this pamphlet will be a serious indicator. For many of us in the Gay world who are afforded some degree of comfort, we live in chains but remain blind to this. We live in chains, yet we are not slaves. In other corners of the Gay world, conditions are much more dire and desperate.

So, it depends on the global Gay community whether this political booklet is, for the time being, only a political novel. If the present generation is still too dulled by their lives at the margins, another better, more advanced generation will come along. Those Gay, Lesbian, Bisexual, and Transgender individuals who want a state of their own will have one, and deservedly so. My hope is that those of you who are reading these words will live long enough to see with your own eyes the creation of the Gay State—your democracy that will be just over the horizon and ready to welcome you home!

"In no instance have... the churches been guardians of the liberties of the people."

James Madison

"The empires of the future, are the empires of the mind."
                                                    ~ Winston Churchill

Foreword.
by Ted Becker.

The Origins of *The Gay State* and an Introduction to Garrett Graham.

The Gay State, 2010.
Garrett Graham's Guide to Creating *The Gay State: The Quest for an Independent Gay Nation-State and What it Means to Conservatives and the World's Religions.*

Garrett T. Frasier Graham's booklet *The Gay State* was first published in March 2007. It sold out of its limited run and after a revision, was re-edited and re-released in November 2008. Now, for its third edition, it will be re-released internationally in 2010. It heralded the coming of the age of the global Gay Independence movement. A widely fractured ideal of a Gay nation-state has been forming on the Web since the late 1990's, advocating for various niches within the Gay movement, but no group had a coherent plan worthy of tactical implementation. Graham's plan for creating a Gay State, arrived at after contemplating other solutions as well, provided the practical primer for groups seeking an autonomous state. It has been widely praised for offering a blueprint for establishing a philosophical ideology. After shaping his ideology and sharpening the concept, Mr.

Graham provided the practical program of Gay Independence and led to the first Gay Statehood Congress in Washington, DC in 2007, with another scheduled for 2010.

Born in New York in 1959, Graham was educated in the United States and Europe. He worked in law and as a political activist and on Capitol Hill in Washington, DC, London, and Amsterdam before entering business. He invested in international real estate and a number of businesses including a publishing house in Manhattan before selling it in the early 2000's. Throughout his life, Graham travelled extensively, having homes in Europe, the States, and in the Pacific.

Even prior to 2007 and the first production of *The Gay State*, Graham observed an increase in the degree of the homophobia that is rampant and widely under-reported in the USA. Once outside the few liberal metropolitan areas and a handful of enlightened states, Gay oppression is wide spread and rarely questioned. Graham became involved with Gay Rights organizations in his liberal and enlightened home of Manhattan. In personal and professional dealings with like-minded internationalists, Graham recognized that while Europe showed great progress in recognizing the legal rights of Homosexuals, there was nothing to alleviate the imbalance imposed by the ruling majority in the U.S. And while a few select nations on the globe allowed for equal Gay marriage, and a few select states in the US allowed for Gay Marriage "ceremonies," in the States they were stripped of most of the federal protection laws afforded to married non-Gay couples.

More to the point, greater than 95% of the world's population lives under oppression due to their sexual orientation, if not outright threats of murder, beatings, and imprisonment for two adult Homosexuals expressing their love for one another in the privacy of their own homes. More than 80 countries on Earth still consider Homosexuality as an abomination and illegal act, with penalties ranging from public floggings to prison sentences of five to ten to fifteen years. Some countries still allow men discovered to be Gay to be stoned to death. Other nations enforce a more "humane" death sentence for engaging in

Homosexuality. Graham recognized that these most extreme forms of oppression occurred in developing nations with colonial pasts.

Yet the impact of ruined lives, careers destroyed, families lost, and financial ruin still occurred in the most "advanced" nations by virtue of cultural intolerance and lack of protection under the law. In this new Millennium, parents, as reprehensible as it is, were known to kill their own children to save the "honor" of the family name. Protests swept across the United States in 2009, a backlash to whatever advancement the progressives had made in support of Gay issues and other liberal causes. Throughout the United States, Family Values parades and demonstrations were held in the summer of 2009, with marchers shouting "Death to Fags!" Posters were inscribed, "Thank God for giving AIDS to Gays" and paraded around in front of St. Patrick's Cathedral on Fifth Avenue in New York City. Gay Americans fighting for their country in the US Armed Forces in the wars in Iraq and Afghanistan were being drummed out of the military, stripped of their pensions, and given dishonorable discharges because internal government investigations found them to be Gay. As second class citizens, they were less than their heterosexual compatriots. They pay taxes like all other citizens, but were considered second class citizens. Over the decades, this less than full equality has resulted in a wide spread and systemic American "Gay Apartheid."

This culmination of hate motivated Graham to devote thought and effort to the Gay problem. He kept a journal in which he formulated his thoughts, and it showed the evolution of his concepts and political understanding. In his preparations to launch GNN, the Gay News Network, an internet-based daily podcast featuring the Global Gay Nightly News, Graham documented an upswing in the amount of anti-Gay violence being reported around the world.

Graham formalized his concepts through his research, readings, participating in Salons, and brainstorming on the Gay problem. *The Gay State*, he proposed, for the first time, to become a reality in some form, as soon as it could be realistically and effectively be initiated through immediate political action. From the onset, it appeared he was influenced by a history of failed Utopian dreams and his commitment to avoid their pitfalls. He met or conversed with dozens of liberal leaders and gay activists. He studied the founding fathers of other nations, ranging from the United States and Australia to the State of Israel. And he encouraged utilizing the democracy of the internet for Gay internationalists to express their views in the fundamental journalistic questions of what, when, where, why, and who, and the relation to three thousand years of Gay oppression.

Remarkably, Graham learned of others who had attempted and failed in such attempts, only after initiating his idea for a Gay State. He learned about a Gay Homeland Foundation and of a Gay Parallel Republic only after he began traveling about and consulting with others about his ideas and his beliefs that a nation-state may well be the last Gay hope.

The title *"The Gay State"* was probably meant as an ironic play on words, since it was believed by most that there was no one Gay state. It was assumed and believed that most Homosexuals, like the non-Gay Heterosexuals, were first and foremost allied with their native fatherland and then considered their Gayness as a secondary condition. This turned out to be exactly the opposite. As Gay men and womyn thoughtfully pondered their place in the world, many, if not most, came to see that their Gayness was their primary identifier. Men and womyn determined their Gayness cut clear through to their very being. Many aspects of one's life revolve around one's innate Gayness. And for this their fatherland would savagely beat and imprison them or, in the very least, suppress their liberty and foist upon them untold discrimination. In *The Gay State*, Graham proposed a modern solution to the Gay question. He believed that attempts at assimilation of Gays into national societies of birth were in vain, as the majority in each country decided to which degree Gays would be tolerated, if at all. This simply took the realm of freedom out of the hands of Homosexuals wherever they be. The persistence of anti-Gay sentiments determined that the Gays would always be an outsider in their lands of birth, and only the creation of a Gay state, a matter that would be of interest to both Gays and non-Gays, would be the most viable solution in bringing about an end to the global Gay problem.

The Gay State proposed that diplomacy would be the primary way of attaining the Gay State. Graham called for the organized transfer of Gay communities to the new state. As for the location of the state, Graham said, "We shall take what is given to us, what is negotiated by our Founding Fathers and what is selected by public opinion." We have no time to devote centuries in battle merely to occupy land and defend the borders. In an effort to assertively get on with things, we will purchase our land. Our territory, our homeland, will be acquired like any other business purchase. Freedom and strength will bring peace and affluence.

Graham's The *Gay State* included innovations that would include several firsts in the history of Man. This would be, as far as history shows, the first fully recognized and independent Gay state on Earth. It would become the first "Green" nation, conceived after the realization of global warming, and predicted climate change on a massive scale and the deployment of clean technology. It would be a secular nation offering equality for all citizens – whether Gay, Lesbian, Bisexual, Transgender, or non-gay Heterosexuals. Graham was interested in building a society where free enterprise and state involvement went hand in hand. It would become a truly global society, taking residents from every conceivable corner of the globe. And this Gay State would be modern, sophisticated and technologically advanced. It would be guided by centuries of nation-building as its teacher and would endeavor to avoid the many pitfalls most other countries had made.

The Gay State established Graham as the leader of the Gay Independence movement and the "father of global Gay independence." His concepts also provoked considerable opposition, in particular from the assimilationist Gays of the United States and liberal Europe. The book became required reading for all Gay independence activists and was taken as the basic platform of political Gay independence.

Graham anticipated the internal conflict that followed even within the Gay movement. The struggle to coalesce international activists around the concept of a Gay state clashed with egos more concerned with protecting the embodiment of local and regional gay rights organizations. Acting in a coordinated manner beyond their limited scope might sacrifice their funding and jeopardize their donor base, and they mistakenly feared that in time, it would threaten their very existence. Meanwhile, external opposing forces from the conservative political world and the religious world preferred that the Gay problem not become nationalized at all, but simply be exterminated.

The arguments against nationalism came from those opposed to Gay independence:

> *"In a world ravaged by war, poverty and unspeakable human suffering, the Gays are not the only people in the world who are in a condition of distress. Here I would reply that we may as well begin by removing a little of this misery, even if it should at first be no more than our own. Among the many suffering in this world to varying degrees, the global Gay community has within its ranks the vitality and wherewithal to amend a great deal of its circumstances if given the opportunity to right its own ship.*
>
> *It must be said that in this new millennium it is unwise to tear apart the fabric of international diplomacy and create new divisions and distractions between people; we ought not to raise fresh barriers, we should rather make the old disappear. But men who think in this way, they are the utopian visionaries not a wit concerned with our Gay agenda; and the idea of a native land will still arouse passion for millions when the dust of their bones will have vanished in the winds. Universal brotherhood is so far removed from human reality as to not even be a beautiful dream."*

Quite accurately, Graham foresaw the sort of objections that some in the Gay community would raise to the idea of Gay Independence:

It might more reasonably be objected that I am giving a reason and a target to anti-Gay hate speech when I say we are a people—one people; that I am hindering the assimilation of Gays in the regions of the world where Gays have become accepted and endangering it where it is an accomplished fact, insofar as it is possible for a solitary writer to endanger, obstruct or hinder anything! This objection will be especially brought forward in the liberal pockets of America. It will probably also be made in some liberal European countries. It is to Graham's point entirely that even in these liberal oases, society will diminish their Gay rights and repeal their equality to some degree whenever given the opportunity. The pendulum will continue to swing. State after state in the US, our rights were granted by the Courts and then unceremoniously taken away from us in a popular vote by the citizenry. This is testimony to the fragility of the acceptance of a minority that has been a scapegoat for religious persecution since time immemorial.

These objections were raised by Graham repeatedly at numerous conventions including the Coalition to Consider the Formation of a Gay Pre-State, gathered in New York as well as while presiding over the Council of Founding Fathers for the Free People's Federation of the Gay States, which took place on Fire Island in the summer of 2009.

If, however, Graham foresaw the tremendous antagonism of the mainstream Gay leaders to his unilateral doctrine to one Gay independent state, which threatened to supplant local and regional influence of the Gay communities by a new political and ideological framework, he was careful not to mention this issue, perhaps because he understood the need to cultivate the allegiance of these movements and their not inconsequential political and lobbying clout.

Graham has studied and understood the motives that compelled the modern anti-Gay forces to act:

Modern anti-Gay thought is not to be confused with the age-old religious persecution of the Gays that has been the basis of most brutality foisted upon them over the last two to three thousand years. The abuse does often take a religious bias in most less advanced countries, but the main current of the aggressive movement within the advanced nations has now changed. In the principal countries where this contemporary anti-Gay thought prevails, it does so as a result of the backlash brought about from the successful immersion into the larger culture that Gay communities have achieved. In the less developed nations where nearly all Gay citizens are forced to conceal themselves is typically where one finds the most religious intolerance and where religion effects laws that persecute the Gay community.

In conclusion, Graham wrote:

"I can nearly hear the Celestial Choirs of Angels singing! And what glory! What joyfulness and freedom awaits those who fight unselfishly for the cause!

Therefore I believe that a wondrous generation of Gays, Lesbians, Bisexuals, Transgender persons, and non-Gay Heterosexuals will spring into existence, free from the emotional torture and psychological shackles that have plagued our people for centuries.

Let me repeat once more my opening words: The Gays who wish for a State will have it. We shall live at last as free people on our own soil and will die peacefully in our own homes.

The world will be freed by our liberty, enriched by our wealth, magnified by our greatness.

And whatever we attempt there to accomplish for our own betterment, will react powerfully and beneficially for the good of humanity."

Graham was not a racist and did not base his conception of the Gay peoples on racist ideas of nationalism, but rather on cultural and historical development. He described himself not as American or Caucasian, but as a "Gay internationalist." While he saw himself as an "everyman," he had great respect for Gay activists and the formal process of recruiting like-minded souls and motivating them to fight for a cause. Graham understood that to garner support from the masses, he would want the endorsement of the leaders of these organizations from around the globe, who were the *de facto* organizers of Gay society. He wrote:

...We shall first of all ask for the cooperation of our leaders from every nation around the globe.

...Our Gay activist leaders, on whom we especially call, will devote their energies to the service of our idea and will inspire their community by advocating it through their various levels of communication. For their service, they will be amply rewarded. They will not need to address special meetings for the purpose; an appeal such as this may be uttered as part of their general minutes in assembly, posted in their monthly newsletters and posted on their websites. Their courage, commitment, and endorsement secure their place in history in bettering the lives of their people on their patch of earth. Thus it must be done. In all historic movements, great men and womyn have stood up and come forward to advance the righteous cause. We feel our historic affinity only through our Gayness and faith in one another. We know straight through to our core that we are in a struggle for the Ages. And in spite of having long ago absorbed the languages of different nations to an ineradicable degree, we will come together as a people – one people.

Graham realized that the curse of ethnocentrism has infected almost all nations on Earth. In its purest, most basic form, ethnocentrism is the belief that one's culture is the best and is superior to all others. Although he is an American by birth, his world view and his extensive travels taught him to be something other than "the ugly American" with a narrow America-centric view. Having lived an adulthood of discrimination as an "out" member of the Gay community, in various parts of the world, he understood the emotions attached to being considered less than equal, both in his nation of birth as well as in his travels. In his search for equality he believed we should not compete with other minorities for the "most oppressed" category.

Graham completely rejected the race theories of some of his contemporaries in America and other Euro-centric corners of the world. This Gay State would not become an "exclusive club" for people of one race or national birth origin. It must not become a de facto American State or a European State or a state only for Intellectuals or the Affluent. He became increasingly aware of the existence of Gay peoples yearning to be free from every continent. The inequality and suffering around the globe pained him deeply. News of more beheadings of young teenage men, boys really, with their whole lives ahead of them, suddenly and brutally vanquished from this earth, filled him with sorrow and his inability to stop it. But Graham persevered with his vision of a safe and peaceful place such men and womyn could call home; the Gay State—whatever its official name, and there will be much discourse in this decision —as a modern, sophisticated and cosmopolitan state where many citizens spoke multiple languages and understood the primary language of the world was his own native tongue of English. His own biases, as much as they existed, and any degree of Ethnocentrism he may have concealed, did not play a role in his selecting English as the official language for the new state. Instead, practicality ruled and the desire to see the new Gay State achieve a degree of acceptance and general affluence in matters of business and commerce. In his notes, he wrote:

> *"I believe we will be able to fashion one of the most advanced, integrated and educated nations in history. It is not now, nor will it be, uncommon among our people to speak two, three, four or more languages. Our dedication to respect all peoples and heritage will make our practices a beacon for the world. In as much as a culture can survive anywhere, it will survive here. Our teachers and cultural programs will see to it."*

In this Gay State, Graham envisioned the government of the new state to be a democracy with some socialist aspects to ensure equality to all citizens, whether one is a seasonally unemployed musician from London, a Wall Street millionaire, or a dishwasher from Bangladesh. He modeled the social service programs of the new state's major population centers on the contemporary cities of Amsterdam, Stockholm, Oslo, and Zurich. Free health care, free day care, free transportation, free security pensions, and free meals are aspects that all citizens can be assured of. Graham envisioned a multi-pluralistic democracy in which all Homosexuals, Bisexuals, Transgender individuals, and Heterosexuals had equal rights. And that while non-Gays will be a minority in this Gay-state and therefore the only nation on Earth where the Heterosexuals are the minority, they will be afforded every equality granted their fellow Homosexual countrymen.

For the Gay state, Graham addressed his vision to his Gay global audience. Through his first and second printings and its accessibility on the web, countless copies have been distributed to every continent on earth.

The Gay State might not have emerged at this time in history as a viable concept and world wide movement if Graham had not taken active steps to implement its program. Because of his contacts and organizational skills, Graham was able to initiate several conferences and symposiums that focused on the Gay independence movement. He initiated the Coalition to Consider the Formation of a Gay Pre-State in New York in 2007. He was placed as a delegate for the Free People's Federation of the Gay States, held on Fire Island in the summer of 2008, and again in Fire Island Pines in the summer of 2009, which was in many ways the seminal moment and key event in the coming of age of the Gay independence movement. Graham's contribution to a notion that had been fancied for several millennia was to physically and concretely establish a unified Gay independence movement that made a public statement of its political ambitions and settlement program known to friends and foes alike. At the moment the global Gay community dared to speak its truth out loud, there would be no retreating.

Graham wrote *"Insofar as we have endured unspeakable acts of brutality as one people and have survived global oppression on every front,*

*collectively as one people, we now must ask the question: How do we write
the history of a secret? Our individual survival so often called for hiding
from the world our true identities, and our deepest selves. As of now, the
hiding is over. We are stepping firmly into our future."*

Millions of Homosexuals have been persecuted in the last two
millennia. Murder and executions, imprisonment, public stonings and
floggings and even beheadings, countless Gay bashings long before
the term was part of our current lexicon, have impacted the personal,
private as well as public psyche of Homosexuals everywhere. There are
millions of people living invisible lives, keeping their fleeting moments
of happiness shrouded as if never will it reveal itself from the shadows.

Graham determined that if Gays around the world were to be
afforded protection, they must first be free. Our brothers and sisters
must not only be free from arrest and persecution, but simply free to be
themselves. If gays were to build their own society, they must embrace
returning to performing productive work, regular, "normal," work-a-day
jobs and be committed to a democratic society. There would be a need
for a superior military and sewage workers as there would be a need for
administrative clerks and trolley operators. In this gay state, not everyone
could contentedly occupy the stereotypical positions of hair stylist and
fashion designer or Broadway dancer or florist. Stereotypes our oppressors
are prone to denigrate. Enough of our citizenry must step forward to do
the necessary, mundane and back breaking work of nation building. The
rewards for such toiling will be life affirming, but even the strongest men
and womyn would be pushed to the brink of resignation if not fueled by
the self-realization that they were creating something historic that would
belong to the Ages. To Graham's vision, the Gay state is a democratic
society. And per Graham's leadership and implementation of his vision,
it could become, through a determined effort, an advanced technological
society. The Congress, he wrote, will use the most inspiring documents
the modern world has ever known to commit to Graham's vision of a
secular, liberal democracy which would inspire the nation's Declaration
of Independence and its own Bill of Rights.

Graham has appealed to the philanthropists to join the Gay independence movement. He found his most ardent allies, however, among the impoverished masses and the working class from the developing and under developed worlds. Side by side, Graham and the founding fathers penned a program for attaining a Gay state. And throughout the multiple committees and Congresses that have been held or will take place in the near term, Graham will continue to meet with leaders of the global Gay community in North America, Europe, Asia, Australia and South America, to flush out the charters and finalize fiduciary agreements for holding accounts including the plan for The Gay National Trust and The Gay National Development Fund and to oversee their implementation.

Readers may come to see Graham as I do; as a secular "Saint." For all the ways he cares about those suffering around the world and his efforts to end it. Even more so, is Graham's insistence for independence without advocating for violence against those who persecute us. He strives to make the world better than it is. Garrett Graham's planned concept for a free and independent Gay state remains a plan not yet realized. Yet it continues to generate strong interest and commitment from people around the world. The time will come when the right mix of courageous leaders come together and demand equality for all Gay people. May you who read these words be alive to see our independence become a reality.

Ted Becker.

"Fourscore and seven years ago our fathers brought forth on this continent, a new nation, conceived in Liberty, and dedicated to the proposition that all men are created equal."

Abraham Lincoln

"Take the first step in faith. You don't have to see the whole staircase, just take the first step."

Rev. Martin Luther King, Jr.

Chapter One.
The Initial Concept of The Gay State.

Dear Gay Patriots and our non-Gay Allies:
You hold in your hands the world's first truly global Gay Manifesto. It is the call to arms of our people from every nation on the planet. Read it and come together. And know that we have the power to live our lives free from the murder, abuse and executions, free from life of imprisonment, ruined lives and financial ruin, free from seeing our loved ones hacked to death and set on fire and the absolute, utter despair that the Straight majority imposes upon us. It doesn't have to be this way – no longer must we wear their chains – get their boots off our necks and it's time for us to take our freedom. In solidarity for our Gay brothers and sisters everywhere, Garrett Graham

~

I am always amazed and enormously frustrated when I ponder how six billion people currently occupy Earth, often crammed into urban cores, punctuated with unimaginable poverty and squalor. The overwhelming majority find day-to-day life to be a struggle, often filled with more misery than joy. So why, I wonder, do nations of the world seek out and punish Homosexuals when they should be focusing on their grinding poverty, massive starvation rates, and abysmal Gross Domestic Product? For Gays, Lesbians, Bisexuals, and Transgender people, they are merely guests in the lands of their birth. Their hosts seem to tolerate their presence at best and root them out for extermination at worst. I won't attempt to educate the reader in all aspects of the global denigration of Homosexuals and will instead trust the reader knows that this exists, to whatever degree we can discuss at a later time. A brief summary by nation will appear in a later chapter.

The more outspoken Gays who have taken to marches are the ones who have fought for, earned, or feel entitled to their rights to speak freely. The specter of having one's "freedom" snatched away at any time is, for many of us, uncomfortable to ponder for too long. In the United States, for instance, some Gay rights are granted in limited geographic areas, and then within a short period of time, the straight majority usually becomes aroused for whatever reason, and our rights are then taken away—repealed by the non-Gay majority. Some say we depend for sustenance on the nations who are our hosts, and if we had no hosts to support us, we should die of our decadence and deviancy or starve from our collective inefficiencies. Do you, reader, believe this? More to the point, do you accept it as a truth? This is a point that shows how unjust accusations may weaken our self-image and our self-knowledge. The oppressed always believe the worst about themselves.

Global economics, for instance, is based on consumption of goods, now more than ever. Global interdependence is nearly complete. Every day of the year, there are new products being introduced throughout the world. The quality of life for peoples, without regard of their sexuality, has vastly improved. We need not wake from a long slumber, like Rip van Winkle, to realize that the world is considerably altered by the production of new commodities and services. Consider the average life spans of those still among us and possibly reading these pages; in so short a time frame, amazing technological progress has been made, ushering daily life habits that someone from just one century ago might not even recognize. So much have things changed, yet remained the same. Who amongst us, however, would not forsake all of the technological marvels to save the life of a loved one? Who amongst us would not want to live a life of freedom, to love our cherished partner fully? Our "hosts," it turns out, may allow us to exist, but they don't allow us to prosper too much. We can be consumers and we can be laborers, we can even be professionals and celebrities, but we cannot be who we are. We cannot love our Gay partner or our Gay culture. The exception being only a handful of countries where Gays endure their own various forms of inequality, are the best off amongst us. And in nations where our hosts do not put us to death or imprison us for our Gay love, they often prefer that we hide it. To them, our Gay love is distasteful and should not be on display for others to see. If a heterosexual couple were to hold hands at a restaurant over a candlelit dinner, it would be approved of. If a Gay couple were to behave in the same way, they would be accused of "flaunting" their "lifestyle." We are in the final conclusion tolerated, but not allowed to be fully human.

If Gays were to assemble as a group, would they not have the skills to feed and house themselves? Do they not have the grit to do the dirty work required in fashioning a community? Don't we, as a group, have the flair for commerce, the imagination to create and innovate? Can't we manage to pull together even the most lackadaisical among us to establish a well-oiled machine? Don't we collectively offer all that is needed to run an amazing machine and still have excess parts in our collective inventory? The global majority, the non-Gays, see us as unfit or unwilling to perform manual labor of any import. We're believed to be too weak of mind to be strong of body. No, we should not require another nation to live on. We do not need to feed off of our hosts like a bacteria. We do not depend on the circulation of old commodities because we are inventors and innovators, and together we will produce new ones.

The world as we know it is inhabited by a great many ignorant people. Later I will list groups that would be opposed to our very being.

But you already have a list very close to your heart of those who have most endeavored to hold you down. Many on that list are among the most backward-thinking who absurdly exaggerate the traits of some of us. They wish to make us out to be many things beneath their standing. And I will not indulge such ridiculousness by attempting here to refute each and every verbal arrow they have slung at us. Doing so would only continue to perpetuate our self-belief that we are somehow less than the heterosexuals that for centuries and millennia have kept their boots on our necks.

Everything rational and everything sentimental that can possibly be said in defense of their ignorance has been said already. If a speaker's audience is incapable of comprehending him, one may as well be a preacher in an empty hall. And if one's audience is broad and high-minded enough to have grasped all that is to be said, then the sermon is unnecessary and redundant. I believe in the ascent of man to higher and yet higher grades of civilization, but I consider this ascent to be desperately, miserably slow. Were we to wait until average humanity had become as charitably inclined as to embrace our participation within their cultures, we should wait beyond our day, beyond the days of our children, of our grandchildren, and of our great-grandchildren. But the world's spirit comes to our aid in another way.

These last decades have given the world a wonderful renaissance by means of its technical achievements, but at the same time its miraculous improvements have not been employed in the service of humanity. Distance has ceased to be an insurmountable obstacle, yet we complain of insufficient space. Yet for all of this "advancement," the misery of the Gays is an anachronism – not because there was a period of enlightenment one hundred years ago, for that enlightenment reached in reality only the choicest locales. Beyond the fashionable neighborhoods of DuPont Circle and Chelsea, the average life for a closeted Gay person remains abysmally small, repressed, and lonely.

I believe the cell phone camera was not invented for the purpose of increasing the multi-functionality of the cell phone industry, but for capturing injustices around the world that could shine light on those dark places. I believe that electricity was not invented for the purpose of illuminating the private clubs and houses of worship of those who repress us, but rather for the purpose of throwing light on some of the dark problems of humanity. One of these problems, and not the least of them, is the Gay question. In solving it we are working not only for ourselves, but also for the many other over-burdened and oppressed beings.

Yes, post-"Will and Grace" where Gay people are brought into our homes by the means of television, even if only to make us laugh (and mostly *at* Gays, not with them,) the Gay question still exists. It would be foolish to deny it. It is a remnant of Biblical times, which civilized nations do not even yet seem able to shake off. Only a few nations on earth have even attempted to show a generous desire by way of emancipating us. Be clear, as you may be surprised, that in most under developed nations, in some of the more advanced European nations, and, in fact, even in huge pockets of the United States, we remain second class citizens at best. Yes, the Gay questions exist wherever Gays live in perceptible numbers. Where it does not exist is where the suppression of Gays is so dominantly overwhelming, that few brave souls declare to the world who they really are.

There is no country on earth where we do not exist. The governmental leaders who proclaim they have no Homosexuals within their borders are under the mistaken belief that they have either deported or executed them all. But we are able when necessary to blend in with non-Gay Heterosexuals, so it is unlikely that all of our brothers and sisters were rounded up so that none of us have survived. And lastly, of course, is the undeniable fact that Heterosexuals simply keep making more of us. By biological and genetic facts of life, millions more of us populate the planet every year. As long as the non-Gays keep breeding, our numbers will continue to grow.

Migration patterns have shown that we tend to move to those places where we are not (or less) persecuted. And by virtue of being there, our presence produces persecution. This is the case in every country, and will remain so, even in those highly civilized nations – for instance, the Netherlands – until the Gay question finds a solution on a political basis. So even in the Netherlands, long considered the most benevolent of global hosts to the Gay community, is now undergoing a striking and unsettling explosion in anti-Gay violence and increasing persecution. We again are faced with the reminder that our safety and the value and worth placed on our being are in the hands of others. Now two Gay men that hold hands in Amsterdam or share a quick kiss on the cheek in the very heart of Rembrandtplein face the specter of violence against them. Gays, in this, the most Gay-liberated and accepting nation on earth, now cannot stop or control the brutal and savage Gay-bashings that play out at the hands of religious fundamentalists in the most Gay of all Gay-friendly cities on the planet.

I believe I understand anti-Gayism, which is really a condition that can be initiated from the earliest stages of infancy. While the actions perpetrated by the young can be the simplest forms of hatred, the movement can be surprisingly complex when carried out by adults. I consider it from a Gay standpoint, yet without fear or hatred. I believe that I can see what elements there are in it of socio-economic standings, common trade jealousy, of brutal sport, of inherited and intensely indoctrinated prejudice, of religious intolerance of varying extremes, and also of pretended self-defense. I think the Gay question is no more a social than religious one, notwithstanding that it sometimes takes these and other forms. It is a national question, which can only be solved by making it a political world question to be discussed and settled by the civilized nations of the world in joint counsel.

We are a people – one people.

We have honestly endeavored, in nearly all instances and by all accounts, mostly everywhere, to merge ourselves in the social life of surrounding communities and to preserve the faith of all of those who suffered before us. But we are not permitted to do so. In vain we are loyal patriots to our birth nations, our loyalty in some places running to extremes; in vain do we make the same sacrifices of life and property as our fellow citizens; in vain do we strive to increase the fame of our native birth lands in science and art, or her wealth by trade and commerce. In countries where we have lived for centuries, we are still denied the same rights as newly arrived immigrants. The majority may decide, at the whim of their choosing, who among us are the strangers, the inferiors and less-thans; for this, as indeed every point which arises in the relations between nations, is a question of might. In the world as it now is, and for an indefinite period will probably remain, might precedes right. Military might over-rules moral righteousness. It is useless, therefore, for us to be loyal patriots, as were the Huguenots who were forced to emigrate, or the Jews of Europe and the Orient, who sought a land to settle in peace and acceptance. If we as Gays, could only be left in peace…

But I think we shall forever suffer at the hands of the Heterosexual majority, and we will not be left in peace. Oppression and persecution cannot exterminate us. Of the thousands of tribes over the history of Man, few have survived such struggles and sufferings as we have gone through. The oppression of our people has been so thorough, and the efforts to divide us have successfully kept us from rising. Our oppressors have exterminated the weakest among us, and to our detriment, that has not made us stronger. Our lack of unity has played into their hands. New and more Gays have continually joined our ranks, but it's not as if through Darwinian measures we have grown resistant to their attacks. And so, decade after decade, we have merely continued to survive in many corners of the globe. Of course as most readers know, in the Western nations this was not the case. For much of the Gay community, our prosperity in material possessions increased along with the general population.

I am embarrassed to say many of our fellow Gays who advanced intellectually and materially entirely lost the feeling of belonging to an oppressed people relegated to second or third class status. Wherever our political or material well-being has lasted for any length of time, we have assimilated with our surroundings. For many, this meant laughing along with our oppressors when the Gay culture and movement are attacked. This is not something we should discredit our brethren for doing. Their efforts to "get along" helped ensure the degree of comfort and affluence they had personally attained, and toward that goal there is no criticism. Most of us cannot name a politician where we live who has gone out on a limb to support us in attaining any Gay-centered political power. Outside of a few Gay enclaves, politicians see no value in allying with our causes. Doing so is tantamount to political suicide in much of the world.

For old prejudices against us still lie deep in the hearts of the people. For proof of these, we need only listen to commoners where they speak with frankness and simplicity; proverbs and fairy-tales are both anti-Gay. Children are taught from the youngest ages that their behavior must comply with their assigned gender. "Boys don't cry," "Stop acting like a little girl," and "you want to grow up big and strong, don't you?" are spoon-fed to children beginning at a very young age. The sentiments, however, are equally strong in their implications that the opposite sentiments are not viewed as favorable. A nation is everywhere a great child, which can certainly be educated, but its education would, even in most favorable circumstances, occupy such a vast amount of time that we could, as already mentioned, solve our own problems by other means long before the process was accomplished.

There is the issue of assimilation. In some manners relating to personal affectations, many of our brothers and sisters cannot wholly or naturally blend in and be mistaken for members of the non-Gay society. Matters relating to dress, language, and customs also tend to be giveaways for many of us. The reader understands that of course we can all do our very best to blend in [read "hide who we really are, because that is not good enough"]. But, the objective here is to demonstrate how our community can first be true to itself. No one seems to ever ask the Heterosexuals in our midst to give thought and effort every day to try to fit into our Gay culture and, above all, conceal who they really are;

and truthfully, for the vast majority of non-Gays around the world, the mere suggestion stirs their indignation.

Gay culture cannot be watered down or diluted by assimilation. Homosexuality cannot be diluted through assimilation the way some might suppose a particular religion can. Others have promoted that bi-racial intermarriage would dilute the White race or the Black race, and some contend if we only had one race, most of the societal tensions would melt away. These arguments on their individual merits are preposterous and should be stricken out of hand. Gays, however, cannot be watered down through intermarriage. A primary identifier of Homosexuality is the sexuality part. If the sexuality of Homosexuality was acceptable enough to be part of inter-marriage, there would be much greater acceptance of the global Gay community, and that would probably render the necessity of a Gay State as null and void. Again, the process of assimilation occurs through a blending that takes generations, if not centuries. In several thousand years, assimilation has not produced the favorable results one might hope for in countries where Gay people are imprisoned, whipped, beaten, and fined for being Gay. This is what is occurring in the majority of the nations on Earth and is still legally sanctioned and approved of and carried out by governments in more than 80 of the nations around the world! We must not wait another 3,000 years; we can't wait another 3,000 years, and to willfully wait a fraction of that term is shameful. Those of us living in comfort would have the blood on our hands of our brothers and sisters given up to an oppressive system. We must fight for our freedom.

Because I have drawn this conclusion with complete indifference to everything but the quest of truth, I will probably be contradicted and opposed by Gays who are in easy circumstances. Affluence tends to help us forget the early struggles. This must be human nature. The claims of those who feel that their private interests are endangered can safely be ignored, for the concerns of the poor and oppressed are of greater importance. But I wish from the outset to prevent any misconception from arising, particularly the mistaken notion that my project, if realized, would in any way injure the property, position, and affluence now held by Gays. I shall therefore explain everything connected with rights of property very fully. Whereas, if my plan never becomes anything more than a piece of literature, things will merely remain as they are.

It might more reasonably be objected that I am giving an excuse for the existence of Anti-Gayism when I say we are a people – one people, that I am hindering the assimilation of Gays where it is about to be consummated and endangering it where it is an accomplished fact, insofar as it is possible for a solitary writer to hinder, or endanger anything! This objection will be especially brought forward in the Netherlands, Belgium, Norway, Canada, and even in pockets of the United States. It will probably also be made in other countries, but I shall answer on the Dutch and American Gays beforehand, because these afford the most striking examples of my point.

However much I may acknowledge the power of personality – powerful individual personality in philosophers, leaders, inventors, statesmen, or artists, as well as the collective personality of a historic group of human beings which we call a nation – however much I may appreciate personality, I do not regret its disappearance. Whoever can, will, and must, let him disband from our ranks and disassociate from us. But the distinctive nationality of Gays throughout the world, neither can, will, nor must be destroyed. It cannot be destroyed, because external enemies do not have the means necessary. It will not be destroyed; this is shown during thousands of years of suffering. It must not be destroyed, and that, as a descendant of numberless Gays who persevered, I am trying once more to prove in this booklet. Whole branches of our Gay world may whither and fall, but the root system embedded deep remains.

If all or any of the Dutch and American Gays protest against this Gay State concept on account of their own "assimilation," my answer is simple: The whole thing does not concern them at all. They are the Gay Dutchmen and the Gay Americans, all well and good! This is a private affair for the Gays alone. No one will force anyone to join our cause. The movement toward the organization of the Gay State that I am proposing would not of course harm Gay Dutchmen nor Gay Americans, just as it would not harm the "assimilated" of other countries. It would, on the contrary, be distinctly to their advantage. For they would no longer be disturbed in their "chromatic function," as Darwin puts it, but would be able to assimilate in peace, because the present anti-Gayism would have been stopped or significantly lessened forever. They would certainly be credited with being assimilated to the very depths of their souls, if they stayed where they were after the new Gay State, with its superior institutions, had become a reality. The "assimilated" would profit even more than their Heterosexual-majority citizens by the departure of the faithful Gays, for they would be rid of the most antagonistic, disquieting, incalculable and unavoidable rivalry of the Gay working class and the proletariat, driven by class struggles and political pressure.

Nations around the world might still hold the Gay culture in disdain, but be gladdened to see us in sizable numbers leave their borders permanently. The end of struggle and discomfort on both sides will allow for humanity to exhale. There should be a home for all of us and now, for the first time, Gay men and womyn will have their place as well. The religious right in Holland and America should join in the growing chorus of farewells as we leave their shores. Recent news coverage in the United States has the religious right devoting more time in protestations towards the Gay community than they zero in on Muslim fanaticism, the Taliban, the belligerent governments threatening nuclear annihilation, or on Heterosexuals violating the "sanctity of marriage" in which 50% of all American marriages dissolve—many by adulterous action. With our departure, the Christian fundamentalists will have a great deal of free time on their hands. Who then will they set their sites on? It would be a great irony to see charitable organizations offering "relief" to assist in the resettlement of Gays to their new Gay State. Their "philanthropic" undertakings would be comical if not for the fact it is covering centuries of oppression in which countless lives were destroyed. And thus, many an apparent friend of the Gays turns out, on careful inspection, to be nothing more than anti-Gayites, attempting to remove us from their vicinity, disguised as philanthropy. We will take their philanthropic offerings and thank them and offer our blessings in return. Then we will move on to a new life of freedom.

There have been attempts at colonization over the many years and sometimes by truly benevolent men, interesting attempts though they were, have so far been unsuccessful. I do not think that this or that man took up the matter merely as an amusement, that they engaged in the emigration of poor Gays as one indulges in viewing a sporting event or playing poker. The matter was too grave and tragic for such treatment. These attempts were interesting, in that they represented on a small scale the practical forerunners of the idea of a Gay State. Most establishments or concepts were Utopian in nature. They were centered on individuals rather than key concepts of liberty. Most were communal in nature, and avoided the serious business of nation-building.

No serious attempt has garnered scholarly attention in or out of the Gay world until now. However, even these failed, early attempts were useful, for out of their mistakes may be gathered experience for carrying the idea out successfully on a larger scale. They have, of course, done harm also. Every failed attempt or circumstance that concluded in unsatisfactory outcomes caused Gays themselves to entertain doubts in the Gay men on the usefulness of Gay abilities. Reasonable men and womyn may overcome these doubts by the following simple argument: What is impractical or impossible to accomplish in a small enterprise, need not necessarily be so on a larger, grander scale. A small enterprise may result in loss under the same conditions which would make a large endeavor flourish. A stream cannot even be navigated by a canoe; the river into which it flows, however, carries massive and stately cruise liners of magnificent proportions. On a small scale, a canoe gets stuck in the mud flats; in the other, the *Queen Mary* glides by in all of her opulence.

No human being is wealthy or powerful enough to transplant a nation from one habitation to another. An idea alone can achieve that, and this idea of a Gay State may have the requisite power to do so. The Gays have dreamt of this vision of peace all through the long nights of their history. It is now a question of showing that the dream can be converted into a living reality.

For this, many old, outgrown, confused, and limited notions must first be entirely erased from the minds of men. Dull brains might, for instance, imagine that this exodus would be from civilized regions into a virtual Siberia concluding into more primitive living than they endured under their oppressors. That is not the case. It will be carried out in the midst of civilization. We shall keep the most treasured of our customs and foster new and more meaningful ones; we shall reap the benefits of our universal health care, where in our prior home there was none; we shall leave behind the hard scrabble life of incessant work and poverty for a life with meaningful vocation with ample compensations; we shall not be vanquished to a lower ranking, but will rise to a higher station; we shall surrender our fears of persecution to live in freedom and liberty that extols the virtues of the Gay community; we shall not be required to leave our old homes until the new one is prepared for us, and we shall not live in drab scrap metal huts, but we shall build new more beautiful and more modern houses and possess them in peace and safety. Those who go first will realize the most to gain; those who are now desperate who feel there is nothing to lose will go first; after them the poor; next the prosperous; and last of all, the wealthy. Those who go in advance will raise themselves to a higher grade, equal to those whose representatives will shortly follow.

Nation-building requires Patriots; men and womyn who resolve to put their shoulder to the stone for all of those who will follow. Thus, the exodus will be at the same time an ascent of the classes. We shall offer all citizens dual citizenship. They need not renounce their citizenship of birth; they will be able to hold dual passports and come and go with diplomatic ease. We know Gays worldwide will view this new Gay State as their homeland, whether they relocate immediately or not. Pilgrimages to the new Gay State will be the vacation objectives for tens of millions of fellow Gay brothers and sisters. Countless others will see our Gay State as their second homes of choice—as their "seasonal residences." Even more people will complete their careers and relocate to enjoy their gay retirement in our new Gay State.

The departure of the Gays will involve no economic disturbances, no crises, no persecutions; in fact, the countries from which they relocate will revive to a new period of prosperity. There will be an inner migration of non-Gays into the positions occupied by the Gays. As stated earlier, the Gays who choose to remain behind will also benefit from the diminishment of their local rank and file. The outgoing current will be gradual, without any disturbance, and this initial movement will put an end to much anti-Gayism. The Gays will leave of their own accord at the time of their own choosing with fond farewells and will be received with the same favorable welcome and treatment accorded to all foreign visitors. The exodus will have no resemblance to a flight, for it will be a well-regulated movement under control of public opinion and the Founding Fathers of the Gay State. The movement will not only be inaugurated with absolute conformity to law, but it cannot even be carried out without the friendly cooperation of interested Governments, who would derive considerable benefits from it.

Security for the integrity of the idea and the vigor of its execution will be found in the creation of a corporate body, or a corporation. This corporation will be called "The Society of Gays." In addition to it, there will be a Gay holding company representing each continent and region of the planet which will focus on economic and human service work. The personal character of the members of the corporation will guarantee its integrity, and the adequate might of its capital will ensure realistic and timely proceedings. Both of these matters will be explored in detail in later chapters.

These introductory remarks are merely intended as a hasty reply to the mass of objections which the very words "The Gay State" are certain to arouse. In the coming weeks and months we shall proceed more slowly to meet further objections and to explain in detail what has been as yet only indicated, and we shall try in the interests of this pamphlet to avoid making it a dull exposition. Short, punchy chapters of fact will therefore best answer the purpose. Frequent updates for those who file a citizenship request will be e-mailed to all interested parties.

If we wish to substitute a new building for an old one, we must demolish before we construct. I shall, therefore, keep to this natural sequence. In the first and general part I shall explain my ideas, remove all prejudices, determine essential political and economic conditions, and develop a plan.

In the central part, which is divided into three principal sections, I shall describe its execution. These three sections are as follows: the Gay Company, Local Groups, and The Society of Gays. The Society comprised of the Founding Fathers is to be created first, the Company last, but in this exposition the reverse order is preferable, because it is the financial soundness of the enterprise which will chiefly be called into question, and doubts on this score must first be removed. We know that our opposition, including external threats from the Heterosexual world and other adversarial concerns from local and regional Gay groups who view a greater and larger organization as threats to their fiefdoms, will seek to diminish our efforts. We know that some will disregard our concepts out of hand, and we know they will seek to mischaracterize our financial projections.

In the conclusion, I shall try to meet every further objection that could possibly be made. My Gay readers will, I hope, follow me patiently to the end. Some will naturally make their objections or displeasure clearly known. But of those of you who stay with me through my written efforts, you will, I trust, have your doubts dispelled, and I will ask you to give your allegiance to the cause.

Although I speak of reason, I am fully aware that reason alone will not suffice. Old prisoners do not willingly leave their cells. We shall see whether the youth whom we need are at our command – the young, who irresistibly entice the old and chiseled veterans, carry them forward on strong arms, and transform rational motives into enthusiasm, for it will be the young and the not-yet-born who will reap the most bounty in our new freedom and liberty.

"The fact is that more people have been slaughtered in the name of religion than for any other single reason. That, THAT my friends, is true perversion".

Harvey Milk

"First they ignore you. Then they laugh at you. Then they fight you.
Then you win."

~ Mohandas Gandhi

Chapter Two.
The Global Gay Question
(Some say "Problem.")

N o one can deny the gravity of the situation of the global Gay community. Wherever they live, they are more or less persecuted. They need not be gathered in large numbers. Individual and small groups are sometimes even easier and greater targets of more severe brutality due to their perceived weakness. Their equality before the law, granted by statute, has become a dead letter. Internationally, in the majority of nations, they are debarred from filling even a moderately high position, either in the military or in any public and private capacity. They are also sought out in attempts to throw them out of business. Undercover agents of national police agencies infiltrate Gay groups so they might weed out, isolate, and destroy any individual with potential to rise economically or socially. Orchestrated attempts by Heterosexuals are carried out to terrorize business owners with ongoing harassment, vandalism, threats to the lives of employees and customers alike, and investigations by every government agency that has any administration over their practices. More than half of the nations that exist as of this writing do not even pretend to protect gays according to the law. Gay entrepreneurs are sought out in attempts to drive them out of business: "Don't buy from the fags!" In America, Gays have secured the right to rent an apartment in only half of the US, and for the rest, they can be forced from their apartments at any time for being Gay. In that same vein, many of the US states allow Gay people to be terminated from employment if their secret is discovered.

Attacks from Heterosexual conservative community leaders, in assemblies, in the press, in the pulpit, in the street, on journeys – for example, their exclusion from certain hotels – even from recreation areas – ebb and flow. "They're thieves; they are unethical; they are immoral; keep your children away from them;" the character assassinations go on and take root. Lies told often enough become gospel. The forms of persecution vary according to the countries and social circles in which they occur. In the United States, Gays who are exposed have been in the past, and in some places continue to be, forced out of their homes and can be terminated from the workplace. In Amsterdam, The Netherlands, gay-bashings occur in even this, the gayest of cities. In European, Asian, and African countries too numerous to list in this chapter, Gays have been beaten to death when they are determined to be Homosexual. In nearly every country on Earth, Gays find themselves the recipient of violence whether it comes in the form of thorough beatings, public whippings, or public stonings as punishment for their activities, even within their own homes. In a NATO-member country (perceived to be among the more modern and forward thinking nations), parents murdered their own Gay child in order to protect the family's honor" and "good name." Throughout the world Gays are shut out of the so-called best social circles and excluded from clubs. Many of the finest and most prestigious apartment co-operatives in Manhattan will not rent or sell apartments to Homosexuals. Governments have imposed fines on Homosexuals greater than a year's salary in some cases and have handed down sentences of five, ten or fifteen years of imprisonment for their Homosexual conduct.

The President of Gambia has organized squads to infiltrate hotels, root out Gay activity, and arrest criminals. The alleged Homosexual is given 24 hours to leave the country permanently or face imprisonment and death by beheading. In Jamaica, machete-yielding mobs have attacked Gays. In Haiti, as in a number of other countries, Gays have been set on fire and burned to death. And in America, the land of the free, Gays have been beheaded and dismembered and their remains partially burned. And in some American states, Gay teenagers, still children, are raped and murdered or beaten with lead pipes while adults look on. And in 2009, hate crimes in the United States based on sexual orientation have soared eleven percent for the year 2008. This is not an attempt to list all grievances and wrath the world has served to the global gay community. It is, in fact, not even scratching the surface.

There will be, I am sure, some reader, perhaps a Gay reader who has achieved a level of success and comfort, who prefers not to think of the wrath that is falling upon his or her less affluent and less fortunate brothers and sisters. He will say, "Oppression? There is no oppression." Every incident, every beating, every death will be a rare incident, he will say. Such incidents number into the hundreds of thousands per year. But do not, gentle reader, convince yourself as some have that the violences just mentioned are the rare exceptions. To do so would be deluding yourself and ignoring the facts. Some of the most liberal among us are the most likely to misread the current state of the global Gay community.

I do not intend to arouse sympathetic emotions on our behalf. That would be foolish and futile. I shall content myself with putting the following questions to the Gays: Is it not true that in countries where you live, the punishment exacted for being Gay goes beyond economic punishment? Is it not true that middle class Gays are threatened and targeted only because of their sexual orientation? Is it not true that the passions of the mob, which are often comprised of the so called "moral majority," are incited against our wealthier Gays, whether out of resentment, jealousy, prejudice, or some other rationale? Is it not true that the poor endure greater sufferings (socioeconomically as well as emotionally) and incidents of being ostracized as children through adulthood because of what they are? I think that this external pressure makes itself felt everywhere. In our economically upper classes it causes discomfort, in our middle classes continual and grave anxieties, in our lower classes absolute despair. In our community, psychological and emotional problems are deep and wide spread. The mental illness is not because we are Homosexual. The mental illness is because of the verbal and emotional abuses inflicted upon us each and every day of our lives, year after year, often for a lifetime and often in the most subtle of ways. The shame for this condition is not ours, my Gay brothers and sisters, but should instead be placed squarely on the abusers.

The rage and hostility clearly enunciated against our Gay brothers and sisters are so often based in houses of worship. The pious are armed with their beliefs and their self-righteousness. To them we are to be pitied, mocked, and targets of rabid desire to rid their communities of us. So I shall now put the question in the briefest possible form: Is it not time that we finally "get out," take our freedom, and start anew? Or may we yet remain? And for how long?

I am not suggesting we abandon our communities to accommodate our oppressors. I am saying that we must fulfill our individual destinies. We must form our nation for our own mental health, our physical well-being, and for the self-affirmation that we deserve to be equal among the world's great nations, that we deserve to prosper, determine the quality of our lives based on our own resourcefulness and to live in peace, freedom and liberty. If you believe in a God, then you may know too, that we are also God's children. Know that we are prefect in God's eyes, and know that we are just as he made us. Celebrate this!

Let us first settle the point of staying where we are. Can we hope for better days, can we maintain our self-possession patiently, can we wait in pious resignation until the princes and peoples of this earth are more mercifully disposed towards us? I say that we cannot hope for a change in the current feeling. And why not? As a people, we have endured thousands of years to get to where we are. How many more generations of our brothers and sisters and of our children and grand children will be denied the promise of a full life afforded to virtually every other category of people? Even if we were as near to the hearts of princes as are their other subjects, they could not protect us. They would only feed popular hatred by showing us too much favor. By "too much," I really mean less than is claimed as a right by every ordinary citizen, or by every race. The nations in whose midst Gays live are all either covertly or openly anti-Gay. The United Nations and good people everywhere would rise up if this degree of human rights abuses were exacted upon the Jews or Christians or racial minorities around the world. As long we remain divided and do not come together as a people, we are too conveniently ignored. It is an unconscious tactic similar to "divide and conquer."

The common people have not, and indeed cannot have, any historic comprehension. They do not know that the sins of the Biblical times are now being visited on progressive nations throughout Europe and North America, as well as every other corner of the globe. We are what our Gay Ghettos made us. We are what our Heterosexual oppressors have made. We excel in particular endeavors and characteristics because societal conditions in part drove us to it. The same process is now being repeated. We must free ourselves from the incessant barrage of negative reinforcement. We must raise several generations of Gay youth who have not had their psyches pulverized for their lack of worth. Then and only then will the demons of a tortured past begin to dissipate.

PREVIOUS ATTEMPTS AT A SOLUTION.

The artificial means heretofore employed to overcome the troubles of Gays have been either too petty – such as attempts to remain in our assorted Ghettos and eke out a life as best we can – or colonize within the same governmental systems that willfully oppressed us when we were members of the public at large – or ill conceived plans to integrate into the general populous where our community was severely diluted to the point of losing our identities to the whims of our Heterosexual masters. So, what is achieved by transporting a few thousand Gays to another country? Either they come to grief at once and consider returning to the lands of their native birth, or they prosper. The danger of past movements has been in their small thinking. Their limited views had limited their potential, all while trying to work under the rule of their oppressors. We must seek our own freedom to fail—to embark on a historic quest where our collective destiny is in our hands. Our success or failure is ours alone. We cannot look to an oppressor to provide the excuses for our misery.

CAUSES OF ANTI-GAYISM OR HOMOPHOBIA.

First, allow me to clarify the use of the term Homophobia. As it is widely and commonly understood, a phobia is a fear of something. Homophobia would imply a fear of Homosexuals. Many consider such a fear is borne out of ignorance. Popular culture in the West has morphed the term Homophobia to also mean dislike or hatred of Homosexuals. In much, if not most of the world, the definition has not yet altered itself to this degree. Hence, the world understands what is meant when we use to prefix "anti-." Therefore, we use the terms anti-Gayites and anti-Gayism. Readers understand these terms. General consensus throughout the world understands precisely what is meant by these terms.

We shall not again touch on those causes which are a result of temperament, prejudice, and narrow views. To put the subject in a historical context, one must recognize prejudice against minorities. In determining our exact numbers, contemporary researchers have put our population numbers as statistically between as low as 3% of the population to as high as 10% of the population. (These statistics discount views that say those less than fully identified as Heterosexual account for upwards of 20% of a population.) Even if the average is taken, Gays are outnumbered on an average of 95 Heterosexuals for every 5 of us. Of the five of us, several are afraid of losing their families and suppress their Gayness so they are not found out. Others, from terror and fear for their lives, live as impostors and pass themselves of as Heterosexuals, being married to opposite sex people, having children, and in doing so, perform a grave injustice to themselves and the other lives entangled in a web of lies. In the end, a smaller percentage of Gays are willing to risk themselves and their relations with family to be honest about the person they were born to be. As such a small minority, these Homosexuals were and continue to be easy scapegoats.

In Biblical references, our standing was not helped by those who viewed us as a problem. Their accusations and rhetoric painted a condemnation that has only grown among the so-called pious over the last two thousand years. Religious conservatives have promoted our oppression for so long it is often not even recognized as such. Many believe it is a deserved outcome for our human defect. This is the bill of goods sold, and some Homosexuals are indoctrinated into this homophobic way of thinking. Homosexuals of a certain faith sometimes try to find a place for themselves at the table of their local church, synagogue, or mosque. The more liberal houses of worship may continue to marginalize their Gay members as well as their participation, but to their credit, make the effort to extend the fellowship of hospitality to all within their house of worship. They may allow their tithe-offering Gay parishioners the feeling that they "belong," while in reality, the Church hierarchy accepts their contributions, but marginalizes their participation under the motto of "Hate the Sin, but Love the Sinner." Those houses of worship that do not offer this liberal sensibility may in its most generous forms, see the Homosexual as one damned to Hell and view him as a pathetic figure to be pitied for his or her malady.

How many of us would see the favor of being this lone and disparate character? It is another strong influence that takes its toll upon those of us who are called to a higher power and in seeking divine providence come to the realization that others in the larger community see us as "less than." In more extreme denominations, there are movements to "fix" the Homosexual, that is, to undergo psychological retraining to rid yourself of these desires. Time and time again, in well publicized cases, this form of therapy does not work in the medium or long term—that something innate within our soul, will once again, find its way to the surface. All of these messages from religious institutions result in significant degrees of self-loathing among Gay men and womyn. Repeated negative reinforcements are eventually believed by those who are repeatedly subjected to the vitriol.

The passage of time may have further cemented our standing in most nations around the world. The civilized nations of the world have begun to acknowledge us, but they have largely not even begun to awake to the inhumanity and discriminatory practices we as a people have endured all around the world since time immemorial. History is forgotten and overlooked, and the extent to which we have lived a great portion of our lives as disenfranchised people is often not considered. It was no longer possible to remove our disabilities in our old homes, our given lands of birth. For we had, curiously enough, developed while in our Gay Ghettos and neighborhoods into a bourgeois people, and we stepped out of it only to enter into the fierce competition with the middle classes. Hence, in the more progressive societies, our emancipation set us suddenly within this middle-class circle, where we have a double pressure to sustain, from within and from without.

The Heterosexual business class generally tolerates us along with our considerable skills and talents and allows for our efforts to benefit us as long as we and our skills first and foremost benefit the Heterosexual world. Many upper class Gays have moved away from traditionally Gay neighborhoods and into dominantly Heterosexual neighborhoods. In some of the world's more progressive communities, an effort for complete immersion was begun by Homosexuals of a certain class. There was a time in this historic cycle when it was fashionable to have a Gay in the neighborhood. Heterosexuals wore their tolerance of us as if it were a fashion accessory. Small pockets around the world acted as if Gay were the "new cool." And then the pendulum swung. Laws were passed in the United States to cement our second class status. Laws that protected Gays living in a straight world began to be repealed.

Gay people were being evicted from their homes by their landlords. In thirty of the fifty United States, Gays were afforded no protection to either housing or employment. Employers could freely and willfully fire their Gay employees.

Yet on the flip side, in some American cities, for the first time, Gay Americans were allowed to marry. Then the uproar from the "moral majority" was so deafening, that within a very short time, laws were passed ruling a Homosexual marriage as invalid. In fact, as of this writing, there is no Gay couple in America that is receiving full and equal Social Security, Federal, and taxation benefits. If Gays wanted to get married and be equal to their non-Gay fellow countrymen, the government would force one of the two people to undergo a sexual reassignment surgery. Only after this operation was successful would two people be allowed to marry and have that marriage recognized by the federal government. Their physical anatomy must comply with historic standards. This apparently satisfies the outcries from the non-Gay populace. Yet in religious houses of worship, the couple would continue to be discriminated against, cast as deviants and nonconformists. As of this writing, there are several states within the United States that allow for Homosexuals to have a marriage "ceremony." This does not afford Homosexual couples the same rights as Heterosexual married couples, however. There are in fact, over one thousand rights that straight married couples have that gay married couples do not. Ongoing litigation in the courts continues to remove even this token marriage ceremony. California, one of the most liberal states in the US, has repealed the right for Gays to marry. Another state, Maine being the most recent, has followed suit and repealed laws that afforded Gays any semblance of equality and protection.

Hence, our march to equality since the dawn of man finds itself with a very long way to go. As long as we, as a people, allow our freedoms to remain in the hands of our historic and oppressive majority, we will not be free, equal, or hold the keys of liberty. We must be content with the crumbs of liberty that are left for us on the table.

EFFECTS OF ANTI-GAYISM

The oppression we endure does not improve us, for we are not a wit better than ordinary people. It is true that many of us do not love our enemies, but he alone who can conquer himself dare reproach us with that fault. Oppression naturally creates hostility against oppressors, and our hostility aggravates the pressure. It is impossible to escape from this eternal circle.

"No!" some soft-hearted visionaries will say: "It is possible! Possible by means of the ultimate perfection of humanity."

Is it necessary to point to the sentimental folly of this view? Anyone who would found their hope for improved conditions on the ultimate perfection of humanity would indeed be relying upon a utopia. I referred previously to our "assimilation." I do not for a moment wish to imply that I desire such an end, and I must report that I now see assimilation more of a detriment to our overall movement. Our national character as Gay people is too unique and rare that, in spite of every degradation, is too fine to make its annihilation desirable. We might perhaps be able to merge ourselves entirely into surrounding people, outside of our Gay ghettos and into more distant communities, if these were to leave us in peace for a period of two generations. But they will not leave us in peace. For a little period they manage to tolerate us, and then their hostility breaks out again and again. The world is provoked by our prosperity and creativity because it has for many centuries considered us to be an easy target and, as a group, less than them. Thus, whether we like it or not, we are now and shall henceforth remain, a historic group with unmistakable characteristics common to us.

I do not desire to inflame liberal indignation to support our cause. This is reality for us and not extreme rhetoric. These conditions afflict all Gay people to some degree. But to the extent that Heterosexual majorities have affected our Gay community, so much of it has been through the psychological tools of ridicule, shunning, and intimidation. Sarah Schulman is one of the world's leading voices in the field of familial homophobia and with profound clarity and insight, details the devastating impact this brutality exacts on our Gay brothers and sisters. To be treated as a pariah, as a deviant or as pure evil by ones own family causes a psychological wound and inflicts untold pain on the human soul, unlike any of the other abuses endured by Gays.

Males lacking in sufficient degrees of masculinity are ridiculed and teased even as children, which often draws children more inwards. Calling boys "girls" often damages their already fragile self esteem and only encourages many to be as their oppressors see them. Bullying young children and adolescents is a form of hate speech and intimidation, and thus begins the cycle of a lifetime of a damaged self-worth. In every major city on earth that holds Gay Pride Parades, the media shows up to televise the event. Of course the cameras focus on the flamboyance of the affair. Outrageous costumes and men cross-dressing in various and wild stages of undress make for great television. Half naked men marching in their leather hot pants and boots only encourage the Heterosexuals who view the proceedings to think "there they go again!" "They're wicked! And decadent!" And the cycle perpetuates itself. The style in which some Homosexuals dress is akin to a uniform of sorts. This clone-like use of apparel or hair styles can act as a self-identifier. Historically, it allowed Gay men and womyn to find one another in very repressed societies. One would wonder if they weren't oppressed or acting out from years of subtle abuse and if their personal affectations would be as plain or mundane as the Heterosexual community in the absence of said abuse.

We are one people – our enemies have made us without our consent, as repeatedly happens in history. Distress binds us together in spirit, yet so apart is our distance and so fragmented politically and linguistically we have not unified as one. Still we have our voice, and our strength is gathering. Yes, we are strong enough to form a State and indeed, a model State. We possess all human and material resources for the purpose.

This is, therefore, the appropriate place to give an account of what has been somewhat roughly termed out "human material" or "human capital," the values derived from our work. But it would not be appreciated until the broad lines of the plan, on which everything depends, have first been marked out.

THE PLAN

The whole plan is in its essence perfectly simple, as it must necessarily be if it is to come within the comprehension of all. And very simply, the plan is this: let sovereignty be granted us over a portion of the globe large enough to satisfy the rightful requirements of a nation; the rest we shall manage for ourselves.

The creation of a new State is neither ridiculous nor impossible. We have in our day witnessed the process in nations that were not members of the middle class, but poorer, less educated, and consequently weaker than ourselves. The governments of all countries "scourged" by Gayism and the occurring anti-Gayism will be keenly interested in assisting us to obtain the sovereignty we want.

The plan, simple in design, but complicated in execution, will be carried out by two agencies: The Society of Gays and the Homotannia Land Company. The Society of Gays will do the preparatory work in the domains of our Four Arts - science, industry, humanity, and nature—which the Homotannia Land company will apply practically, as well as organize commerce and trade in the new country.

We must not imagine the departure of the Gays to be a sudden one. It will be gradual, continuous, and will cover a number of decades. All citizens of the global Gay community that relocate will be known as members, and all members must apply to relocate. Among the first to relocate will be those who will be destined in history as the Patriots of Homotannia. Whether they are the poorest, the richest, or most desperate among us, they will arrive first and do much of the back-breaking construction that goes along with building a new nation from nothing. They will cultivate the soil, secure our borders, and through fortitude, enable the land to be environmentally and ecologically as ready to create a nation as possible. In accordance with a preconceived plan, they will construct roads, bridges, sidewalks, a medical clinic, airstrip, harbor, new government buildings, and build their own dwellings. Their labor will create trade, trade will create markets, and markets will attract new settlers, for every man and womyn will go voluntarily, at his own expense and his own risk. The labor expended on the land will enhance its value, and the Gays will soon perceive that a new and permanent sphere of operation is opening here for that spirit of enterprise which has heretofore met only with hatred, disdain, and antagonism.

If we wish to found a State today, we shall not do it in the way which would have been the only possible way a thousand years ago. It is foolish to revert to old stages of civilization, as many occupiers and colonists have done in recent decades. We will be among only a handful of nations that will purchase their land. It will be a commercial transaction with both buying nation and selling nation each agreeing to the terms. There shall be no force, no bloodshed, no thievery, and no taking what we are not entitled to. Our operations will be from a position of honor and righteousness, and from it we will build a nation based on humanistic ideals. Our culture will embrace an ideal that is more stately and bolder than ever adopted before, for now we possess means, money, and materials which men never before possessed.

The emigrants standing lowest in the economic scale will be slowly followed by those of a higher grade. Those who at this moment are living in despair will go first. All will go of their own free will and of their own accord. There will come a point not too far into the establishment that all new members will be required to offer an entry fee or to work off the value of the fee through the ongoing construction needs. In time, every new member will pay an entry fee of some modest monetary sum. This will, in part, offset the considerable expenses of establishing a cohesive society. For the first two years, this as yet unnamed new Gay state will, for all intent and purpose, resemble one of the largest construction sites of our time, under the direction of the Society of Gays and the management of the Homotannia Land Company. Upon arrival, all new members will receive free housing, free meals, recreation, health care, English language training, job and career training, seminars on how the new nation is being constructed, and opportunities to participate. They should willingly and enthusiastically desire to participate in such a manner. After a brief period on our Arrivals Campus, they are free to pursue their own and individual interests apart from the needs of the State. Those who wish to contribute as Patriots toward the development of the country are exempt from any such fees. Those who choose not to work in this manner are free to decline and pay this entry fee instead.

Whether someone chooses to relocate in the initial stages or not is up to the individual and the application process. However, everyone who may at some point desire to relocate at some distant time in the future should take the opportunity and have their names added to our pending membership roster list sooner rather than later, as there could come a time when we will not be able to take all who wish to join us. With 6 billion people on earth, one could argue that we would become a nation of upwards of 600,000,000 people. That is more people than in all of Europe and approximately double the population of the United States. Our real life expectations are on a different scale entirely, and we see only hundreds, then thousands, seeking initial citizenship. Land management will obviously determine eventual maximum potential. The new state will not resemble a refugee camp, but initially will be managed, with military precision and corporate objectives, so that a modern and prosperous homeland can be readied.

This pamphlet will open a general discussion on the Gay Question, but that does not mean that there will be any voting on it. Such a result would ruin the cause from the outset, and dissidents must remember that allegiance or opposition is entirely voluntary. Anyone who will not willfully follow us, particularly during the settlement period, should remain behind.

Let all who are willing to join us, fall in behind our banner, and fight for our cause with voice and hand and pen and deed.

Those Gays who agree with our idea of a State will attach themselves to the Society, which will thereby be authorized to confer and treaty with Governments in the name of our people. The Society will thus be acknowledged in its relation with Governments as a State-creating power. This acknowledgment will practically create the State.

Should the Powers declare themselves willing to admit our sovereignty over a neutral piece of land, then the Society will enter into negotiations for the possession of this land. Here two territories and three options come under consideration:

A Caribbean archipelago, land currently within Brazil, or a third option…

In both settlement choices, important experiments in colonization have been made, though in our case there was the mistaken principle of a gradual infiltration of Gays. An infiltration is bound to end badly. It continues until the inevitable moment when the native population feels itself threatened and forces the government to stop a further influx of Gays. This lack of autonomy leaves us in the same dire circumstances which we have found ourselves all along—no clear form of independence. Immigration is consequently futile unless we have the sovereign right to continue such immigration. We are to be a free and independent people and afforded the same international rights to cooperate and self-determine.

The Society of Gays will negotiate with the present masters of the land, putting itself under the protectorate of the United Nations, if it proves friendly to the plan, or some other agreeable protectorate and defense agreement. We could offer the present possessors of the land enormous advantages. Massive injections of monetary payments are used to acquire the land. In addition, the Gay State could assume part of the public debt, build new roads for traffic, which our presence in the country would render necessary, and do many other things. The building of our State would be akin to one of the world's largest construction projects, and this commerce would undoubtedly spill over into surrounding economies. Thousands of jobs will be created to supply what our Gay State will need in terms of establishing an infrastructure. Major infrastructure projects which could last for decades will open new markets to regional industries and companies. The creation of our State would be beneficial to adjacent countries as would the upgrade in infrastructure with 21st Century techniques, and our commitment to Green technology would inevitably improve their sphere of influence. Our global tribe of Gays consists of notorious vacationers and travelers. Our demographic is among the highest income producers in the world and has one of the highest amounts of disposable income on the planet. Therefore, neighboring countries would benefit from an eager and amiable group of high income travelers seeking new vacation destinations. Neighboring countries could see their tourism revenue spike and remain high for years to come as our Gay brothers and sisters from every corner of the Earth come to visit our and their new "homeland."

CARIBBEAN OR BRAZIL?

Shall we choose the Caribbean or Brazil? Or should we consider a third way? We shall take what is given us, considering what we can afford and what is selected by Gay public opinion. The Society will determine these fine points.

Brazil is one of the most fertile countries in the world, extends over a vast area, and has sparse population and a mild climate. The Brazilian Republic would derive considerable profit from the cession of a relatively small portion of its territory to us. The present relations of openly Gay individuals have certainly produced some discontent in predominantly Christian countries, such as those in South America, and it would be necessary to enlighten the Republic on the intrinsic differences of our new movement. Yet Brazil stands out among most nations in that it is enlightened. Its society recognizes the positive role that the Gay community offers. Rio de Janeiro and Sao Paulo are two cities that have benefited in substantial ways from their internal and domestic Gay communities. Our location in what is now the rural and uninhabited northern quadrant of Brazil would prove to be mutually beneficial for both countries.

The Caribbean is a popular vacation destination, and as such it ranks high on our list of desirable Gay locations. The very name of the region would attract our people with a force of marvelous potency. If an island or archipelago or piece of territory can be obtained from the numerous uninhabited islands which are estimated to be in the hundreds, from one of the nations or territorial protectorates, we could establish a base from which we could provide a fantastic monetary benefit to neighboring Caribbean nations. Of course all of the monetary payments our Gay State makes for the land, whether initial payments or those over the coming decades, are only one portion of the equation. Our tourism-based economy will bring in a successive wave of high income visitors that are loyal to our niche— visitors who arguably would not normally be spending their vacation dollars in any Caribbean country without the close proximity of the Gay State.

A THIRD OPTION…

We remain open to a viable third option. Countries with lower standards of living could be greatly enhanced by parceling a portion of territory for what might be defined as a handsome sum. Nations with lower GDP's would see immediate benefits to welcoming a prosperous and peace loving society as a neighbor. The benefits are immediate, intermediate, as well as long term and could vastly improve the lot for some existing nations who prior to acquiescing a portion of land in a sale to the Gay State, had few prospects for improving the livelihoods of its citizens. In all cases we endeavor to find agreeable terms so that both buyer and seller nations are winners and are satisfied by the outcome.

WITH REGARD TO SIZE:

In terms of the land mass required to launch the new Gay State, bigger is not necessarily better. The land mass must be sufficiently large enough to assure us of our sovereignty. Using New York City as a benchmark; the birthplace of the modern Gay rights struggle and as a city that has welcomed probably more foreign immigrants that any other city on the planet, consider the number of countries on earth that are no larger than this one American city. Two nations are actually *smaller than Central Park* (the Vatican and Monaco.) Seven countries are *smaller than the island of Manhattan*. And *51 nations* are no larger than the city of New York. Add to this mix, the modern techniques of urban land planning, our use of "Green" technology and the strategies of efficient land use and the new Gay State can begin with considerable advantages.

We should endeavor to remain a neutral State and as an international educational center, and, bearing in mind that our citizenry come from every nation on earth, we would remain in solidarity with all free and peaceful nations which would have to guarantee our existence. We will work diligently to improve the dialogue among all peoples of the Earth. Now in our 21st century of documented mistreatment at the hands of Heterosexual governments from around the globe, we extend an olive branch to all. Our nation will be a secular one that honors all people, all faiths as we recognize their colorful histories. We will of course be a nation offering freedom, peace, and liberty to Gays, Lesbians, Bisexuals, and Transgender people. But we will also offer a home to non-Gays who wish to join us in this historic experiment and, of course, secure for them also equality, peace, freedom, and liberty. Continuing to fight the grievances of the past serves no useful purpose. We will seek freedom and peace for the mutual advancement of our peoples.

DEMAND, MEDIUM, TRADE.

I said in the last chapter, "The Homotannia Land Company will organize trade and commerce in the new country." Let me make a few remarks on that point.

A plan such as mine is at great risk if it is opposed by "practical" people. Now "practical" people are as a rule nothing more than men sunk into the groove of daily routine, unable to emerge from a narrow circle of antiquated ideas. Consider for a moment the state of the world, see the wars, the starvation, and the poverty, even the lack of suitable drinking water around the world, and see where the "practical" people have taken us! At the same time, their adverse opinion carries great weight and can do considerable misdeeds to a new project at any rate until the new thing is sufficiently strong to throw off the "practical" people and their moldy notions to the winds.

In the earliest period of automobile industry, some "practical" people were of the opinion that it was a passing fad, and as fanciful as it was, they did not see the need to build superhighways connecting our cities. "Superhighways through remote farmlands? Preposterous!," they said. They did not realize the unavoidable truth which now seems obvious to us – that travelers do not produce the highways, but conversely, the highways produced the automobiles; the latent demand, of course, created a market, and the highways fueled the industries that revolutionized global economies and created a solid middle class in nations throughout North America, Europe, and eventually, to every continent on Earth. Now may be the time to rid the world of the combustion engine, but for decades of advancement, it did serve a purpose.

The impossibility of comprehending how trade and commerce are to be created in a new country, which has yet to be acquired and cultivated, may be classed with those doubters and "practical" persons concerning the need for highways. A "practical" person would express himself in this fashion:

"Granted that the present situation of the Gays is in many places undesirable and discriminatory and aggravated day by day; granted that there are a great many nations that would like to see the Gays reduced in number within their borders; granted that there exists a desire to emigrate; granted even that they emigrate to the new country—how will they earn their living there, and what will they earn? What are they to live on when there? The business of many people cannot be artificially organized in a day."

To this I should reply: We have not the slightest intention of organizing trade artificially, and we should certainly not attempt to do it in a day. But, though the organization of it may be monumental, the promotion of it is not. And how is commerce to be encouraged? Through the medium of demand. The demand for a Gay State is recognized, the medium created, it will establish itself.

If there is a real earnest demand among the global Gay community for an improvement in their status; if the medium to be created – the Homotannia Land Company – is sufficiently powerful, then commerce will extend itself freely in the new country.

"I have nothing to offer but blood, toil, tears and sweat."
~ Winston Churchill

Chapter Three.
The Homotannia Land Company.

The Gay Company is partly modeled on the lines of a great land-acquisition company. Inspired by the exploratory nature of the Dutch West Indies Company, the Homotannia Land Company shall perform other than purely colonial tasks. The overseers to the Land Company will be the Society of Gays, which will provide the wisdom and moral compass for the development of a nation and will be comprised of peoples from around the world.

The Gay Company will be founded as a joint stock company, subject to American jurisdiction, framed according to American laws, and under the protection of the United States. Its original principal center will be Washington, D.C., with an Operations Base in New York. I cannot tell you how large the Company's capital should be; I shall leave that calculation to our numerous financiers and economists. But to avoid ambiguity, I shall put it at $5.0 billion US; it may be either more or less than that sum. The form of subscription, which will be further clarified, will determine what fraction of the whole amount must be paid at once.

The Homotannia Land Company is an organization with a transitional character. It is strictly a business undertaking and must be carefully distinguished from the Society of Gays.

The Gay Company will first of all convert into cash all necessary funds held in the National Gay Development Fund, as well as the National Gay Trust. The method adopted will prevent the occurrences of crises, secure every man's property, and facilitate any inner migration or emigration from homesteading Heterosexuals which has already been indicated.

PURCHASE OF LAND.

The land which the Society of Gays will have secured by international law must, of course, be privately acquired. Provisions made by individuals for their own settlement do not come within the province of this general account. But the Company will require large areas for it own needs and ours, and these it must secure by centralized purchase. It will negotiate principally for the acquisition of fiscal domains, with the great object of taking possession of this land "over there," without paying a price too high. A forcing of prices is not to be considered, because the value of the land will be created by the Company through its organizing the settlement in conjunction with the supervision provided by the Society of Gays. The latter will see to it that the enterprise does not become a banana republic, but a newly developing nation.

The Company will sell building sites at reasonable rates to its officials and allow them to mortgage these for the building of their homes, deducting the amount due from their salaries, or putting it down to their account as increased recompense. This will, in addition to the honors they expect, be additional pay for their services.

All the immense profits of this speculation in land will go to the Company, which is bound to receive this indefinite premium in return for having borne the risk of the undertaking. When the undertaking involves such risk, the profits must be freely given to those who have borne it. But under no other circumstances will profits be permitted. Financial morality consists in the correlation of risk and profit. There will be more than sufficient security, as well as financial observers to maintain strict monetary policies.

BUILDINGS.

The Company will thus barter houses and estates. It must be plain to any one who has observed the rise in the value of land through its cultivation that the Company will be bound to gain on its landed property. This can best be seen in the case of enclosed pieces of land in town and country. Areas that are not built up increase in value through surrounding cultivation. The men who carried out the extension of Paris made a successful speculation in land which was ingenious in its simplicity; instead of erecting new buildings in the immediate vicinity of the last houses of the town, they bought up adjacent pieces of land, and began to build on the outskirts of these. This inverse order of construction raised the value of building sites with extraordinary rapidity, and after having completed the outer ring, they built in the middle of the town on these highly valuable sites, instead of continually erecting houses on the extremity. The latter was the technique typically used in the sub-urbanizing of America, persistently building out and stretching into vast distances.

Will the Company do its own building or employ independent architects? It can and will do both. It has as will be shown shortly, an immense reserve of working human labor power, which will not be sweated by the Company, but transported into brighter and happier conditions of life, will nevertheless not be expensive. Our geologists will have looked to the provision of building materials when they selected the site to the towns. What is to be the principle of construction? Initially, materials that are indigenous to the region—presumably wood and lumber, until iron and stone are readily available.

WORKMEN'S DWELLINGS.

The workmen's dwellings (which include the dwellings of all operatives) will be erected at the Company's own risk and expense. They will resemble neither the melancholy workmen's barracks of 1900's industrial towns, nor those miserable rows of shanties which surround factories; they will certainly present a uniform appearance, because the Company must build cheaply where it provides the building materials to a great extent, but the detached cottages and bungalows with little gardens will be united into attractive groups in each locality. A timeless style of architecture will be used so that this residential district will have the same inviting appeal in thirty years that it would have today, and certainly not be diminished by current architectural fads. For initial Patriots who come to build the land, these cottages may well be the finest accommodations they have ever known.

The natural formation of the land will rouse the ingenuity of our young architects, whose ideas have not yet been cramped by routine; and even if people do not grasp the whole import of the plan, they will at any rate feel at ease in their loose clusters. The National Center, which is a building that will house The Dining Hall and a multitude of amenities for the Patriots, will be seen from a distance and a point of reference for all workers, whether in distant fields or in the heart of what will become the first city center. This complex will include a dining hall, medical clinic, salons for conversation and lounging, satellite television rooms, recreation rooms, and a physical fitness center. There will be light, attractive classrooms for language training, cultural immersion classes, and career training. The Continuing Educations schools will teach some of the Patriot's trades and skills that will serve them throughout their lives in Homotannia and set them up for prosperity and success in their personal and professional lives.

The Workmen's dwelling and the National Center will all be built with an eye on the future. As our population grows and our nation branches out, these original buildings will become the New Arrivals Processing Campus (NAPC.) To establish an order and to maintain security, new arrivals will receive a thorough medical examination and undergo appropriate briefings so that all members are involved, aware, and enthusiastic of our future goals. The understanding is that building a new nation is no small thing, and the responsibilities and obligations in doing so are great and require that we all work toward the same goals.

Drunkards, drug addicts, criminals, and those whose intentions are not conducive to the group will be dealt with. This processing can perhaps be thought of as a "boot camp" of sorts. Certainly it is more boot camp than country club. These newly arrived Patriots have come to work and to build a future, and we want to give them the security of knowing we have a well thought-out plan. Such would be a rationale that any large corporation would employ in constructing any remote and massive development. After a suitable period of time, these Patriots will relocate into more permanent housing for the remainder of their service to the country. They will be followed by other incoming members for their initiation and processing. And so on and so on.

We are, however, speaking merely of the buildings at present and not of what may take place inside them.

I said that the Company would build workmen's dwellings cheaply. The fixed costs would be comparatively low, not only because of the proximity of abundant building materials, not only because of the Company's proprietorship of the sites, but also because of the non-payment of workmen.

American farmers, and members of the Amish community, have worked on the system of mutual assistance in the construction of houses and barns for centuries. It may sound as if a childishly amicable system, but it still is employed in the 21st century. While an admittedly somewhat clumsy process, the model achieves all families having a home of their own, the farmhouses are erected, and all of this model can be curtailed along on much finer lines.

UNSKILLED LABORERS

Our unskilled laborers will come from all corners of the globe and from every continent. This original collection of Patriots will be housed in tents while they construct their dwellings. They will be obliged to build with wood in the beginning, because metal, steel, concrete, and stone may be in short supply.

Compensation for terms of service will depend on the length of term a Patriot devotes to the State. Think of it in terms of signing an employment contract for a predetermined period of time or joining the Armed Forces for an initial two, three, or four-year period. If a Patriot joins us with a one year commitment and completes the term satisfactorily, he will be allowed to remain in the State free of any entry fee. A Patriot who completes such a two-year term will be exempt from the entry fee, as well as receive exemption from annual payments for the next ten years. Should someone stay for three years, the State will provide them with an internationally accredited college education upon completion of their term. For five years of service, a single individual will receive a small apartment with no mortgage, in essence a free home for life, in exchange for his five years of service. If someone devotes ten years to the service of the State, a pension will be provided at the age of retirement. Lastly, for someone who stays twenty years and more, the rewards are a full pension and other benefits.

Like a military college or a fine private boarding school, certain conduct is expected of all members. Life will be structured and will instill in all Patriots a sense of pride in one's accomplishments, a belief in diligently working to achieve a common good, and to learn skills that will enhance the rest of their lives. In this way we shall secure energetic and able men, and these men will be practically trained for life by their agreed upon years of service and under good discipline. I said before that the Company would not have to pay these unskilled laborers. But what will they live on?

On the whole, I am opposed to the barter-type system (where workers are forced to buy any personal provision from a "company store,") that is exorbitantly priced to benefit the company. Such was the commerce used in miserable working conditions around the coalmines of West Virginia, northern England, and throughout the developing world. But such a modified system will need to be applied in the case of these first settlers. The Company provides for them in so many ways that it may take charge of their maintenance. In any case, the company store system will be enforced only during the first year or so and will benefit the workmen by preventing their being exploited by small traders, landlords, etc., that will begin to appear in this free society.

During their service to the State, the workers will receive a number of benefits at no cost to themselves. They will receive free housing, free meals in the National Dining Hall, free recreation, free health care, free language training, and free vocational and technical skills. They will receive a stipend or chits based on their work which they can use to exchange for goods, sundries, and the like within the Company stores.

By the end of Year One, or sometime during Year Two, our first retail center should be ready for occupancy. Independent retailers and entrepreneurs will operate their establishments within these leased spaces, providing their goods and services to the general public. This will be the initial stages of free commerce and capitalism within the new Gay State.

THE EIGHT HOUR DAY.

There was a time in human history when individuals worked slavish hours to eke out a living. By the mid to later 20th century, industrial nations instituted the concept of an eight hour work day. Now in the early part of the new millennium, economic pressures have eaten away at this labor principle in many places. Now in many of these same industrialized countries, people often work more than 55 to 65 hours a week with no additional pay compensation. And in many other nations around the world, long days and long weeks have always been the norm.

The Gay State is based on humanistic ideals and equality for all. We believe an eight hour day is reasonable given the amount of tough, difficult, back-breaking work that will be performed. Each man is expected to give his all, as if he were in battle. Wood-cutting, stone breaking, digging ditches, and construction of sewage systems are only the beginning of the hard physical labor. So rest will be essential in order to maintain in the long haul.

Laborers will have their working day split into two shifts. Instead of working eight hours straight through, they will work the first four hours, followed by a four hour break. During the break they can have their meal and take a rest, attend to personal matters, and catch up on their studies. They will return to their assignment for another four hour shift, at which time they will relieve another crew of workers who will go on their break. After the two four-hour shifts have been completed, the laborer will break for a meal and attend language training. This will be followed by a period of vocational and technical training and studies. In all, an average of four-plus hours per day should be devoted to studies and personal improvement. This system should ensure all laborers a solid seven to eight hours of sleep per day. Through this schedule, a sound man can do a great deal of concentrated work and achieve more and better results. In addition, all men will receive one to one and a half days of no labor within a seven day period, to rest, recreate, and pursue personal interests, whether utilizing the library, watching television, or enjoying a sporting event with the other men or womyn. It is their free time to enjoy as they wish.

The organization of all this will be military in character; there will be commands, promotions, and pensions, and the means of providing these pensions will be discussed below. The Society of Gays and the Homotannia Land Company will uphold the virtues of equality and liberty, and through concentrated work, the newest citizen among us will achieve a lifestyle many only dreamed of.

The eight hour day will be the call to summon our people in every part of the world. All must come voluntarily, for our nation must indeed be the Promised Land for the global Gay community. Drunkards and laggards will be dealt with as we all must carry our weight.

Whoever works longer than the eight hours will receive their additional pay in overtime in cash. Seeing that all their needs are supplied, and that those members of their families who are unable to work are provided for by transplanted and centralized philanthropic institutions, they can save a little money. We want to encourage the native drive to work and prosper and get ahead because it will, in the first place, facilitate the rise of individuals to higher grades; and secondly, the money saved will provide an immense reserve fund for future loans. Overtime will only be permitted on a doctor's certificate and must not exceed three hours per day or twelve additional hours per week maximum. For our men will eagerly work in the new country, we will be lining up to receive their entrance, and the world will see then what an industrious people we are.

PARTNERS AND DEPENDENTS.

In the initial stages there will be only adult men and womyn. The quarters will be in the style of military barracks and not suitable for family arrangements in the initial stages. In time, partners will be encouraged to join as well as dependents, whether they be aged parents or their dependent children. We shall educate the children as we wish from the commencement, but I will not go into this now.

My remarks on Workmen's dwellings and on unskilled labors and their mode of life are no more utopian than the rest of my plan. Everything I have spoken of is already being put into practice all around the world, though often on an utterly small scale carried out by private business enterprises.

RELIEF AID BY LABOR

In a free society, citizens are allowed to fail. We will enact safety measures to prevent any Patriot from being tossed onto the heap of human failure. This principle is to furnish every needy man with simple, unskilled work such as chopping wood, washing laundry, preparing meals, and doing assorted manual labor tasks. These are necessary tasks that will need to be done. This is a kind of reverse, "prison-work before the crime" scheme, done without loss of character. It is meant to prevent men from taking to crime out of want, by providing them with work and testing their willingness to do it. Starvation must never be allowed in a humane society. A home and a degree of comfort should be available to every man. Their despair in some countries drives men to suicide, for such suicides are the deepest disgrace to a civilization which allows "rich men to throw table scraps to their dogs."

Relief by Labor provides everyone with work. In the early stages, all new and arriving Patriots are a part of the Homotannia Land Company. There will be some, as human nature requires, who are unable to meet the minimum standards of working together, enjoying harmony and seeing assignments through to completion. These are men and womyn who travelled great distances to be a part of a historic enterprise, but now find that they are not cut from the suitable cloth to advance. These people who reject the invitation to participate may elect to depart of their own free will. Or they can stay if they choose. In these early stages, we cannot afford the luxury of putting an able bodied person on the dole, to stand idly by while the rest carry his burden. So the government, which would normally provide a stipend to the unemployed, now gets something in return. And the unemployed is not forced to beg for table scraps, and by virtue of his work, will earn fifteen times more than were he to stand on street corners begging for handouts, all the while forsaking ones dignity.

There is a moral side to the relief by labor concept. The Society of Gays has adopted its own Eleven Corporal Works of Mercy which were established at the Congress of Fire Island in 2009. They were assembled by the founding fathers and mothers of Homotannia and include the following: 1. feed the hungry, 2. give drink to the thirsty, 3. give shelter to those in need, 4. visit the sick, 5. show good grace and humanism to the downtrodden, 6. honor the dead, 7. leave our world cleaner than we found it, 8. humility to those less fortunate, 9. offer a kindness to others, 10. pay someone a compliment, and 11. teach a man to fish.

While such benevolence conflicts with private industry in established nations, there is room for such a plan in a new society. We know that Man has free will. Some men function contrary to their best intensions. More still function in a way that damages their better interests. For such men who commit an action that renders them unsuitable to continue their work as Patriots, they are free to leave the country, or they may be able to stay and participate for a period of time in our Relief by Labor plan.

For, above all, we require enormous numbers of unskilled laborers to do the first rough work of settlement, to lay down roads, plant trees, level the ground, build the public utilities and necessary infrastructure to enable international commerce. All this will be carried out in accordance with a large and previously agreed plan.

COMMERCE.

The labor carried out in the new country will naturally create trade. The first markets will supply only the absolute necessities of life—cattle, grain, working clothes, tools, arms – to mention just a few things. These we shall be obliged at first to procure from neighboring states or from those nations who we have entered into protectorate status with. But we shall make ourselves independent as soon as possible. The Gay entrepreneurs will soon realize the rewarding business prospects that the new country offers.

The army of the Company's officials will gradually introduce more refined requirements of life. (Officials include officers of our defensive forces, who will always number about twelve percent of our colonists. They will be sufficiently numerous to quell mutinies, for the majority of our colonists will be peaceably inclined.)

The refined requirements of life introduced by our officials in good positions will create a correspondingly improved market, which will continue to better itself. The partnered individual will send for his or her other half and for any children and the single individual for parents as soon as a new home is established "over there." The Irish who immigrated to the United States always proceeded in this fashion. As do the Jews who continue to settle in Israel. As soon as one of them has daily bread and a roof over his head, he sends for his people; this has been the story of America, for family ties and bonds of friendship are strong among us. The Society of Gays and the Homotannia Land Company will unite in caring for and strengthening the family still more, not only morally, but materially as well. The officials will receive additional pay on marriage and on the birth of children, for we need all who are there and all who will follow.

FAMILY DWELLINGS AND OTHER CLASSES OF DWELLINGS.

I described before only workmen's dwellings built by themselves and omitted all mention of other classes of dwellings. Let me briefly touch upon this matter. The Company's architects will build for the poorer classes of citizens also, being paid in kind or in cash; about 100 different types of houses will be erected and, of course, repeated. These beautiful types will form part of our public relations and marketing campaign. The soundness of their construction will be guaranteed by the Company, which will, indeed, gain nothing by selling them to settlers at a fixed sum. And where will these houses be situated? That will be shown in the section dealing with local groups.

Seeing that the Company does not wish to earn anything on the building works, but only on the land, it will desire as many architects as possible to build by private contract. This system will increase the value of landed property, and it will introduce luxury which serves many purposes. Luxury encourages arts and industries, paving the way to a level where affluence begets affluence.

Well-to-do Gays who are now obliged in their old residences to secrete their valuables and to hold their Gay parties behind lowered curtains will be able to enjoy their possessions in peace "over there." Due to such lower building costs, wealthy Gays will be able to live in mansions and luxury beyond what they had in their nations of birth. They will be stared at from all continents on the earth with such envious eyes; it will soon become fashionable to live "over there" in beautiful modern houses. The positive press from every corner of the world will only further increase the demand for one of the asylum and citizenship slots.

SECURITIES OF THE COMPANY

What assurance will the Company offer that the abandonment of the project will not cause Patriots their impoverishment and produce economic crises?

I have already mentioned that honest anti-Gayites will support the emigration of Homosexuals out of their country. They have less concern of what becomes of the Homosexuals as long as they depart from their territory. Of 195 nations and 6 billion people to draw from, there is a numerical certainty that we will achieve our necessary numbers to keep the interest and momentum at maximum hum. However, this is an experiment in our liberation the world has never before witnessed. It is a significant historical event that new members are a part of. They are staking their future and taking a chance. Yes, there is risk, and those that join us the earliest will reap the greatest rewards when we succeed.

We are offering dual passports to all of our members. This is important because there are some nations that require you to choose one over the other; to denounce the old when you join the new. The Homotannia Land Company does not see the necessity in this. Keep the passport from the land of your birth. In a land of freedom, liberty and equality, we want you to be loyal to our efforts, but in the modern world, come and go as you see fit. For most, life will be so pleasurable in the new Gay State, that they would be willing to defend their new home if asked. And in part due to our expected geographic location, millions of our Gay brothers and sisters whose lands of birth are in cold weather climates, they especially will welcome a passport and a home base in our warm weather locale.

If at some point new members decide our new nation is not what they wanted in a country, they at least have the option of departing to whatever life they had prior to joining us.

These are, of course, purely calculable matters. It will have to be considered and decided how far the Company can go without running any risks of failure. And the Company itself will confer freely with Finance ministers on the various points of issue as it conducts its foreign relations and issues with regard to immigration and commerce. Ministers will recognize the friendly spirit of our enterprise and will consequently offer every facility in their power necessary for the successful achievement of the great undertaking.

Further and direct profit will accrue to Governments from the transport of passengers and goods. Where they are held by private companies, the Homotannia Land Company will receive favorable terms for the transport, in the same way as does every transmitter of goods on a large scale. Freight and carriage must be made as cheap as possible for our people, because every traveler will pay his own expenses.

As soon as an airstrip is ready for use in our new nation, Homotannia Land Company will begin operating a charter service, connecting our new land to a major airport hub. This would depend on its ultimate location, but at this stage, let us say that the major hub will be Miami, Florida. New members to the new nation could be thought of as co-owners and as such, receive steep discounts for their travel to and from our hub city. Provisions could be shipped quite inexpensively and initially, tariffs will be suspended for members bringing their personal possessions into their new homeland. Members will be afforded deeply discounted or free air travel to and from Miami in a manner of a weekend furlough to break the monotony and exhaustion of such regimented and vital assignments. This booklet is not the place to touch on the details of such a monster expedition. The plan will be judiciously evolved out of the original plan by many able men, who must apply their minds to achieving the best system.

SOME OF THE COMPANY'S ACTIVITIES.

Many activities will be interconnected. For example, the Company will gradually introduce the manufacture of goods into the settlement which will, of course, be extremely primitive at their inception. Clothing, linen, and shoes will first of all be manufactured for our own emigrants, who will be provided with new suits of clothing at various emigration centers. Design and fashion, perhaps in clothing or furnishings, are obvious gifts of our people and one could presume a fair amount of work could be performed off shore for design houses in the US, Europe, Brazil, and beyond.

Even the manufacturing of the new clothing for our initial workers will have a symbolic meaning. "You are now entering a new life." The Society of Gays will see to it that long before the departure, and also during the journey, a serious yet festive spirit is fostered by means of lectures, cocktail receptions, dinners, Q&A's, and prayers for our new undertaking. On their arrival, the emigrants will be welcomed by our chief officials with due solemnity, but without foolish exultation, for this Promised Land will not yet have been conquered. But these people, many coming from economically stagnant circumstances, not to mention the societal oppression, will be thankful for the fresh start and should already see that they are at home.

The clothing industries of the Company will draw from the deep, rich information base of the Gay community. Several internationally-renowned fashion designers will be called upon as fellow Gaymen to fashion the uniforms for our new country. We will have, I am confident, the finest looking workers and civil servants in the Western Hemisphere. Our military, our law enforcement, immigration and border patrol, as well as sanitation workers and New Arrivals Processing Greeters will appear sharp and professionally attired. It will further the sense of pride our new members will feel for their Gay State.

PROMOTION OF INDUSTRIES.

The duties of the Homotannia Land Company and the Society of Gays cannot be kept strictly apart in this outline. These two great bodies will have to work constantly in unison, the Company depending on the moral authority and support of the Society, just as the Society cannot dispense with the material assistance of the Company. For example, in the organizing of the clothing industry, the quantity produced will at first be kept down so as to preserve equilibrium between supply and demand, and wherever the Company undertakes the organization of new industries, the same precaution must be exercised.

Individual enterprise must never be checked by the Company with its superior force. We shall only work collectively when the immense difficulties of the task demand common action; we shall wherever possible, scrupulously respect the rights of the individual. Private property, which is the economic basis of independence, shall be developed freely and be respected by us. Our first unskilled laborers will at once have the opportunity to work their way up to private proprietorship. And, as more new members join us in our Gay State, an immense class of entrepreneurship will emerge.

The spirit of enterprise must, indeed, be encouraged in every possible way. Organization of industries will be promoted by a judicious system of duties, by the employment of cheap raw material, and by the institution of a board to collect and publish industrial statistics.

In this same spirit of enterprise, it must be wisely encouraged, and risky speculation must be avoided. Every new industry must be advertised before establishment, so as to prevent failure on the part of those who might wish to start a similar business six months later. Whenever a new industrial establishment is founded, the Company should be informed, so that all those interested may obtain information from it. Without hindering free trade and without building the barriers of nationalism, we will promote and patronize the businesses that have invested in our new Gay State. Prior to the first free elections, the

Society and the Homotannia Land Company will respect free trade issues. However, an element of protectionism will seek to secure our fledgling new markets and enterprises during the initial 18-24 month period of our construction phase.

Industrialists will be able to make use of centralized labor agencies. The industrialists might, for example, send an email for 100 unskilled laborers for three days, three weeks or three months. The labor agency would then collect these 100 unskilled laborers from every possible source and dispatch them at once to carry out the agricultural or industrial enterprise. Parties of workmen will thus be systematically drafted from place to place like a body of troops. These men will, of course, not be sweat-shopped, but will work our customary eight hour day, and in spite of their change of locality, they will preserve their organization, work out their term of service, and receive commands, promotions, and pensions. Some establishments may, of course, be able to obtain their workmen from other sources if they wish, but will not find it easy to do so. The Society will work to maintain the harmony between the needs of industry and the rights of the workers.

As the founding fathers have put serious effort into selecting industries which could be concentrated on, there is no shortage of possible options. The likely success is quite positive. As in any industry, it is not beneficial to announce these plans in advance so that one's competitors can get a jump start. Suffice it to say, variables such as the final location of the Gay State will be a determining factor, yet the prospects hold spectacular potential.

SETTLEMENT OF SKILLED LABORERS.

It is clear that what can be done for unskilled workers can be even more easily accomplished for skilled laborers—the artisans and journeymen and licensed trades people. These will work under similar regulations in the factories, and the central labor agency will provide them when required.

Independent operatives and small employers must be carefully taught on account of the varying quality control standards of varying countries from which our workers will arrive from. Independent workers will be provided by the Society's agency. The local operative or department, for example, will notify the central office: "We want so many carpenters, computer programmers, welders, etc." The central office will publish this demand on its web site or on the bulletin boards at the National Center. Workers with the appropriate skills will apply for the work and will be dispatched to the job site.

METHOD OF RAISING CAPITAL.

The capital required for establishing the Company was previously put at what seemed an absurdly high figure. The amount actually necessary will be fixed by financiers and will in any case be a very considerable sum. There are seven ways of raising this sum, all of which the Society will take under consideration. The Society will be formed by our best and most upright men, who must not derive any material advantage from their membership. Although the Society cannot at the outset possess anything but moral authority, this authority will suffice to establish the credit of the Homotannia Land Company in the nation's eyes. This Company will be unable to succeed in its enterprise unless it has received the Society's sanction; it will thus not be formed of any mere indiscriminate group of financiers. The Society will not permit experiments with insufficient means, for this undertaking must succeed at the first attempt. Any initial failure would compromise the whole idea for many decades to come, or might even make its realization severely damaged for generations to come.

The seven methods for raising capital are as follows: 1) Through Non-Governmental Organizations; 2) Through Departing-Nation Grants; 3) Through international subscriptions from global Gays and supporting Heterosexuals; 4) Through international Corporate Sponsors; 5) Through personal memberships; 6) Through big, small and private banks; and 7) Through Grants offered by supporting international nations.

The funds that will be raised will be divided between The National Development Trust and the National Development Fund, which will release monies to the various projects as the work and construction dictates. The Society of Gays will oversee both accounts and release the disbursements as required to the Homotannia Land Company, which will oversee all development.

The great accountants and financiers, moreover, will certainly not be asked to raise an amount so enormous out of pure philanthropic motives; that would be expecting too much. The promoters and stock holders of the Company are, on the contrary, expected to do a good piece of business, and they will be able to calculate beforehand what their chance of success is likely to be. The Society of Gays will be in possession of all documents and references which may serve to define the prospects of the Homotannia Land Company. The Society will in particular have investigated with exactitude the extent of the new Gay movement, so as to provide the Company promoters with thoroughly reliable information on the amount of support they may expect. The Society will also supply the Company with comprehensive modern Gay statistics, thus doing the work of what is typically referred to as "due diligence." Some of our prospects might, perhaps, even try to oppose the Gay independence movement through their secret agents. Such opposition we shall meet with relentless determination.

DEMOCRATIC REPRESENTATION.

In the first two years, the Homotannia Land Company will be a physical and substantially large construction site. It will be operated like a business with a military style organizational chart. During this period there will be a necessary hierarchy of leadership. Unfortunately, in this initial period when the whole world is watching, we must execute ourselves efficiently and with harmony to achieving our collective objectives.

Ruling by committee is not an option in the early stages when the land is in essence a construction site. Leadership and responsibility to the plan is required at this early stage. Those who are not willing to support the process should not come or wait until the initial hard work is done.

In a stage of initial growth that should be reached in approximately two years, we will be open to accepting settlers who will go about living in a democratically elected land and to prosper according to their abilities and drive. The structure of national representation has not yet been fully developed. This will be done by the founding men and womyn of the Society of Gays. At prior Congresses in New York and Fire Island, members have developed a representation chart as to how all citizens of the Gay state can have their voices heard and their desire to participate fulfilled.

Our citizenry is coming to our Promised Land from all corners of the globe. We all will bring with us the societal norms from our nations of birth where we have resided. We will embody the cultures and ceremonies that make us, to some degree, who we are. The Gay state will strive to honor the best of what all citizens bring to our new land. Granted, some of our cherished cultural mores may be embedded within us, and we may harbor, whether knowingly or unknowingly, attitudes that are detrimental to ourselves as a people. Most of our new members will be individuals who have had stressful and negative reinforcement about who they are foisted upon them for most of their lives and may not even be aware of how damaged their self esteem and self image have become. For these many people, our new Gay state will utilize the services of professional therapists and counselors for free counseling sessions during their initial immersion stage. The Gay State will cooperate with all new members to strive to limit the attitudes beholden to self-loathing Gay people from tainting our positive views of living freely in peace and harmony. I will touch on more of this later.

As a people with varied backgrounds, our representation will take into account 1) the country we claim as our nation of birth; 2) the continent we have come from; 3) the sexual classification or familial status with which we most identify; and 4) there will be representation for our citizens based on the geographic area in which they reside in our new Gay State.

International Geographic Representation. In the early stages, we will have a Representative from every major region of the earth. There will be a Minister of 1) North America; 2) South America; 3) The Caribbean/Latin America; 4) Western Europe; 5) Eastern Europe; 6) The Middle East; 7) Central Asia; 8) South Asia; 9) East Asia; 10) Northern Africa; 11) Southern Africa; 12) Austral-Zealand; 13) Oceania; and 14) Homotannia proper. Each of these Representatives will have an equal vote. These Ministers will be appointed by the President and the Administration, similar to any Ambassadorial postings. In the event of a tie vote in the Assembly, the Prime Minister will have tie-breaking power. This body will ensure that no one region dominates in our new Gay State. It will not become a de facto American state, nor will it become a colony of purely Western European interests. A lone citizen from Oceania will not be shut out of the system in his new country. This way, we all will have a say when our Parliament convenes, and all of our voices will be heard, without an unnecessary gridlock.

Sexual Classification/Familial-Individual-National Status. Our new found peace and liberty affords us the opportunity to address issues that, never in the history of civilization, have free citizens been allowed to identify by their chosen gender and of their own accord. The Gay State is the only and first nation on earth in which the majority of its citizens are Homosexual. It is conversely the only nation on earth where non-Gay Heterosexuals are a minority people. As we are a secular nation, offering equal status to all its citizens in voting and rights, we have established a preliminary legislative body to recognize the many shades of the Gay rainbow. Representatives will be duly elected to represent the people by the following societal categories: 1) Gay Men; 2) Lesbians; 3) Bisexuals; 4) Transgender individuals; 5) Transvestites; 6) Military Bears; 7) non-Gay identifying Heterosexuals; 8) Single individuals; 9) Married individuals; 10) Families; 11) Young Adult community; 12) Elders; 13) Part-time residents; 14) Full-time residents; 15) Newly Arrived citizens; and 16) Established citizens. Each of these Senators will have an equal vote of one. The Vice-President and the Administration will have tie-breaking authority.

Community Board Representation. The Gay State is being founded on the precept of equality under the law. This protection includes the rights for equal quality of life as far as the Gay State can oblige its citizenry. Every resident should have equal access to free health care, transportation, and dining privileges in the National Dining Hall, just as there should be free access to recreational opportunities, green space, quality schools and quality of available public works. Toward the attainment of this goal, the Founders have identified fourteen communities that will be among the first built in the new Gay State. The particular names as they have been plotted for development have not yet been ratified by the Coalition of Founders and can be changed but for this purpose, here is the list as it stands as of this writing: 1) Cascade, the Government District; 2) New Amsterdam; 3) New Chelsea; 4) Rainbow Hill; 5) Hanging Gardens 6) Cherry Grove; 7) Fire Island Boardwalk; 8) New World City, including the International District; 9) Fort Cammermeyer; 10) Marina District; 11) Coconut Cove; 12) Banana Bay; 13) Eros Islands; and 14) Four Seasons BioDome. Each of these districts will have one duly elected Representative for each 5,000 people residing within its boundaries, to the House of Congress. The Vice-President and the Administration have tie-breaking authority.

USE OF LAND.

The Gay State will strive to be self sufficient in every way possible. With regard to its land management, the Department of Agriculture will attempt to grow as much of the food necessary to feed all of its citizens. Through intensive farming and utilizing the most modern techniques available, we will employ terraced farming where necessary, and vertical farming where available, such as on Rainbow Hill and the Hanging Gardens. Strict land control will emphasize certain agricultural districts. Also, per land control policies, strict zoning laws will eliminate all urban sprawl and maintain commercial zones and residential districts within the planned urban borders.

Only in as far as the Homotannia Land Company plays a role in the establishment of these policies will it play a role in exercising such issues during the first two years when the Land Company is in operation. Within two years, it is expected urban planning has progressed to the point that large swaths of territory will be relinquished to civil authorities and a formal transfer of power to the new Gay states elected officials.

"America boasts that it is the 'land of liberty' while simultaneously crushing the human spirit through its uniquely American Gay Apartheid. This is not even close to being considered good enough"

~ Paddy McKinnon

"It is not fair to ask of others what you are not willing to do yourself."
~ Eleanor Roosevelt

Chapter Four.
Gay Groups of Every Color, Both Local and Afar, We Have Earned Our Stripes.

O UR TRANSMIGRATION.
Previous chapters explained only how the emigration plan might be executed without creating any economic disturbance. But so great a movement cannot take place without inevitably rousing many deep and powerful feelings. There are old customs, old memories that attach us to our homes and our lands of birth. We have cradles and graves, and we have to find individual ways of dealing with these separation issues. Our cradles we may elect to carry with us, they will embolden our future, filling us with optimism of what lies ahead. Leaving behind the graves of our fallen families and friends will be the hardest sacrifice. But with global travel, global telecommunications, and instant messaging, goodbyes do not have to be permanent; yet goodbyes must occur and cannot be avoided.

Economic distress, political pressure, and societal vilification had already driven many of us from our communities of birth. Families that found us disgraceful, community leaders that reviled our presence, and our church elders and employers who ostracized us from belonging had already forced many of us to seek greener pastures—perhaps larger cities where we could at least enjoy the company of other, likeminded people. Our Gay State is the answer to the question "Where will our presence finally be accepted and give us a place to call home?"

We shall, however, give a home to our people. And we shall give it to them with as much careful consideration as possible, preplanning to make any inconveniences as gentle as we could manage. Just as we wish to create new political and economic relations, so we shall preserve as sacred as much of the past that is dear to our people's hearts.

Hence a few suggestions must suffice, as part of this plan will most probably be condemned as visionary. Yet even this is possible and real, though it now appears to be something vague and aimless. Organizations, political departments, and passionate leadership will make something rational of the Gay State concept.

EMIGRATION OF GROUPS.

The reality of life for many in the global Gay movement is that they have spent a lifetime hiding who they really are, sometimes to simply survive, other times to keep the love of their parents and families. They have not forged strong alliances, sometimes out of fear they would be found out and punished for being Gay, sometimes because their isolated lives have deprived them of forging relationships with others in the Gay community. Therefore, those who find the inner strength to leave their troubled existence behind and venture out to a more liberating future will often be making the trip alone.

Through our international representatives and network of supporting agencies around the globe, we will forge networks in every country. We will afford prospective members the opportunity to meet other future members from their old country. They may elect to travel together or not, but at least shortly upon arrival, they will at least have a small network of individuals from the native lands of birth that they will already have built a bond with. However, no man or womyn will be coerced into joining such a group from his former place of residence. In fact, some people may opt to leave all remnants of their former lives behind them altogether, and if they choose to disassociate themselves, that should be their privilege.

Since each person will travel at his or her own expense, he or she will naturally travel at whatever class he or she prefers. Most will arrive by air; whether by commercial airlines or by our charter planes that will travel to and from Miami. We will facilitate our new members in every way possible, acting with all the hospitality we can muster. It benefits the plan, as well as the arriving members, to have all concerned in an upbeat and positive state of mind.

The Company will welcome all scheduled arrivals to our shores. A very thorough and modern Immigration and Customs Department will be established. All new members will undergo a period where they will be ensconced in our New Arrivals Processing Campus. It will be reminiscent to a country club, by some standards. While members are housed and fed, they will undergo a thorough physical, receive health care, take a battery of tests, be placed in language training classes, and begin career counseling. Most will be housed in comfortable but not extravagant accommodations. As more prosperous emigrants follow, they may elect to reside in our Distinguished Visitors Quarters upon arrival until suitable accommodations of a more permanent nature can be arranged.

It would be unnecessary, if not monotonous, to point out at this stage all of the elements that will be required to go along with a monstrous bureaucratic movement of this scale. Every man or womyn that attaches himself or herself to the national idea will know all of the details as the relocation draws near and will come to terms with how he or she might want to implement his or her resources. The international representatives and our internet webinars in various languages will spell out all of the particulars in due time. Finally, whatever discomfort or inconveniences all of us may endure in the resettlement phase will pale to the freedom and liberty we will experience for a lifetime. Though I do not want to minimize anyone's concerns, the hardships, as temporary as they will be, will be no worse than what some of us have endured in the countries we emigrate from. Those who are unwilling to roll up their sleeves and join us in building a nation should wait a few years into the experiment or stay behind.

OUR INTERNATIONAL LEADERSHIP.

Every nation will become a source of new members for our Gay State. We will develop our leadership structure within each of those 195-plus nations from Homosexuals with appropriate education or professional credentials. For example, everyone that emigrates from Estonia will have made contact with our Estonia Representatives, either in person or via e-mails or telephone. When these individuals reassemble in our Gay State, they will gather under the same leadership if they choose. Our international leadership, on whom we especially call, will devote its energies to the service of our idea and will inspire its ranks to commit themselves to our plan. It will be devoted to serving the needs and issues that face those under its tutelage. Our unity for what we are and what we have collectively endured may have been diluted through our various languages and customs, but these obstacles will be overcome by our shared desire for freedom.

Our international representatives will receive regular communication from both the Society of Gays and the Homotannia Land Company and will announce and explain these dispatches to their potential new members. The Gay State and all members of the Gay global movement will pray for us and our perseverance, and a desire to succeed will rise up in a constructive manner that the world had never before witnessed.

REPRESENTATIVES OF THE LOCAL GROUPS.

The local groups will appoint small committees of representative men and womyn under their Local Director for discussion and settlement of local affairs. The attention paid to a hierarchal organization will remedy many miscommunications from language barriers.

The extent that the Company endeavors to provide new members with familiar vestiges of their prior residence stops with their domiciliation. To promote a nation-state where old allegiances do not breed the fostering of the ethnic strife we are attempting to eradicate, new members will not be assigned initial housing immediately adjacent to one's former countrymen. We want to avoid having ethnic communities deteriorate unto themselves. We will prevent those less affluent neighborhoods from morphing into the ghettos which eat at one's soul. And we will discourage the development of racial enclaves or cliques based on ethnicity. Their assembly in public or private is neither encouraged nor discouraged, whether in restaurants or in parks. The Company will establish in New World City an "International District," and nations will be afforded their own avenue with a cul-de-sac that contains a green-space park. On the avenue, they will open their shops, restaurants, bars, and services. This will be encouraged and will foster our promotion to the world's travelling public that we are a cosmopolitan, international destination, the likes of which has never before been presented to the world. It has the potential to become a world class tourism and shopping/dining/recreation and resort destination.

Detractors have called this both a "foolish notion" and a "scheme." It is not a foolish notion that law abiding citizens of the world can come together and live in harmony. The United States was founded on the principle of freedom, and dating back hundreds of years, a Catholic could live next to a Jew, and a Norwegian could live next to a Spaniard. Others have called the "International District" a scheme and an imitation to Disney's EPCOT village. To this I say, as a new country, we can break the old molds. We can try something different. We can become a unified center of internationalism. Residents and visitors alike may option to breakfast in a Parisian Cafe, shop in Hong Kong, lunch in Italy, spend the afternoon watching Cricket matches in India, celebrate a "happy hour" in America, and dine lavishly in Brazil before dancing the night away in Argentina. By our accounts, celebrating the "joie de vivre," or joy of life, of all countries and respecting their heritage is an acceptable undertaking. It is also the best way to eradicate the scourge of ethnocentrism.

The Company will undertake an unprecedented level of support for its new members. Many nations that have been in existence for hundreds of years have not evolved enough to offer the array of services that our Gay State will provide from the earliest stages. We consider this service to our fellow man to be a right and a privilege for both the giver and the receiver. In a new society, these organizations can be evolved from our modern consciousness and may be based on all previous social experiments. This matter is very important to us because so many of us have lived our lives being marginalized by unresponsive governmental authorities.

OUR CARE FOR THE ELDEST AND THE DISABLED AMONGST US.

The true moral compass of a nation is in how it treats the weakest among them. For this Gay State this includes our disabled and our elderly. Let our care and compassion for the disabled and the elders among us be our hallmark of respect and love. Some of our new members will come as elders, and we will embrace them as family. Some of our new members will arrive disabled, and some will become disabled after arriving. Like any loving and supportive family, we will provide for these individuals. And like family, these individuals will do whatever they can to assist those who care for them. This may mean following their physicians' orders precisely. It may mean going to physical therapy when they would prefer to nap or watch television. It means doing for themselves what they are able to do. The Society will arrange for whatever amenities or services are within its grasp. For many of our newest members, our level of medical care will be superior and offer more compassion than what they have emigrated from.

We will do what we can to keep our seniors and physically challenged in their own homes. When necessary, we will relocate them into assisted living facilities or into full service nursing campuses. Some nations allow the elderly to die out of shame and abandonment. The Gay State, in its goal to be a compassionate society, will let all men and womyn enjoy the pride of contributing to society and performing some task that makes their participation useful to the greater good. We see a certain moral salvation in remaining productive.

PROFESSIONAL AFFILIATIONS AND LIFE STYLE CLUBS.

Who amongst us does not wish to be liked? The grizzled curmudgeon may not care a wit to a neighbor's thinking, but still wants the loyalty of a spouse or support of a friend. We are most often liked by those who appreciate our interests and abilities. To foster clubs that serve a recreational or philosophical purpose, we will have dozens of clubs that might be of interest to new members. These clubs will range from professional, social and financial, to religious, spiritual, or hobby-oriented. There will be clubs for professionals—the Accountants' Club, the Barristers' Society, the Law Enforcement Association, the Hoteliers' Association, the Sales and Marketing Networking Club, etc., etc. There will be such clubs for hundreds of professions and avocations. Through these organizations, active professionals and engaged retirees will have a platform for keeping abreast of their career interests and a place to meet other likeminded professionals. They foster relationships and build community.

Business people young and old, just starting out and those fully established, will find their livelihoods enhanced by participating. There will be dozens, if not hundreds, of clubs for all people with likeminded interests: The Cricket Clubs; the Soccer (Football) Clubs; the Chess Club; Book-Reading Clubs; the Political clubs; the Board and Games Clubs; the Radio Controlled Airplane Association; The Restaurant Club; the Tai Chi Club; The Karate Club; the Bicycling Club; the

Movie-Lovers Club; The Australia Club; The Argentina Club; the Japan Club; etc. As I said, there could be hundreds of such clubs to serve our members, and serious input would come from the members themselves by virtue of their interests, etc. Any participation is strictly voluntary.

In fact, all Gays who find themselves persecuted and seeking new opportunities who now escape from oppression in their native country to earn a living in a foreign land will assemble on this soil so full of promise and potential. The bravest will get the best out of this new Gay State. But there we seem to have touched on one of the difficulties of my plan – even if we succeeded in opening a world discussion on the Gay Question in a serious manner – even if this debate lead us to a positive conclusion that the Gay State were necessary to the world – even if the powers assisted us in acquiring the sovereignty over a strip of territory –how do we transport masses of Gays without undue compulsion from their present homes to this new country? Their emigration is surely intended to be voluntary. Here our Diplomatic Corps, the cooperation from non-governmental organizations, and the insistence that a process be followed will prevent some nations from causing a mass exodus— something in our infancy we are unprepared to handle. The reality is, in many countries, we will leave one at a time, like a dripping faucet; our absence will not be noticed until the sink is about to overflow.

Religion. It is a practice that for thousands of years has historically been a major source of oppression for our people. I do not want to hurt anyone's religious sensibility by words which might be wrongly interpreted. Almost all people of the Gay global movement have been persecuted by the faiths in their countries of origin. These organized religions, the vast majority of them though not all, have pitied us, shown contempt, persecuted us, and played a part if not an active role, in our imprisonment, beatings, having our lives destroyed, or putting our brothers and sisters to death. We were the recipients of extreme bigotry and intolerance. We will not condemn our souls by following in their self-righteous footsteps. We will invite all houses of worship to follow along with our new members to this, the world's first Gay state. We do this in the name of equality and of our commitment to an open society. But we will not allow houses of worship to spew their hate on our soil. We will not permit their hate mongering and intolerance to be foisted upon us in our Gay homeland. Religions that wish to join us are welcome. Their messages, however, without squelching freedom of speech, must be of tolerance, love of man, and the betterment of society. Anything less than speaking to our better angels is a crime against humanity. Our citizens have travelled great distances to escape homophobia and/or anti-Gayism, and they do not wish to bring institutions of intolerance with them. And the agents of intolerance that would spew their hate are unwelcome, whatever denomination over which the clergy presided.

All of the organizations and clubs above provide our members with an improved quality of life. They derive enjoyment, pleasure, purpose, and camaraderie from these affiliations. They also perfect a skill, and the sharing provides teachable moments to their fellow members. Being involved in one's community will be an encouragement from our leaders to all of our members. It contributes to community solidarity.

THE PHENOMENON OF MULTITUDES.

Great exertions will hardly be necessary to spur on the movement. Anti-Gayites provide the requisite impetus. They need only continue doing what they have done for the last several thousand years, and they create the desire to emigrate. Gays will seek an opportunity to live in a free, democratic land with equality for all and liberty. Currently there are upwards of 600,000,000 Gay men and Lesbians presently living on earth. There is an additional untold number of Bisexuals and Transgender individuals. How many of those might seek a more prosperous and freer life? If half of one percent chose freedom and liberty, which is to say that 99.5% of the world does not choose to join us, we would have in excess of 3,000,000 people applying for citizenship. This does not include the numbers of non-Gay Heterosexuals who would like to live in our nation.

Of those 3,000,000-plus individuals seeking entry, our ability to absorb new members is limited. Initially we will be limited due to land management and the construction site as managed by the Land Company. However, we anticipate having 5,000 to 8,000 new citizens in year one. By year two, the population will increase to 15,000. By year three, we will increase to 25,000. In year four, our population number will top 40,000. And we will complete year five with a total of 60,000 citizens. Again, these numbers are based on our anticipation of budgetary constraints and the land management issues that may constrain us. Until a land mass is secured, we are at best speculating. We could conceivably have the capacity for many thousands more. In contrast, Israel could not quickly house all of the world's Jews, Ireland could not accommodate all of the world's Irish. However, an analysis of the numbers and percentages does not seem to put the viability of the plan into question. As there will likely be constraints in funding, there will be limited land to accommodate all of our people. It would seem clear that, unfortunately, we could not accommodate all Gay people seeking to emigrate. That Heterosexual people keep breeding and making more Homosexuals means we will never run out of a fresh supply of new emigrants to keep the health and vitality of our Gay State strong and robust.

Initially, the Gay State will require strong, able-bodied Patriots to perform the hard work of building a nation. The poorest, who have nothing to lose, would drag themselves there, if need be. Our message to them should be strong and clear: Come to our new Gay state however you can. But come! I maintain, and every man may ask himself whether I am not right, that the pressure weighing on us arouses a desire to emigrate even among the prosperous strata of society. Now our poorest strata alone would suffice to found a State; these form the strongest human material for acquiring a land, because a little despair is indispensable to the formation of a great undertaking.

But when our initial settlers increase the value of the land by their presence and by the labor they expend on it, they make it at the same time increasingly attractive as a place for settlement to people who are better off.

Progressively higher classes will feel tempted to join our historic "Gay State." The expedition of the first and poorest settlers will be conducted by Company and Society conjointly and will probably be additionally supported by existing philanthropic societies to the Gay Rights causes. These "poor" classes I keep referring to are the true heroes. We will build a great society on the backs of these Patriots. They will be remembered in history as patriots who helped change our world.

For all of mankind in general, and for our people in particular, we must give hope.

OUR HUMAN CAPITAL.

There are more mistaken notions about Homosexuals than concerning any other people. And we have become depressed and discouraged by our historic sufferings that we ourselves repeat and believe their mistakes. One of these is that we have only a mad desire for sexual perversion, and that our promiscuity leads us to have no interests in domesticity. What is not well known nor universally believed is that in some countries we are better educated than the general populace. It is also true that we have higher disposable incomes that the general populace, in part due to our interests in education. The great majority of Gays prefer to cluster in neighborhoods with other like minded people. They have turned their Gay ghettos into someplace chique. In the United States, when the Gays move into neighborhoods suffering from urban decay and urban blight, they begin to morph into desirable areas. When Gays infiltrate a poor neighborhood, the better shops follow them, great restaurants move in, the houses are well maintained, freshly painted, and sprout beautiful gardens. The levels of crime drop precipitously. The gentrification of a neighborhood becomes so complete and successful, that in time, the non-Gays begin to follow them. This has been the pattern in countless Gay neighborhoods. Iconic American neighborhoods include Greenwich Village, Chelsea, The Castro, DuPont Circle, West Hollywood, Midtown Atlanta, and Miami's South Beach, and they are all communities that were down on their luck, plagued with poverty and drugs. Then the Gays moved in; the neighborhoods improved to the point of becoming some of the most desirable neighborhoods in their cities, and then reached the point where the non-Gays began to resettle the neighborhood. They infiltrated, moved in with substantial numbers, and many of the Gays left because of the tension that arose. In their own neighborhoods, regular working class Gays began to feel unwelcome by the interlopers.

Hence, Gay people are by nature willing to take risk; they are innovators and will be diligent in their work. The Society of Gays will be in a position to prepare scientifically accurate statistics of our human potential. The new tasks and prospects that await our people in the new country will satisfy our present handicraftsmen and will transform many small traders and manual workers by presenting opportunities to our Gay citizens that they could never have hoped for in their lands of birth.

The lower class of working Gays consists of good, misunderstood people, who now suffer perhaps more severely than any other. The Society of Gays will, moreover, busy itself from the outset with their training as artisans. They will work with zeal, as Gays are wont to do, to establish our villages and cities as artistic and architectural showplaces. Their love of prosperity and advancement will be encouraged in a healthy manner. Gays can have a thrifty and adaptable disposition and are qualified for any means of earning a living, and it will therefore lead to an explosion in entrepreneurship. Most Gays have historically had few or no dependents, so his or her needs for affluence are borne out of want, not always out of necessity.

DAILY ROUTINES.

Is a reference to the little habits and comforts of the ordinary man in keeping with the serious nature of this booklet?

I think it is in keeping and, moreover, very important. For these little habits are the thousand and one fine delicate threads which together go to make up an unbreakable rope.

Here certain limited notions must be set aside. Whoever has seen anything of the world knows that just these little daily customs can easily be transplanted everywhere. The technical aspects of our day, which this plan will use in abundance to serve humanity, have also been used for the conveniences of our little habits. There are Japanese hotels in London and in the mountain peaks of Peru; Parisian cafes in South Africa and New Delhi; American theatres in Russia and Bangkok; Italian operas in Germany; and the best Dutch beer in Ireland.

When we journey out of Sydney, Las Vegas, Montreal or Berlin, we shall not leave the fleshpots behind.

If sensual pleasures are the pursuit, as with Gay men in particular, a freedom and sexual liberation many have only imagined awaits those who have lived their lives both in the open and hidden behind closed curtains.

Every man will find his customs again in the local groups, but they will be better, more beautiful and more agreeable than before.

When the movement commences, we shall draw some men after us and let others follow; others again will be swept into the current, and the last will be thrust after us.

These last hesitating settlers will be the worst off, both here and there.

But the first, who go over with faith, enthusiasm and courage, will have the best positions and a life that perhaps they dared not even dream of until now.

"I swore never to be silent whenever and wherever human beings endure suffering and humiliation. We must always take sides. Neutrality helps the oppressor, never the victim. Silence encourages the tormentor, never the tormented."

Elie Wiesel

"I submit to you that if a man hasn't discovered something that he will die for, he isn't fit to live."

~ Rev. Martin Luther King, Jr.

Inter-Mission. The World's Most Powerful and Creative Gays and the Greatest Gays in History and Today.

Every author has, at some point in the creative process experienced an adrenaline rush at the exciting prospects that someone or everyone will enjoy the end result. Whether the author is writing a newspaper article or an internet blog, a novella or pamphlet such as this, or a substantial encyclopedia of work, the hope is that the message will reveal itself to willing and accepting readers. For those of you who have attempted to digest this work in one sitting, I offer up this chapter. This section is meant to give your mind a break from the serious business of what role we, and more importantly you, may face in the near future.

In such a serious undertaking as creating a new Gay State, the work will be long and arduous. There will be countless thrills that will make the challenges worthwhile and there will be heartbreaking setbacks, which we will acknowledge, and move forward toward our ultimate goal and inevitable victory. And as a people, one people, we will find solace in each other and will remain true to our vision.

We will seek our inspiration and fortitude, not only from one another, but from the memories of those who have come before us. We will each hold dear to the memories of those who have inspired and comforted us in other trials and tribulations. And we will remember others who have dreamed the dream of a Gay world, where we could thrive in our purpose and live in peace. We will each pray to our Creator or Supreme Being for guidance and support and protection and for the wisdom to always choose the correct path.

And we shall seek the wisdom that has come from our Gay brothers and sisters on whose shoulders we stand. As a people, many of us may have endured earlier lives in aloneness and isolation, but we are no longer on a solitary path. Many trails have been blazed in all areas of life from which we can follow. Great men and womyn, Gays and Lesbians all, have changed history to some degree by their tenacity or their brilliance, their personality or their faith.

As Gay men, Lesbians, Bisexuals, and Transgender Peoples, we have lived in a dark age where we could not be honest about who we were. For most of our Gay brothers and sisters who lived twenty years ago, or two hundred years ago, or even two thousand years ago, they were still able to contribute to the betterment of Mankind while enduring the same degree of persecution, secrecy, or worse. And then the march simply goes on.

Who amongst you – our Gay brothers and sisters reading these pages—will join this heralded list of the world's greatest, most powerful, most brilliant, or most inspiring Gays and Lesbians, Bisexuals and Transgender people in the history of the world?

A SAMPLING OF GAY HISTORIC FIGURES WHO HAVE LEFT THEIR MARK:

Abd Al-Rahman.
> Afghani King. 1880-1901.

Abu Nuwas.
> Arabian Poet, 756?-810.

Achilles.
> Greek mythological hero.

Agathon.
> Athenian Dramatist. 450?-400? BC.

Ai.
> Chinese Emperor. 6 BC-AD

Akhenaten
> Egyptian Pharoah. 1364-1334 B.C.

Alcibiades.(450-404 BC)
> Athenian general-statesman. 450-404 B.C.

Alexander I
> Russian Czar. 1777-1825.

Alexander the Great.
> Macedonian Ruler, 356-323 B.C.

Alexander VI
> Pope. 1431-1503.

Alger, Horatio
> U.S. Author. 1832-1899.

Al-Hakem II
> Cordoban Ruler. 961-976.

Allen, Peter
> Australian Entertainer. 1944-1992.

Al-Mutamid
> Ruler of Seville (Spain). 1069-1090.

Amunullah Kahn
> Afghani King. r: 1919-1929

Anacreon.
>   Greek Poet. 572?-488? BC

Andersen, Hans Christian
>   Danish author. 1805-1875

Anne
>   British Queen. 1665-1714.

Anne Ioannovna
>   Russian Empress. r: 1730-1740.

Anthony, Susan B.
>   U.S. Activist. 1820-1906

Antigonus II Gonatas
>   Greek King. r: 276-239 BC

Antiochus I
>   Greek King. r: 280-261 BC.

Antoinette, Marie
>   French Queen. 1755-1793.

Aristotle.
>   Greek Philosopher. 384-322 BC.

Ashikaga Yoshimitsu.
>   Japanese Shogun. R: 1368-1394.

Ashman, Howard [m] (1951-1991)
>   U.S. playwright-lyricist . 1951-1991.

Auden, W.H.
>   British Poet. 1907-1973.

Augustine, Saint
>   Roman theologian. 354-430.

Augustus. [m] (r: 31 BC-AD 14)
    Roman emperor. R: 31BC-14 AD.

Azaa, Manuel.
    Spanish President. r:1931-1033, 1936-1939.

Bacon, Sir Francis. [m] (1561-1626)
    British Philosopher-Statesman. 1651-1626.

Bagoas.
    Persian slave (to Alex. Great.) 345?-after 323 BC

Baldwin, James
    U.S. Writer. 1924-1987.

Bankhead, Tallulah.
    U.S. Actress. 1903-1968.

Barber, Samuel.
    U.S. Composer. 1910-1981.

Basil II.
    Byzantine emperor. r: 976-1025.

Bates, Alan.
    British-born U.S. Actor. 1934-1992.

Beach, Sylvia.
    U.S. expatriate literary figure. 1887-1962.

Beard, James.
    U.S. Chef and Author. 1903-1985.

Beardsley, Aubrey Vincent.
    British artist. 1872-1898.

Beckford, William.
    British writer and politician. 1760-1844.

Beecher, Henry Ward.
U.S. lecturer and pastor. 1813-1887.

Beethoven, Ludwig von.
German composer. 1770-1827.

Behan, Brendan.
Irish author. 1923-1964.

Benedict IX.
Pope. 1020-1055?

Bennett, Michael.
U.S. choreographer. 1943-1987.

Bernstein, Leonard.
U.S. composer. 1918-1990.

Beyazid I.
Ottoman sultan. r; 1389-1402.

Beza, Theodore.
French theologian. 1519-1605.

Bingham, Mark.
Rugby Player, September 11, 2001 Hero. 1970-2001.

Blackwell, Mr.
Fashion designer; creator of annual "Ten Worst Dressed" list .
20th/21st Centuries.

Botticelli, Sandro.
Italian painter. 1444?-1510.

Buchanan, James
U.S. president; ("speculation") 1791-1868.

Burke, Glenn.
> Ex-Major League baseball player.

Burton, Sir Richard.
> British explorer & scholar. 1821-1890.

Busi, Aldo.
> Italian novelist.

Caligula.
> Roman emperor. r: AD 37-41.

Caravaggio (Michelangelo Amerighi.)
> Italian painter. 1571-1610.

Casanova, Giovanni Giacomo.
> Italian adventurer. 1725-1798.

Casement, Sir Roger.
> Irish patriot. 1864-1916.

Catherine II (The Great).
> Russian Empress. r: 1762-1796.

Charles IX.
> French King. r: 1560-1574.

Charles XII.
> Swedish King. r: 1697-1718.

Charles XV.
> Swedish King. r: 1859-1872.

Cheever, John.
> U.S. writer. 1912-1982.

Christian VII.
> Danish King. r: 1766-1808.

Christina.
  Swedish Queen. 1626-1689.

Claudius I.
  Roman emperor. r: AD 41-54.

Clift, Montgomery.
  U.S. actor. 1920-1966.

Cocteau, Jean.
  French author. 1889-1963.

Commodus.
  Roman emperor. r: AD 180-192.

Conradin.
  Titular King of Jerusalem and Sicily. 1252-1268.

Coward, Sir Noel.
  British playwright, composer & actor. 1899-1973.

da Vinci, Leonardo.
  Italian artist, scientist & painter. 1452-1519.

David.
  Israeli King. 1035?-960 BC

Dean, James.
  U.S. actor. 1931-1955.

Demetrius Poliorcetes.
  Macedonian King. 336-288 BC

Demosthenes.
  Athenian orator. 384-322 BC.

Diaghilev, Sergei.
  Russian impresario. 1872-1929.

Dickinson, Emily.
>U.S. poet . 1830-1886.

Domitian.
>Roman Emperor. r: AD 81-96.

Douglas, Alfred Lord.
>British socialite. 1870-1945.

Earhart, Amelia.
>U.S. aviator, ("speculation,") 1898-1937?

Edward II.
>English King. 1284-1327.

Elagabalus (aka Heliogabalus.)
>Roman Emperor. AD 204-222

Ellis, Havelock.
>British essayist & physician. 1859-1939.

Ellis, Perry.
>U.S. fashion designer. 1940-1986.

Erasmus, Desiderius.
>Dutch theologian & scholar. 1466?-1536.

Euripides
>Greek dramatist. 480?-406 BC.

Ferdinand I.
>Bulgarian King. r: 1908-1918.

Flynn, Errol.
>U.S. actor. 1909-1959.

Forbes, Malcolm.
>U.S. publisher. 1919-1990.

Forster, E.M.
British author. 1879-1970.

Frederick II (The Great).
Prussian King. 1712-1786.

Fredrick II
Holy Roman Emperor. r: 1212-1250.

Gaozu.
Chinese Emperor. r: 206-194 BC.

Gordon, George, Lord Byron.
British poet. 1788-1824.

Grant, Cary.
U.S. actor. 1904-1986.

Gustavus III.
Swedish King. 1746-1792.

Gustavus V.
Swedish King. r: 1907-1950.

Hadrian.
Roman Emperor. AD 76-138.

Hafiz (Shams-ud-din Mohammed).
Persian poet. 1320-1388.

Hamilton, Alexander.
"speculation." American Founding Father & US Secretary of Treasury. 1757-1804.

Hammarskjold, Dag.
Swedish United Nations Secretary General. 1905-1961.

Harmodius.
    Athenian patriot. 532?-514 BC.

Henri III.
    French King. 1554-1589.

Henry, Prince of Prussia.
    Prussian General. 1726-1802.

Hirschfeld, Magnus.
    German sexologist. 1868-1935.

Hoover, J. Edgar.
    U.S. criminologist, Director of F.B.I., 1895-1972.

Hudson, Rock (ne Roy Scherer).
    U.S. actor, 1925-1985.

Hughes, Langston
    U.S. poet & writer. 1902-1967.

Hyde, Edward (Lord Cornbury).
    British Colonial Governor. 1661-1724.

Isherwood, Christopher.
    U.S. writer. (b. England.) 1904-1986.

Jahangir.
    Indian Emperor. r: 1605-1627.

James IV/I
    Scottish/English King. 1566-1625.

Jin Diyi.
    Chinese Emperor. r: AD 336-371.

John XII.
    Catholic Pope. AD 937-964.

Jonathan.
Israeli Crown Prince. 1045?-1013 BC.

Joplin, Janis.
U.S. rock singer. 1943-1970.

Juan II.
King of Castile & Leon (Spain.) r: 1406-1454.

Julius Caesar.
Roman Statesman. 100?-44 BC.

Julius II.
Pope. 1443-1513.

Julius III.
Pope. 1487-1555.

Jung, Carl.
Swiss founder analytical psychology. 1875-1961.

Kamran.
Afghani Emir. r: Early 19th Century.

Keynes, John Maynard.
British economist. 1883-1946.

Krupp, Friederich.
German industrialist. 1854-1902.

Kuzmin, Mikhail.
Russian poet. 1875-1936.

Laaksonen, Touko "Tom of Finland"
Finnish artist. 1920-1991.

Laughton, Charles
British actor. 1899-1962.

Leo X.
Catholic Pope. 1475-1521.

Lian Jianwen [m] (r: AD 550-551)
Chinese Emperor. r: AD 550-551.

Liberace, Wladziu Valentino
U.S. showman. 1919-1987.

Louis XIII
French King. 1601-1643.

Lucius Cornelius Sulla.
Roman Emperor. 138-78 BC.

Ludwig II.
Bavarian King. 1845-1886.

Lully, Jean-Baptiste.
French composer. 1632-1687.

Lynde, Paul.
U.S. actor. 1926-1982.

Magnus VII.
Swedish King of Norway. 1316-1373.

Mapplethorpe, Robert.
U.S. photographer. 1947-1989.

Marlowe, Christopher.
British playwright. 1564-1593.

Maugham, W. Somerset.
British author. 1874-1965.

Mead, Margaret.
U.S. anthropologist. 1901-1978.

Melchior, Lauritz.
    Danish opera singer. 1890-1973.

Melville, Herman.
    U.S. author. 1819-1891.

Michelangelo Buonarroti.
    Italian artist. 1475-1564.

Milk, Harvey.
    U.S. politician/activist 1930-1978.

Milton, John [m] (1608-1674)
    British author. 1608-1674.

Mishima, Yukio.
    Japanese writer. 1925-1970.

Montezuma II
    Aztec Ruler. 16th Century.

Mwanga
    Bugandan (Ugandan) King. r: 1884-1897.

Nero
    Roman Emperor. r: AD 54-68.

Nerva [m] (r: Ad 96-98)
    Roman Emperor. r: AD 96-98.

Newman, John Henry Cardinal.
    British religious leader. 1801-1890.

Nicholson, Harold.
    British author-diplomat. 1886-1968.

Nightingale, Florence.
    British nurse. 1820-1910.

Nijinsky, Vaslav.
    Polish ballet dancer. 1890-1950.

Nureyev, Rudolf
    Russian ballet star. 1935?-1993.

Oda Nobunaga.
    Japanese military dictator. r: 1568-1582.

Olivier, Lord Lawrence.
    British actor. 1907-1989.

Otho
    Roman Emperor. r: AD 69.

Otto III.
    German Holy Roman Emperor. AD 980-1002.

Paul II.
    Catholic Pope. 1417-1471.

Peter the Great.
    Russian Czar. 1672-1725.

Plato.
    Athenian philosopher. 427?-347? BC.

Porter, Cole.
    U.S. songwriter. 1891-1964.

Proust, Marcel.
    French author. 1871-1922.

Przhevalsky, Nikolai.
    Russian explorer. 1839-1888.

Ptolemy IV.
    Greek King. r: 145-144 BC.

Ptolemy VII.
>   Greek King. r: 221-205 BC.

Rama VI.
>   Thai King. r: 1910-1925.

Rasputin.
>   Russian monk. ?-1916.

Richard I, the Lion Hearted.
>   English King. 1157-1199.

Richard II.
>   English King. 1367-1400.

Robespierre, Maximilien de
>   French statesman. 1758-1794.

Rohm, Ernst.
>   German militarist. 1887-1934.

Roosevelt, Eleanor
>   U.S. First Lady. 1884-1964.

Sappho
>   Greek poet. 613?-565?

Schubert, Franz.
>   Austrian composer. 1797-1828.

Shakespeare, William.
>   English playwright. ("speculation,") 1564-1616.

Socrates.
>   Athenian philosopher. 469?-399 BC.

Sodoma, Il (Giovanni Antonio Bazzi).
>   Italian painter. 1477-1549.

Sophocles.
Greek tragedian. 496-406 BC.

Stein, Gertrude.
U.S. writer. 1864-1946.

Takahashi, Mutsuo.
Japanese poet.

Tchaikovsky, Peter Ilich.
Russian composer. 1840-1893.

Tiberius.
Roman Emperor. r: AD 14-37.

Toklas, Alice B.
U.S. author-cook. 1877-1967.

Tokugawa Iemitsu.
Japanese shogun. R: 1622-1651.

Tolstoy, Leo.
Russian author. 1828-1910.

Tripp, C. A.
Psychologist (author, The Homosexual Matrix)

Turing, Alan M.
British mathematician. 1912-1954.

Ulrichs, Karl Heinrich.
German lawyer & gay right activist. 1825-1895.

Valentian III.
Roman Emperor. r: AD 425-455.

Valentino, Rudolph.
Italian-U.S. actor. 1895-1926.

Voltaire.
> French philosopher. 1694-1778.

von Romer, Lucien S.A.M.
> Dutch sexologist. 1873-1965.

Walpole, Horace.
> British writer. 1717-1797.

Warhol, Andy.
> U.S. artist. 1927-1987.

Washington, George.
> U.S. President, ("speculation, ") 1732-1799.

Whitman, Walt.
> U.S. poet, author. 19th Century.

Wilde, Oscar.
> Irish dramatist & wit. 1854-1900.

Wilder, Thornton.
> U.S. novelist. 1897-1975.

William II Rufus.
> English King. 1056-1100.

William III.
> British King. r: 1689-1702.

Williams, Tennessee.
> U.S. playwright. 1911-1983.

Wittgenstein, Ludwig.
> Austrian philosopher. 1889-1951.

Woolf, Virginia Stephens.
> British writer. 1882-1941.

Woollcott, Alexander.
> U.S. journalist & critic. 1887-1943.

Wu.
> Chinese Emperor. r: 140-86 BC.

Yourcenar, Marguerite.
> Belgian author. 20th Century.

Zeno of Elea.
> Greek philosopher. 5th Century BC.

The above list is in no way complete. Any Homosexual omitted from the list should know it was due to scholarly and space requirements and is not intended to allege the person to have been a Heterosexual. Yet even as inconclusive as the list is, our people have left an undeniable impact on world history. There are other works that will far better illustrate our collective talents, in a more comprehensive detail as that is the only goal of those works. I merely want the reader to understand, Gay and non-Gay readers alike, that there is precedence for greatness to emerge from our ranks. Do not doubt our abilities.

Furthermore, all readers must understand that these lists are more for fun, trivia, and general interest than they are to be taken as scientific absolute truths. With the passage of centuries, there is no quantifiable way to determine if someone, whether it be Aristotle, Plato or Marie Antoinette, was primarily Heterosexual, if they have engaged in Homosexual relations as an aside, or if they were primarily Homosexual. Sometimes, the speculation is only based on writings or passages within autobiographies. There have been men and womyn who steadfastly held on to their alleged non-Gay Heterosexuality, over concern their careers or fortunes would vanish if the intolerant non-Gay masses would discover their true dominant orientation. There is naturally the never-ending supposition that many of these men and womyn of a certain status were loathe to be "found out" and concealed their Homosexuality to avoid personal, professional, and financial ruin.

<u>A LIST OF CONTEMPORARY GAYS WHO CONTINUE TO INFLUENCE OUR COMMUNITY AND THE WORLD:</u>

<u>Business.</u>
Christopher Bailey, UK, Designer
Nate Berkus, Designer
Pierre Cardin, Italy, Designer
Ellen Davis, UK, Economist
Barry Diller, US, CEO, IAC/InterActive Group
Tom Ford, Fashion Designer
Sandy Gallin, US, Agent
David Geffen, US Entertainment and Technology
Tim Gill, US, Business and Philanthropy
James Hormel, US, Businessman and Diplomat
Chris Hughes, Facebook Co-Creator
Marc Jacobs, US, Designer
Bruce Lehman, US, Legal
Annie Leibovitz, US, Photography
Bob Mackie, US, Designer
Isaac Mizrahi, US, Designer
Todd Oldham, US, Designer
Rosie O'Donnell, US, Entertainer/Social Visionary
Christopher Radko, US, Fine Arts
Rich Ross, US, The Walt Disney Company
Peter Thiel, US, PayPal Founder and Clarium Capital Management, LLC
Jason Wu, US, Designer
Waheed Alli, UK, Business

<u>Celebrity.</u>
Chad Allen, US, Actor
John Barrowman, UK, Actor
Sandra Bernhard, US, Actress
Dan Butler, US, Actor

Mario Cantone, US, Comedian/Actor
Richard Chamberlain, US, Actor
Margaret Cho, US, Comedian
Judi Connelli, Australia, Entertainer
Alan Cumming, UK, Actor
Frank De Caro, US, Comedian and Radio Host
Ellen DeGeneres, US, Host/Comedian
Portia deRossi, US, Actress
Lea DeLaria, US, Entertainer
Rupert Everett, UK, Actor
Jodie Foster, US, Actress
John Glover, US, Actor
Tim Gunn, US, Designer
Neil Patrick Harris, US, Actor
Tab Hunter, US, Actor
Nathan Lane, US, Actor
Jane Lynch, US, Actress
Kelly McGillis, US, Actress
Sir Ian McKellen, UK, Actor
Cynthia Nixon, US, Actress
Graham Norton, UK, Comedian
David Hyde Pierce, US, Actor
Wanda Sykes, US, Comedian
Lily Tomlin, US, Actress
Tommy Tune, US, Dancer
Bruce Vilanch, US, Comedian/Host
Bruce Weber, US, Photographer
B.D. Wong, US, Actor

Hollywood and Film.
Alan Ball, US, Screenwriter
Clive Barker, UK, Director
Dustin Lance Black, US, Writer/Producer

Bill Condon, US, Director

Russell Davies, UK, Director

Moises Kaufman, Venezuelan-US, Writer/Director

Rob Marshall, US, Director

Sean Mathias, UK, Director

Simon Halls, US, PR firm, PMK/HBH

Kevin Huvane, Creative Artists Agency Partner

Neil Patrick King, US, Producer

Bryan Lourd, US, Creative Artists Agency Partner

Scott Rudin, US, Producer

Gus Van Sant. US, Director

John Waters, US, Director

Influence, Philanthropy & Gay Causes

Gilbert Baker, US Gay Activist and "Betsy Ross" of the Gay Flag

Jeremy Bernard, US, White House Liaison, National Endowment for The Humanities

Chaz Bono (formerly Chastity), US, Activist

Candice Gingrich, US, Gay Activist

Cleve Jones, US, Activist

Larry Kramer, US, Activist/Philanthropist, GMHC and ACT UP!

David Mixner, US, Writer/Political Strategist

Anthony Romero, US, ACLU

Joe Salmonese, US, Human Rights Campaign

Peter Tatchell, UK, International Human Rights Leader

Urvashi Vaid, UK, Arcus Foundation

Journalists/Literature.

Edward Albee, US, Playwright

Richard Berke, US, New York Times Reporter

Ben Brantley, US, New York Times Reporter/Author

Frank Bruni, US, former New York Times Food Critic/Author

Jim Calucci, US, Author

Louis Crompton, US, Author and Historian
Harvey Fierstein, US, Playwright
Fannie Flagg, US, Author
Patrick Healy, US, New York Times Reporter/Author
Andrew Holleran, US, Author
Larry Kramer, US, Playwright*
Tony Kushner, US, Playwright
David Leavitt, US, Author
Arthur Laurents, US, Playwright, Novelist, Screenwriter, Stage Director
Armistead Maupin, US, Author
Terrence McNally, US, Playwright
Adam Nagourney, US, New York Times Reporter, Author
Hillary Rosen, US, CNN & Huffington Post
David Sedaris, US, Author
Sarah Schulman, US, Author/Playwright/Activist
Horacio Silva, US, New York Times Reporter/Author
Liz Smith, US, Journalist
Andrew Tobias, US, Author
Guy Trebay, US, New York Times Reporter
Gore Vidal, US, Author
Alice Walker, US, Author
Sarah Waters, UK, Author
Eric Wilson, US, New York Times Reporter

Media.
Jonathan Capehart, US, Pulitzer Prize Winning Journalist/Television
    Commentator
Anderson Cooper, US, CNN
Evan Davis, UK, *Today* and BBC, Radio 4.
Nick Denton, UK, Gawker Media Founder
Matt Drudge, US, The Drudge Report, "speculation."
Brian Graden, US, President of Entertainment, MTV Networks Music
    Group

Andy Humm, US, Television Host
Andrew Kirtzman, US, Journalist/Reporter
Rachel Maddow, US, MSNBC.
Adam Moss, US, New York Magazine
Michael Musto, US, Village Voice
Martha Nelson, US, Time, Inc.
Ann Northrop, US, Television Host
Suze Orman, US, CNBC
Andrew Pierce, UK, The Daily Telegraph
Doug Shingleton, US, Media Representation
Pam Spalding, US, New Media Internet Blogger
Andrew Sullivan, UK and US, The Daily Dish
Andrew Tobias, US, Finance Writer/Fundraiser
Andy Towle, US, New Media Internet Blogger
Jane Valez-Mitchell, US, CNN/HLN
Jann Wenner, US, Rolling Stone.

Military.
Margaret Cammermeyer, US, Army, Retired, Colonel
LT. Dan Choi, US, Kinghts Out
Jose Zuniga, US, Soldier/Activist

Music.
Clay Aiken, US, Musician
Lance Bass, US, Musician
Melissa Etheridge, US, Musician
Michael Feinstein, US, Musician
Joan Gabriel, Mexico, Musician
Janis Ian, US, Musician
Elton John, UK & US, Musician and Godfather of the Gay World
Adam Lambert, US, Musician
k.d. Lang, Canada, Musician
Johnny Mathis, US, Musician

George Michael, UK, Musician
RuPaul, US, Musician
Emily Saliers, US, Musician, Indigo Girls
Stephen Sondheim, US, Composer
Michael Stipe, US, Musician, R.E.M.
Michael Tilson-Thomas, US, Conductor
Rufus Wainwright, US, Musician

Politics and Government.
Tim Barnett, UK-NZ, Politician, NZ Parliament
Tammy Baldwin, US, Wisconsin Congresswoman
Ben Bradshaw, UK Minister of State for Health Services
Ray Collins, UK, General Secretary to the Labor Party
Angela Eagle, UK Exchequer Secretary to the Treasury
Barney Frank, US, Massachusetts Congressman
Rufus Gifford, US, Finance Director, Democratic National Committee
Michael Guest, US, Ambassador to Romania
Steven Gunderson, US, Former WI Congressman
Nick Herbert, UK Shadow Secretary of State for Environment, Food
    And Rural Affairs
Fred Hochberg, US, Clinton Administration Cabinet, Small Business
    Administration
Ron Huberman, US, CEO, Chicago Public Schools
Pete Mandelson, UK Secretary of State for Business, Enterprise and
    Regulatory Reform
Jim McGreevey, US, former Governor New Jersey
Sir Simon Milton, UK, Deputy Mayor of London for Policy and
    Planning.
Jared Polis, US, Colorado Congressman
Christine Quinn, US, New York City Council President
Dan Ritterband, UK, Director of Marketing for London
Johanna Sigurdardottir, Prime Minister of Iceland
Gerry Studds, US, Massachusetts Congressman

Nancy Sutley, US, White House Council on Environmental Quality
Klaus Wowereit, Germany, Politician, Mayor of Berlin

Sports.
Billie Jean King, US, Athlete, Tennis Champion
Mark LeDuc, Canada, Olympian
Greg Louganis, US, Olympian
Amelia Mauresmo, France, Athlete
Matthew Mitcham, Australia, Olympian
Martina Navratilova, US, Athlete, Tennis Champion
Bob Paris, US, Former Mr. USA and Mr. Universe
Laura Ricketts, US, Owner of Chicago Cubs Baseball Team

Theology.
David Hope, UK, Cleric
Bishop V. Gene Robinson

This list of current and up and coming Gay leaders is only a partial list. Obviously, it only scratches the surface and is certainly not intended to be all inclusive. A larger encyclopedia will be required to list all Gay leaders in 195 countries. For this purpose, the writer chose to focus on primarily English speaking individuals and, more narrowly, primarily within the United States and the United Kingdom.

No omissions or deletions should be misconstrued as any personal or professional slight. Nor do we allege all of those not mentioned are known Heterosexuals. We will be expanding the list on future revised editions into a veritable "Who's Who" of the Gay World, and we welcome correspondence from all those who should be included. E-mails may be sent to: GarrettGrahamAndTheGayState@GMail.com, and we look forward to all future inclusions.

Being recognized as a valued member of the Gay community, you do share the burden along with the rest of us to participate in some way to move the cause along. Millions of your Gay brothers and sisters, the massive numbers who do not bask in any particular public acclaim, can only look to all of you.

On the contrary, our goal here is merely to educate those readers of this booklet who may not be as tuned in to the Gay culture as some others may be.

As we move forward, let no man or womyn from any corner of the world proclaim that we are unfit to develop our Gay State. We can harness enormous talent and intellect, might and creativity to achieve the grandest results.

"I think the first duty of society is justice."
Alexander Hamilton

"Healthy citizens are the greatest asset any country can have."
~ Winston Churchill

Chapter Five.
The Society of Gays and The Gay State.

T hose who ask if we have the capability to sustain a civilization, one need only reel off the list of our people, past and present, from within our ranks who have managed to create magnificent work in this world. Do we have the Human Material? The Human Capital? The answer is apparently yes, and then some. I would add there are few nations that could boast of such a talented and gifted roster of its historic figures and immense talent.

In the build up to the Gay State and in the midst of the heady Pre-State days of philosophical possibilities of building the world's first Gay nation-state, leaders, activists, and members of the global gay community expressed concepts of what could be. There was no shortage of ideas. And in all realms of possibility, we inevitably and eventually invoked the question: "Yes, and does it speak to the advancement of freedom, liberty, democracy, and equality for all of our people?" Can it last? Is there something organic that will benefit mankind long after those of us in this room are gone?

The notion of being free is one that many Gays, if not all at some time have pondered, perhaps as idealistic notions of nirvana as young men or as a vision of wholeness where old Gay men and Lesbians could die in peace. The early stages of any formation of this global Gay independence movement must have begun with the First Congress in New York in 2007. The Coalition of Founding Fathers would grow and then reduce in size as members saw their commitment and their optimism wane. The departure of those less willing to support the movement during the tumultuous times that lay ahead was a step in the right direction. If only Darwinian in nature, it left the core of the movement with stronger, more dedicated, and determined members to see things through to a fruition that benefited all of humanity far beyond their neighborhood causes.

The Second Congress in Fire Island in 2009 was another watershed moment in the early history of the movement. There are few communities on earth that have the peaceful, live and let live attitudes of Fire Island. Commitments were made to further the advancement of the cause beyond exploratory and establishing the necessary steps in the long march to receive independent nationhood.

In the first Congress of Amsterdam in early 2010, just about to take place as these pages go to press, the Coalition of Founding Fathers began to assemble some of the best and brightest leaders of the global Gay community to enlist them in the hard work that would eventually formulate the group that would in time become the first assemblage of The Society of Gays.

What is The Society of Gays? A thorough and exhausting description cannot be accomplished in this pamphlet, and toward that objective, I had other writings that might interest a reader. But to disclose as much about the Society as a reader may wish to know here, let me make this attempt. The Society of Gays is an organization of people who work to advance the cause of Gay independence and strive in their deeds and words, to create a moral and ethical independent state that stresses personal freedom, liberty, democracy, and equality for all Gays, Lesbians, Bisexuals, and Transgender people, as well as non-Gay Heterosexuals who wish to join us in our new Gay nation-state.

The Society is to be comprised of the best men and womyn we can muster for such a massive undertaking. These people must possess the noblest of virtues and the toughness to endure the harshest of environments, as well as the prerequisite courage and tenacity. More on their qualifications will come at a later time. Suffice it to say this is not work for the fair weathered and faint hearted. The function that the Society serves will have its most profound impact in its initial work. After the Homotannia Land Company is formed and its work is completed, the Gay state will launch its first fully elected government (expected within eighteen to twenty four months), and it is in this moment when the Society of Gays will step down and not be responsible for providing the nation's moral and ethical compasses.

The structure of the Society of Gays begins with the appointment of a Cabinet of Officers, who bears the ultimate responsibility for the implementation of all Society actions. The Cabinet is comprised of its President and Vice-President, followed by a Board of Advisors. The Board of Advisors, comprised of nine Gay Patriots, is responsible for twenty five various subjects and departments, committees and sub-committees that influence the outcome of where our nation is headed. The leaders of the departments and committees are known as Secretaries, and sub-committee leaders are given the title of Assistant Secretary.

The areas that the Society devotes most of its attention to are the following:

1.) The Membership Department. It enlists our Gay people from every corner of the globe. It also strategizes to garner favorable world public opinion and support. This department will work closely with the Homotannia Land Company to regulate the pace of new member arrivals and their immersion in to the society. Committees and sub committees will accept and review all application for membership in the initial stages, until, nearing the construction projects of the Land Company relinquish such implementation to the Immigration and Naturalization Department.

<u>2.) The Gifting and Fundraising Department.</u> Only naïve madmen would think the building of a new nation can be created peacefully without the use of capital. Freedom is most often paid for in blood or gold. We will purchase our homeland territory and avoid the violence that comes with unwanted conquest. To make such a peaceful purchase attainable, monies will certainly be raised and expended to advance our cause. The financial arm of our Gay State will include the income producing arms of 1) State and governmental grants; 2) Non-governmental organizations and assistance; 3) International Corporate Grants; 4) Gay Benefactors; 5) the global Gay membership recruitment; 6) Monetary Bank Loans; and 7) Business Development Agreements with and without issues relating to the Homotannia Land Company.

The outgoing and expenditure arms of this department are as follows: 1) Administrative and Organizational expenses; 2) Construction and Development expenses; 3) Public Policy and Relations expenses; 4) Membership and Recruitment expenses; 5) Administering to the Homotannia Land Company and all of their development activities; and 6) Health and Betterment expenses of the Homotannia Land Company and all personnel joining our Gay State.

The Gifting and Fundraising Department will reduce the scope of its activities when the state is formed and the Department of the Treasury assumes such roles.

<u>3.) The Justice Department.</u> The Society will use its moral and ethical compass to ensure that in the initial stages of the Gay State that there will be a guiding force to keep our forward movement on a just and righteous path. Other newly developed states have experienced rampant embezzlement and corruption and raiding of the treasury. Our oversight committees will seek to eliminate any of this. Misappropriation will result in imprisonment. This Department will also work closely with the Homotannia Land Company to ensure it is following proper jurisprudence, which is affording all new members equality under the

law. Operations include the Law Enforcement agencies that will work with the Land Company during its construction phase.

4.) The Standards and Creation Department. We have witnessed in human history countries blessed with majestic geographic surrounding be destroyed by uninspiring human development. We have witnessed the squalor that has become of shanty towns, and beggars scrounging for food in city dumps. This Department will oversee all zoning and architectural development to ensure our new nation will be a shining hallmark to man's ability to recognize spatial harmony and create a society that will become a breathtaking beacon of human ingenuity for millions of people world wide. In a non-religious sense, our Gay State will be a Mecca and pilgrimage not only for the global Gay community, but also for humanity at large.

5.) The Technology Department. We will examine every way possible to break the old binds that limit human potential. We will develop in committees Green Technology that will keep our new Gay State free from the shackles of oil independence. We will establish National fields of Solar Panels that will generate a good deal of our needed energy. Through eco-farming we will be independent and self-sustaining in growing enough food to feed our people. Our Commerce Committees will have five, ten, twenty, and fifty-year Sustainability Plans that will guide our economy and growth with a balanced Smart Plan. We can never be content to take the easy way when we can envision the right way. To elaborate in any greater detail at this point only encourages our detractors to emphasize the impossibilities and challenges, and we will not waste precious time with so much work needing to be done.

6.) The Health and Betterment Department. Some of our readers of this pamphlet may reside in nations where the terms for assisting fellow citizens take on a negative connotation. In such societies, they have bastardized such things as "welfare" and "social services." They are only for the weak among us—the useless, the users, the scoundrels and the lazy, or so some have been indoctrinated to believe. We strive for the betterment of man and all mankind. We take from other nations their tired, their poor, their huddled masses yearning to be free; such words are known all over the world, and in improving life for all of us. This department will oversee the implementation of our Universal Health Care system in its initial stages before it is turned over to the Department of Health Improvement. It will also oversee all socialization and nutrition programs with committees operating the National Dining Halls and Home Nutrition programs for the aged, as well as the clubs and affiliations that benefit our citizenry.

7.) The Transportation Department. This department will work closely with the Homotannia Land Company to 1) organize and assist in the relocation of all new members so that it is done in a timely and well-paced manner; 2) develop the state's local mass transportation and trolley and transportation system including highways, roads, scooter and bicycle paths, walking trails, and sidewalks; 3) oversee the blueprints for the two airports (one commercial, one military) in the State, as well as the various marina and port facilities to ensure they are ecologically sound and aesthetically incorporated into the vibrancy of the communities they serve.

8.) Oversight and Review Board. This quasi-autonomous board will operate to review all budgets and disbursements throughout the Society with regard to how funds are received and expended. It will also review all expenditures granted to the Homotannia Land Company for the operations of its construction projects. It remains vital to our plan that we remain above any suspicion of impropriety. Fraud, graft, and corruption will not be tolerated even through the simplest forms of padding invoices for construction materials. Penalties for such illegalities will be swift and harsh according to the jurisprudence established by the Justice Department.

9. International Service Department. We will seek to establish cordial and ongoing relations with our neighbors and freedom loving nations

all over the globe. We will forge alliances with likeminded peoples in matters relating to defense, as well as keeping our shores clear from organized crime or the scourge of illegal drugs. Diplomacy will provide our people from all corners of the world a buffer should their lands of birth attempt to suppress their desire or ability to relocate to our Promised Land.

These will be the pillars that will uphold the Society of Gays and all of their works. Within the various Departments, a multitude of other agencies will serve our people.

When our Gay State is established to the extent that it resembles the functionality of a working nation, more than that of a refugee and resettlement camp, which it may be portrayed as during the initial construction phase, a full and legitimate government, elected by the people, will assume power and operating authority.

WHY CHOOSE THE NAME "THE SOCIETY OF GAYS?"

There are other names that have a more favorable response to them. Ask any creative marketing person, and you will be bedazzled with the possible play on words. There are also names that are slightly more ambiguous and less likely to arouse feelings one way or the other. And there will be, knowing humanity as I do, names for us that our detractors will make of their own accord, and rest assured that these names will not do us favors.

The Society of Gays was chosen for its accuracy and also for its brevity. It is precise and succinct in whom we are—"The" society. We are "the" one global movement that is working on behalf of Gays, Lesbians, Bisexuals, and Transgendered people everywhere to secure for them their own, new independent nation-state. We are a "Society." By any definition we are a society, an organized group of persons associated together for religious, benevolent, cultural, scientific, political, patriotic, or other purposes. And we are a people – one people. And, the term "Gay"— there is no other word that so favorably describes who we are beyond our sexuality and sexual practices. Gay has been defined as a homosexual, and the word itself has made references to sexual identification at least as far back as the 1600's. This sexual world included homosexuals, too; and Gay as an adjective meaning "homosexual" goes back at least to the early 1900's. After World War II, as social attitudes toward sexuality began to change, gay was applied openly by homosexuals to themselves, first as an adjective and later as a noun. General usage and popular acceptance has never been greater than it has been in the last several decades. Although historically the term was descriptive of both sexes, in modern parlance it often designates only a male homosexual: *gays and lesbians*; GAY remains a term that is acceptable to both sexes. The word has ceased to be slang and is not used disparagingly. Furthermore, Gayness, beyond sexual identification, places an emphasis on the cultural and social aspects of homosexuality.

Popular synonyms for gay are as follows: *1.* gleeful, jovial, glad, joyous, happy, cheerful, sprightly, blithe, airy, light-hearted; vivacious, frolicsome, sportive, hilarious. Gay, jolly, joyful, merry describe a happy or light-hearted mood. Gay suggests a lightness of heart or liveliness of mood that is openly manifested: *when hearts were young and gay.* Jolly indicates a good-humored, natural, expansive gaiety of mood or disposition: *a jolly crowd at a party.* Joyful suggests gladness, happiness, and rejoicing: *joyful over the good news.* Merry is often interchangeable with *gay: a merry disposition; a merry party;* it suggests, even more than the latter, convivial animated enjoyment. *2.* brilliant. Note that these synonyms exhibit none of the negativity we have seen in the lifetimes of some readers, who can attest to their gayness (or Homosexuality) as being officially diagnosed by scientific boards as a deviance and a mental illness.

Hence, as the word GAY is now the standard in its use to refer to people whose orientation is to the same sex, in large part because it is the term that most Gay people prefer in referring to themselves, we will use it as our identifier. We will foist our name onto the world and let it be known that we will not shy away from who and what we are.

There is no shame, no embarrassment in who we are, and as we excel, the world will see us as gifted, benevolent, and good people who have developed a superior nation-state. Who amongst us is not thrilled, delighted, happy, and gleeful to be a part of the new Gay State? We will be among the happiest nations on Earth! The Society of Gays in every way describes who we are as a people, and thus, is the perfect name as we go forward.

WHY CHOOSE THE NAME "THE HOMOTANNIA LAND COMPANY?"

Some readers in the first edition of *The Gay State* interpreted The Homotannia Land Company to be the name of the new Gay State. This is not true, and the official name will be known as we progress.

The Company is first and foremost a land company. Similar to the Dutch West Indies Company, it is a chartered organization to expand with a new colony and to open trade. The purpose of our land company is to develop a new world for our Gay, Lesbian, Bisexual, and Transgendered people, as well as non-Gay Heterosexuals who wish to join us. The emphasis on Homotannia is derived from the fact that our people are everywhere. We can be found in every nation and in every major city on earth. The word Homotannia is play on the name the ancient Romans gave to the people of Great Britain, which was Britannia. And like the historic and mighty British Empire of a past era, the sun never sets on our people. We are still here today, and yet we are everywhere. There is no corner of the globe where we have not survived and endured.

The Term Homotannia is also our attempt to let the world know we will no longer live in the shadows and be marginalized as so many of our brothers and sisters have been. "Homo" no longer needs to be whispered in "polite" and proper circles. It is fundamental to who we are and what we have always been. Some have used the term as a contemptuous name for us. Yet *Webster's Dictionary* refers to Homo as people, men, equals.

We are here, and this, some would call an "in your face" approach, legally chartered name will boldly proclaim our presence, and it will even benefit those who have never uttered those two syllables before with an inkling of enlightenment. Our diligence, our hard work, our good deeds, and our moral and ethical compass will be associated with Homotannia, and the world will be better off for acknowledging who and what we are.

The Homotannia Land Company will build our new nation on land we have secured and will bring in its relocation of countrymen from every corner of the world, young, old, strong or infirmed, the educated and the working class, all Gays who yearn to be free, democratic, and to taste liberty and equality for all. Our inspiration for our identifying terms comes from the Dutch, or should I say the Nederlanders. Or should I refer to them as the people of the Kingdom of the Netherlands, or should I say the people of Holland? To be sure the people of the Netherlands are people from Holland, and they are known as Dutchmen. My point of course is that our precise names we choose for our new Gay State, and the eventual name we use to call out to our new Countrymen, will come in time. While no small issue, it is silly to entangle ourselves over this matter at this time. Now it is unnecessary for any declaration without public opinion, and this I believe will play itself out in due course.

Another example are the office holders and members of F.I.G.S. This is a coalition of the office holders and supporters that work to create a Free, Independent Gay State – FIGS. Over time, these office holders and members have become known as "Figgies." In casual, familiar usage, it conveys a camaraderie that exists between all of those who are a part of our movement and support our cause. Yanks, Aussies, Kiwis and now, Figgies.

THE EARLY ROLES OF THE SOCIETY OF GAYS.

A state is created by the process of a nation's struggle for existence. In any such struggle it is impossible to obtain proper authority in circumstantial fashion beforehand. In fact, any previous attempt to obtain a regular decision from the majority would probably ruin the undertaking from the outset. Internal schisms would make the people defenseless against the external dangers. We cannot all be of one mind, but we can support the leaders who have brought this historic event to the brink of fruition.

This embodiment of the national movement, the nature and functions of which we are at last dealing with, will, in fact, be created before everything else. Its formation is perfectly simple. It began to take shape among those energetic Gays to whom I informed of my concept in New York City at the Gramercy Park during the Salons of the winter of 2006 and onward.

The Society will have a multitude of tasks, for the founding of the Gay State, as I conceive it, presupposes the international aspect of its origins. This third edition of the original booklet is intended to open a general discussion on the Gay question. Friends and foes will take part in it, but it will no longer, I hope, take the form of violent abuse, sentimental vindication, or self loathing internal destruction, but of a debate, practical, large, earnest, and political.

The Society of Gays will gather all available declarations of statesmen, parliaments, Gay, Lesbian, Bisexual, and Transgendered communities, societies, whether expressed on the internet, or in letters, documents of allegiance, speeches or writings, in meetings, newspapers, or books.

Thus, the Society will find out for the first time whether the Gays really wish to create their own Promised Land and whether they are compelled and determined to go there. Every Gay community in the world will send contributions to the Society toward a comprehensive collection of Gay priorities and preferences in their new state.

Further tasks, such as investigation by experts of the new country and its natural resources, the uniform planning of migration and settlement, preliminary work for legislation and administration, etc., must be rationally evolved out of the original plan.

Externally, the Society will attempt, as I explained before in the general part, to be acknowledged as a State-forming power. The free assent of many Gays will confer on it the requisite authority in its relations with Governments.

Internally, that is to say, in its relation with the our Gay people, the Society will create all the first indispensable institutions; it will be the nucleus out of which the public institutions of the Gay State will later on be developed.

Our first object is, as I said before, supremacy, assured to us by international law, over a portion of the globe sufficiently large to satisfy our just requirements.

What is the next step?

THE OCCUPATION OF THE LAND

When nomadic peoples wandered in historic times, they let chance carry them, draw them, fling them without a clarity of how it would most likely come to an end, and like swarms of locusts, they settled down indifferently anywhere—nomads without a base. But our Gay migration must proceed in accordance with management principles set forth from the brightest minds. Thus, we must investigate and take possession of the new Gay territory by means of every modern expedient.

As soon as we have secured the land, we shall send over helicopters or aircraft or ships, as the new lands call for, having on board the representatives of the Society, of the Company, and of the local groups, who will enter into possession at once.

These men and womyn will have three tasks to perform: (1) an accurate, scientific investigation of all natural resources of the country; (2) the organization of a strictly centralized administration; and (3) the molding and development of the land. These tasks intersect one another and will all be carried out in conformity with the now familiar objective in view.

One thing remains to be explained -- namely, how the occupation of land according to local groups is to take place.

In the US, occupation of newly opened territory was set about in naive and almost brutish fashion. The settlers assembled on the frontier and at the appointed time made a simultaneous and violent rush for their portions. When the Jews settled in Israel, the lots in provinces and towns were sold by auction and paid for, not in money alone, but in work.

The Society of Gays and through the Homotannia Land Company will create its own hybrid, borrowing on past principles that offer positive outcomes. During the first two years, as discussed earlier, workmen will go about our construction site, readying it for our new nation and all of those who will follow. These Patriots may be rewarded on individual merit for their back breaking work with permanent housing and other benefits.

Other housing for arriving new members and settlers will be a variety of deed restriction communities, condominium developments that have established rules and guidelines, and there will be independent, free-standing homes which also must conform to general community zoning and guidelines. Most nations can offer up communities that have suffered due to the lack of zoning. We have seen the disastrous effects that come about when a neighborhood has no restrictions to development and activities on the land and proceed even ten or twenty years and you will find a ghetto or squatter camp that will be far more hopeless than anyone could have envisioned at the time of settlement.

The general plan at the end of the initial two years is to have the infrastructure in place. Roads, sidewalks, public squares, utilities, harbors, airports, medical facilities, and the campus to facilitate new arrivals are only some of the projects that will be completed in the initial two-year plan. Urban planners will lay out the initial communities to be established and will continue this work as the nation grows, well beyond the first two years. As mentioned earlier, all new settlers will undergo varying degrees of resettlement assistance within our New Arrivals Processing Campus, particularly in regards to language training, career training, and general assimilation. After several days of immersion, new members will be given a Citizenship training that outlines our general goals and principles as a people. Those who arrive that are more educated and have the financial means may elect, after completing their appropriate level of initial briefings, to settle into longer-term housing and then segue into a home they either choose to purchase outright from the Company or rent as their financial abilities allow.

The Homotannia Land Company will operate a division that concerns itself with land sales. This real estate arm will facilitate the acquisition of residential property and lots as well as commercial and industrial acreage according to zoning regulations. Lands will then be parceled out, from the Homotannia Land Company, to international companies that wish to establish a presence in our new Gay State. They may include for instance, the Four Seasons Resorts of Canada, the Monte Carlo Casino Corporation, or the Wynn Gaming Corporation of Las Vegas, and other entities that will generate employment for our citizens.

Science, The Arts, and Education will be the dominion of our people. In fairly short order, our new nation will have a state of the art medical facility and one or two colleges and universities that are satellite campuses of some of the world's finest institutions, as well as technical and vocational schools. These colleges and universities will offer degree programs to our new residents, as well as Semester Abroad Programs for their students at the mother campuses. Government buildings will be erected to house more of our institutions. Cultural buildings will house our museums and performance and visual arts. They will be centered in our capital city, but will also be erected throughout our nation. Research institutions and prominent academies will be built for our greater national good. Schools, from nursing and day care through secondary and primary, will be constructed to afford high quality, compulsory education for our children, through the age of 17. A preeminent and exclusive Boarding and Preparatory School will be established to offer a first rate education for Gay youth (ages 12 through 18) from throughout the world, and, like our nation in general, our educational institutions will boast an international flair. As a world leader in good health, nutrition, and exercise, our new Gay State will become a preeminent world destination for exclusive fat farms and weight loss programs, emphasizing our commitment to healthy living.

During the first number of years, our Gay State will offer an exempt status to all who worked to create our nation. At some point, based on population and demand, we will begin to enforce an entry fee on all new arrivals. It is not so much a fee to a private country club as everyone in our Gay State will be a member, but a fee for all of the privileges and amenities we will make available to all, free of additional entrance costs and taxations. The free health care, free education, free law enforcement, free nation-wide trolley transportation, free mental health, free use of the national dining hall, the free arrivals-citizen training-immersion classes, these and more are covered by the entry fee. While such an entry fee or annual fee may seem restrictive, we do not anticipate having a residential property tax. Furthermore, many of our other proposed taxes or fees are uncommonly low and advantageous to all residents.

Part-time and seasonal residents who can enjoy all of the best of both worlds will pay an annual residents' fee. This is in place of any residential property taxes. Full time, permanent residents who contribute and are year-round consumers, are also exempt from property taxes and pay an annual fee, although a smaller amount than those who are seasonal or part-time residents. Everything will shape itself quite naturally. All acquired rights will be protected, and every new development will be given sufficient scope.

Our new people will be made thoroughly acquainted with all these matters.

We shall not take others unaware or mislead them, any more than we shall deceive ourselves. The cost of offering these abundant lifestyle benefits must be settled in some fashion without becoming cost prohibitive or resulting in operating deficits. We have sorted these issues out in our industrial components, and from an economist's position, they are handsomely beneficial to all.

Everything must be systematically settled beforehand. I merely indicate this plan in its general terms: our keenest thinkers will combine in elaborating it. Before the slow execution of my plan is carried out to its completion, there will be new social and technical achievement that will benefit our work. The final outcome of the plan will seize every opportunity to improve as time progresses. By these means a country can be occupied and a State founded in a manner as yet unknown to history and with possibilities of success such as never occurred before.

CONSTITUTION.

One of the great commissions which the Society will have to appoint will be the National Federation of Jurists and Constitutionalists. These men and womyn will be charged with the profound task of examining and creating the best form of government in history. Entering such an assignment thinking second best is good enough dooms the process from the start. I believe that a good constitution should hold firm on core beliefs, yet offer some elasticity to suit the times. I think a socialist democracy or a democratic monarchy are the finest forms of a state, because in them the form of state and the principle of government are opposed to each other, and thus preserve a true balance of power. We must believe our government represents our best interests irrespective of the man or womyn in office. I have always felt that monarchal institutions allow for a continuous policy and represent the interests of a historically famous family born and educated to rule, whose desires are bound up with the preservation of the State. But our history has been so fragmented, there is of course no one human King or Queen, Prince or Princess, that unifies our people, and to pretend there is would be laughable, if not so absurdly artificial. The gridlock and self-absorption one finds in modern democracies allows a stagnant and mediocre status quo to endure. Politicians pandering to special interests whose lobbying arm can write large donation checks—this is what has become of the world's largest democracies. For the new Gay State, that is not good enough.

With the pandering that takes place in modern politics, there has been a suppression of worthwhile and inspiring concepts. Utter gridlock and contempt of the system is created when the private interests of the public hold sway over their leaders. Lobbyists successfully influence political leaders, and, in doing so, derail the essence of democracy. Politics must take shape in the halls of Parliament or Congress and work down to the people. No member of the Gay State will be oppressed; every person will be allowed to participate and rise in the process. We wish that our people be ambitious, that everyone will aspire for a greater good, raising himself and raising all citizens in the process. This ascent will support the national idea as well as the State.

As a people, our constitutional devotion to equality will offer better service to its people than any other nation on Earth. All of the nations that have allowed for our persecution will be models of what not to become. We will learn from the abysmal mistakes of others, and we will gain inspiration from those who have lived up to a worthy ideal. Our people in every corner of the globe will be watching, and some will be waiting. They will pray for our success, and while some will be too timid to initially join us, others who are brave of heart will jump to their feet and lend a hand. These are the Patriots who will gladly accept what the Society hands to them. They, the courageous, will be amply rewarded. They will become a part of history's most unexpected success stories and will accept the constitution the Society hands to them. Should any orchestrated opposition attempt to unconstitutionally dominate the rule of law, the Society will suppress it. The Society cannot permit the exercise of its functions to be interpreted by short-sighted individuals who do not hold the greater good as their sole priority. More on the constitution will be forthcoming after the Congress in Amsterdam convenes in 2010.

LANGUAGE.

If a Constitution affords us an operating system, language is then the engine that delivers it. Language can bring us together, but lack of a common language can more quickly divide us. Switzerland is a nation that is successfully tri-lingual. Many of the nations in Western Europe are able to accommodate internationalists with abundant ease. It is a common occurrence for citizens to speak three, four, or five languages. These successful nations will be our role models. It is equally a testament to the ingenuity of the Americans that they have been able to accomplish so much with so little in the ways of linguistic ability. If not for being native born English speakers, history might have turned out differently.

With our eventual and likely resettlement somewhere in the Western Hemisphere, the primary languages one must consider would be English, Spanish, French, or Portuguese. Of the four, the language that arguably has the greatest international usage is English. It is also more so the language of commerce. In terms of nations that are multi-lingual, executives and the educated in French, Spanish, and Portuguese-speaking countries are more apt to choose English as their secondary language than any English speaking country is to be fluent in one of the other three. For the ease of our new members, it is worth noting that English is the official language in 83 countries and is spoken in more than 105 countries, more so than any other language currently in existence.

In that the official language of the new Gay state will be English, there will be multi-lingual signage throughout the Gay state. Nationwide, there will be transportation and public service signs in Portuguese or Spanish and French. Our eventual physical locale may require Dutch to be prominently used in commerce or daily communications. Within the New World City and throughout the planned International District, a *homage* to more than two dozen languages will be in use, including Arabic, Bengali, Chinese (Cantonese), Dutch, Gaelic, German, Greek, Hebrew, Hindi, Indonesian, Italian, Japanese, Korean, Mandarin Chinese, Norwegian, Polish, Portuguese, Romanian, Russian, Swedish, Tagalog, Thai, Turkish, and Vietnamese. Noting that Chinese is the most spoken language in the world, we will emphasize its importance in how our language training institute trains our future linguists. Whatever the time frame, we envision integrating the Chinese culture into our society to a higher prominence. In time, the Homotannia Land Company could become the most fluent nation in the South-Western Hemisphere in Chinese.

As a part of the immersion procedure, all new members will enter the New Arrivals Processing Campus. Language training will become a part of the cultural and assimilation process. Our first arrivals will be some of our most desperate brothers and sisters. Most will be lacking in any substantial formal education and may only speak the language of their local village dialect. We will be vigilant in providing training so that they are successful in following orders and understanding their mission.

CIVICS AND CIVILITY.

Freedom and liberty allow for a greater independence. As a gathering melting pot from every nation on earth, we will have a confusion of varying standards that would result in a dumbing-down found in other nations. We will educate our new members during their New Arrivals Processing Sessions of the standards of civility we strive for in our Gay State. This will include offering up to our citizens and visitors a clean and sanitary environment. Etiquette and manners will be encouraged, and being a polite and courteous society will be our goal. We will offer up, though not require, all of our countrymen and womyn to observe Homotannia's Eleven Sins, Eleven Virtues, and to learn of Homotannia's Corporal Works of Mercy, also known as "The Twelve GayMandments." Some of the world's freest societies allow urination in the streets and spitting on public transportation. New York City, for instance, suffers from the scourge of graffiti on its subways and the facades of its buildings. In Homotannia, such an offense is a crime against civility, and such disregard for fellow citizens results in a sentence severe enough to adequately discourage one from repeating the offense.

In all districts, hamlets, villages, and cities, citizens must remember that we are home to Gays, Lesbians, Bisexuals, Transgender, and non-Gay Heterosexuals alike. In areas that are open to all, a certain respect for humanity and a courteous and respectful decorum is expected. All citizens will find they will have a greater degree of freedom to pursue their pleasures here than anywhere else on Earth. Pleasure, freedom, conviviality, togetherness, and free expression will be sources of great joy for Gays, Lesbians and Transgender people, as well as the non-Gay Heterosexuals amongst us. Districts and parks for each individual subgroup will be operated as a private club atmosphere where everyone will have an unprecedented source of freedom to express themselves. We will lead the world in our liberalization of some laws, while maintaining order through others.

INTERNATIONALLY RENOWNED WOMYNS TERRITORY.

David Landes of Harvard University is the renowned author of *The Wealth and Poverty of Nations.* In this groundbreaking work, Landes argues that the nations that secure the legal rights of womyn and support their equal status, tend to be the nations that have an affluent standard of living and it serves as a gauge of an economies growth potential.

"To deny women is to deprive a country of labor and talent…and in doing so, it undermines the drive to achieve among the boys, men and other women." Landes goes on to write there is nothing more dilutive to drive and ambition than the sense of entitlement.

But there is no more widely dispersed sense of entitlement than the ingraining of the "old boys network" among half of the population that they are superior, which Landes argues, reduces their need to learn and do. We see this in the US where men are now out-earned and out educated by the female population.

This kind of distortion is inherently uncompetitive and it is the result of the subordinated economic status of women in the Arab world, in Africa and virtually every underperforming nation on Earth, reports Landes in this groundbreaking work.

To implement Landes' work as the Gay State moves forward and to further elevate the rights of womyn after centuries of societal attempts to undermine their economic power, the Gay State recognizes womyn have endured multiple layers of undeserved discrimination.

As a first among modern western cultures, the Gay State will allocate a territory that will be exclusively for womyn. In this community, Sappho Island, will reside Lesbians, non-Gay womyn who wish to participate in this community, Bisexual womyn and Transgender members of the community. Male residents within this designated district, would be the minority (under-age) children and elderly parents living within the same household. Male visitors would be granted visitors passes for a specific length of time. Other than any necessary male civil servants or public officials, the district would provide an environment for Lesbian womyn from all over the world to enjoy the ambience and lifestyle the modern world has never seen.

The womyn of Sappho Island would of course retain their full citizenship of the larger Gay State and would retain all rights and responsibilities of all other citizens of the Gay State. The womyn who are either residents or visitors of Sappho Island will come to see this locale as unique in all the world, unique in its designation as both a benefit and privilege to their Gay State experience.

Lesbians world wide have often endured the double discrimination at the hands of both non-Gay Heterosexuals, as well as from male-dominated cultures and authorities. The Homotannia Land Company will establish the world's first nation in the world that is primarily Gay. To further enhance the comfort of our sisters who wish to live in a community that is largely free from male influences, we have earmarked at least one community to become predominantly but not exclusively "womyn only." Cherry Grove, a predominantly Lesbian community will offer direct ferry access to Sappho Island, an exclusively womyns-only island community. The first of its kind in the modern age, will allow men to visit, but they must be issued passes to do so. While all males may come and go and visit Cherry Grove at any time of their choosing, there is only limited, permanent "male" residential housing within Cherry Grove, so that it can retain it feminist sensibilities.

For the larger portion of all land, civility reigns and is no different than many of the world's most affluent, liberal Gay enclaves that are modern, aesthetically pleasing, progressive, clean, neat, safe, and open to all.

VIEWS OF POLITICAL CONSERVATIVES AND THE RELIGIOUS.

We know that Homosexuals have been societal scapegoats for conservatives and religious fundamentalists since time immemorial; this we know has been a frequent claim. For those with only a contemporary reference, it is accurate for all intent and purpose. But there was once a period of time when Homosexuality had an honored place in society for more than a millennium, in the days of early Greece. This was followed by a "kaleidoscope of horrors" which lasted more than 1,500 years, right up to the "madness of 19th century Europe" and today.

Louis Crompton of the University of Nebraska has authored one of the most comprehensive works on Gay history. *Homosexuality and Civilization* is a book that is a "must read" for anyone who wishes to understand the historic perspectives of today's global Gay community. "During the Middle Ages and the Renaissance, harsh legal sanctions against homosexuality routinely found their justification in Christian teaching. Angry sermons spewed their contempt and hate, predicted catastrophes and blamed sodomites when they occurred, incited mobs, called for stonings, and expressed gratification when these took place," Crompton tells the reader.

The ongoing savagery of atrocities ranged from Spain's Ferdinand and Isabella burning sodomites and confiscating their estates, to Henry VIII of protestant England, through his agents, using the charge of sodomy to justify the pillaging of the monasteries. And except for the madness of the Nazi's which claimed the extermination of tens of thousands of Gays, nowhere on Earth have more Gays been executed and imprisoned than in Venice—in the prison adjacent to the Bridge of Sighs. Travel books and tour guides do grave disservice to all global Gay visitors by rendering such a great carnage as unworthy of even a mere mention. The American sensibilities of several staff members were offended and they reported that in Venice there should be nothing less than a memorial for the atrocities waged against the Gays, but alas it's fitting that our mass extermination parallels the reality of how so many of us have lived—invisibly.

While non-Gays have gorged at the table of Gay persecution for centuries, it still continues today unabated. In the past, Crompton tells us, "cruel and unjust institutions such as slavery were, in the not-too-distant past, defended by theologians, including Protestant clergy in the US. But the clergy today decries the crimes of slavery and anti-Semitism and America's Southern Baptists for the endorsement of slavery and segregation practices." Slavery existed in North America (before the US was a nation) for a mere 246 to 305 years, depending on early shipping records that transported Africans in the 1500-1600's. The brutal oppression has been foisted on Homosexuals for two to three *thousand* years. And yet it remains so largely overlooked by the Heterosexual masses.

When nations all around the world can no longer point to Gays for their downfall, who then will they blame? We acknowledge that their views are incompatible with who we are as a people. What is uncertain is how these groups will view the formation of the world's first and only openly Gay State. Will they resent our departure? Will they see our emancipation as an even greater threat and our success as a determination that they have misjudged us for the past thirty centuries? Will they hope we will see the light and find redemption while on this path? Will they support its development, so that our people will leave "their" homelands? Will they wish us well—allow us to live in peace and cheer as we become one of the globe's most modern and manageable nations? One thing is certain in our current condition of modernity in the west, and that is that one can only be modestly hopeful about the future though the controversy will be long and impassioned. Scholarship, general academia, and popular culture have brought to light the "long sad record of oppression and abuse, and men and women who call themselves Christian can no longer plead ignorance or avoid the burden of a deplorable, long obscured past," as Mr. Compton puts it.

In that the new Gay state will never again allow hatred and intolerance to enter our homeland, we will be vigilant in our quest for equality and virtue. As a people we honor tolerance. But we will not invite bigotry and hate onto our shores. We know there are countless good and decent people of faith, and there are conservatives who do not wish to squelch the freedom and liberties of others to satisfy their narrow views. And to those who embrace our nationhood, they are welcome to participate in our great experiment. They will not be among the surprised citizens of the world who witness our loving families, our care and adoration for our elders, the love and nurturing we have for our children, the faithfulness and commitment we have for our married spouses. They will not be surprised by our love of country and our willingness to defend it by participating in necessary military maneuvers. We will invite them to join us as we celebrate our faiths and devotion to honoring something larger than ourselves. And they will see our creed to forgive but never forget the atrocities committed against us in the names of religion.

RELIGION AND THEOCRACY.

The coalition of Figgies (members and supporters of FIGS – a Free, Independent Gay State) of the new Gay State do not wish to make blanket statements regarding the intentions of all people who believe in and follow the precepts of a particular faith. There is no intention to hurt or insult anyone in the pages of this small booklet. There may be in time a full accounting of all deeds done for and to our fellow Man, whether in this world or another, and so it is not my place to neither pardon nor condemn the actions of those who believe they are following the word of God, or whatever name may be given to their Supreme Being.

Neither is this booklet meant to sugar coat the atrocities that have occurred against the global Gay community. Since Biblical times, one could strongly argue that organized religions have orchestrated a primary role in the persecutions of Gay men and womyn in every nation on Earth. Even the United States, founded on secularism and freedom of religion, has suffered from its narrow view of humanity. One of the most liberal regions within the United States, the state of New York, has in its 400-year history, imprisoned Homosexuals and sentenced Homosexuals to death for no other reason than their sexuality. Around the world, accountings of public stonings and public floggings until death are countless since time immemorial.

At what point could one argue that religion left to the devices of Man, is an enemy to freedom and philosophical ethics? It would be silly to try to change the minds of the devout and pious in these few paragraphs. For new members who have a familial history of attending the services of a particular faith, we will honor their customs in their lands of birth, in so far as allowing houses of worship in our Gay State. The condition to this of course, is that they can practice their freedom of speech, but they cannot use their pulpit to spew their hatred of our people in our own home—love, peace, charity, and noble virtues, yes. None but the self-loathing amongst us needs or wants to hear of our supposed shortcomings from our oppressors. The history of organized religion and its brutality and obscene degrees of suffering that it has inflicted on us shall not be forgotten. The belief among many in the Gay community is that "God" made us perfectly and as he saw fit. Nothing fundamental in our make up necessitates a change.

There are those that believe that God or Allah, if of any sexuality at all, could likely be Gay. How God or Allah expresses its respective sensuality or sexuality if at all, we can not comment as we were not there. Some think Satan is the Hetero in the mix, cluttering up necessary breeding with sinning and a breeders lust. Others believe that Jesus was Gay, as were many members of his inner circle. Some believe Mohammed was a self-loathing Gay man, while secretly practicing his Homosexuality. Others believe our Creator positioned the male version of a "G spot" internally for a reason – so that it could only be reached through anal penetration. Both science and determined practice has concluded that such anal stimulation results in multiple male orgasms. Still others, primarily Muslim Homosexuals have commented that a Gay Mohammad promised most of his non-Gay followers 77 virgins for acts of bravery and sacrifice. What Mohammed did not tell his "straight" followers is that they would be rewarded with 77 male virgins. I suppose, if this is true, the joke is on them. As the author of this booklet, I am not professing to be an expert in theology. Like the religious over many centuries, none of us were actually alive when the Bible or Koran were written so all views must be met with some speculation if not skepticism. Therefore, I can not confirm the accuracy of the above third party opinions with regard to the above statements. The point to it all of course, is that when laws are made to accommodate a particular philosophy or religious view at the expense of others, any could be on the winning or losing side. This is why law built on faith should be avoided. Equality. And freedom.

Many millions of Christians, Jews, Muslims, and people of other faiths will be surprised to know that there are millions of people in the Gay, Lesbian, Bisexual, and Transgender community who believe that God speaks to them through their faith. Religion is practiced, and the faiths of our families remain essential to many Gay people. Yet the intolerance within the tenets of Christianity, Islam, and Judaism, along with dozens of other, smaller faiths, leave millions of people in the Gay community conflicted. Yet, make no mistake, and I now speak directly to the religiously inclined non-Gay Heterosexuals all around the world: our people that comprise the diverse Gay spectrum believe strongly in their God and their faith and will follow their teachings in the spirit of God's love and spiritual devotion. We leave it to the non-Gays to make their amends to their God, for having passed judgment on others and ridiculed what God has created. Let us hope that God will have mercy on their judgmental souls and that all humanity can live in peace.

While this is intended to reflect upon all of the world's major religions, we acknowledge that each and every one of them has left its mark on history. To speak to the vast majority of readers in English-speaking nations that will read this edition, civility throughout the world owes an enormous debt to Christianity. Its works of compassion, its educational services and impressive contribution to the world's treasury of great art, music, and timeless architecture must be acknowledged, as Louis Crompton pointed out in *Homosexuality and Civilization*. And we must, he added, "recognize the church leaders who worked for peace and the alleviation of human oppression." And so we value their works and their contribution, but are again reminded of the quote from Martin Luther King, Jr., *"In the end, we will remember not the words of our enemies, but rather the silence of our friends."* Where were you at every family shunning, at every village Gay bashing, at the brutal assaults on our souls? Where were you when we were imprisoned for loving someone? Where were you when we lost our homes, our employment, and our futures? Where were you when our Gay sons were beheaded and burned alive by angry mobs, and where were you when we were sentenced to death? Where were you for the last three thousand years, and why did you not speak in our defense?

As to the finer points of our Constitution regarding religion, our Gay State will officially be a secular nation. There will be an emphasis on the goodness of people, a stress on Humanism and Philosophy, and supporting our Corporal Works of Mercy. Other religious organizations may gather as well in their houses of worship and conduct their practices as desired by our citizenry. The leaders of these religions, be they Rabbis,

Priests, Imams, and those of other titles, will confine their activities to their houses of worship, just as our military will be confined to its barracks and bases. They will be honored for the roles they play, but will in no way be allowed to interfere with the role of a secular and civilian government. Let no house of worship posture itself as being better than any other. We are all equal and free.

LAWS.

Our laws will revolve around the laws of human rights and will be similar to those of other modern societies. When the practical nature of finalizing the particulars is upon us, we will utilize the wisdom of our Council of Jurists to establish the words and principles that should guide all of the actions of our people.

The Society of Gays and their work within the Department of Justice will make these laws known to all.

THE MILITARY.

We are a peaceful people. We are generally law abiding, discounting the 80 nations that make our very existence illegal. We also will be friendly to our neighbors and, through our friendships, forge a trust that improves our collective defense, commerce, and quality of life. The nations that surround us will come to view our presence favorably, and we will look out for them as any good neighbor would. Our neutrality will be known to all, as will our fierce determination to defend our borders. We have waited thirty-plus centuries for our own homeland and will not surrender quietly our new found freedom.

We in the new Gay State know there are forces in the world that despise our freedom, our liberal views, and our social democratic ways. We will not flinch. We will steel our spines and do what is required to make a historic change. Make no mistake, there is a clarity of purpose here and a steely resolve to make a safe and free home for our people. We will defend ourselves mightily. And toward this end, we will always be prepared. Our military will be strong, modern, and well trained. Our efforts will lie in a superior Army, Navy, Air Force, Marines, and Coast Guard.

Our Gay State will require eighteen months of compulsory service from all of its citizens between the ages of 17 to 21. Young men and womyn may be assigned to general military service or to our peacekeeping and national service causes. During this time, they will acquire defensive skills and learn military strategies. We will be strong of mind and body and will conduct ourselves as civilized members of the international community. The military training will also provide career training with a military specialty that may enhance one's civilian resume. After completing the initial term of service, each citizen will complete two weeks per year in training for the following three years. Citizens will then follow up with one 7 day training session for the next five years. No one will be compelled to perform military service beyond the age of 35 unless they are career military personnel or we are in a period of warfare that requires everyone's participation to defend our nation.

Like Switzerland, we will require all trained citizens to keep a military weapon in their places of residence. The weapon is not allowed outside of the residence without proper authorization, and violations of this will result in a severe punishment. Under no circumstances will we become a nation of violence like the United States, nor will we allow savage mobs to intimidate our citizenry.

PHYSICAL FITNESS.

A healthy body promotes a healthy mind. And a healthy body enables life to be pursued with zest and vigor. And as the state provides universal health care for all of its citizens, it is to everyone's benefit to keep a lid on the costs associated with health care. Toward meeting that goal, the

Gay State will initiate physical fitness clubs throughout the nation-state. All citizens will be required to attend three physical training sessions per week. Twenty one (seven weeks of) unexplained absences are allowed per year. In addition, all citizens who are out-of-nation will be exempt from the requirement.

Those who miss more than twenty one sessions per year will be required to provide a physician's certificate or incur a monetary fee for each session they are absent. This fee will go towards our nation's increased expenditures in our health care arena, brought on by those who do not at least attempt to maintain their optimal physical and mental health.

Those who do not wish to participate in their own health maintenance and do not wish to participate in lowering health care costs for all citizens are not required to join in our physical fitness clubs. They may elect to pay an annual sum to be determined at a later date; it will be approximately equal to the cost of a person's health insurance premium that is otherwise provided by the state.

THE FLAG.

For more than twenty years the world has had a Gay flag. It was often flown as a voluntary identifier for Gay residences out of pride and for businesses to attract customers or to display their solidarity to the Gay community. And, as a Gay State, we will need a flag. If we desire to lead many men, we must raise a symbol above our heads.

I suggest we utilize the existing flag of our people. It is already being flown in countries all around the world. The Rainbow Flag, as it has been called, was created by Gilbert Baker, the so called "Betsy Ross" of the gay movement. To differentiate our nation-state's flag from the current rainbow flag that is known for its commercial endorsements, as well as from all of the non-Gay oriented rainbow flags in existence, I have suggested to Baker that we keep the Rainbow Flag on one portion of our State flag and, on the other, smaller portion, we have a crest of some sort or a graphic that identifies our Gay, Lesbian, Bisexual, and Transgender status. It should perhaps be on a background of white or yellow to signify our hopefulness, our peaceful nature, and the purity of our fresh start. Our people will gather in our Promised Land under the banner, and as such, there should be a component that emphasizes its international aspect.

RECIPROCITY AND EXTRADITION TREATIES.

The new Gay State must be properly founded, following all diplomatic protocol and international standards with due regard to our future honorable position in the world. The Society of Gays and the Homotannia Land Company will exercise rigor that all new members depart from their nations on good terms. Priority will be given to those who submit, along with the requisite applications, an official testimonial from the local authorities, certifying that they have left their affairs in good order. In lieu of this, such as in the case where a new member experiences extreme and aggravated anti-Gayism, a candidate must submit five verifiable letters of reference, either personal or professional. If in all cases, if an upright and solid applicant has led a hidden life, measures will be taken so that a candidate can bypass such bureaucracy and still come to our Promised Land.

There have been insinuations made to the Founding Fathers that the nations that most revile our Gay people will want our experiment to utterly fail. Toward that end, an effort will be made to flood our new homeland with the worst of their murderers, thieves, organized criminals, and imprisoned masses. (A similar situation played out in the United States in an operation known as the Mariel Boat Lift. Thousands of Cuba's worst convicts were sent on boats to the shores of South Florida, and they became a serious issue that the United States was forced to deal with.) These people, some Gay but mostly non-Gay, NOT shining examples of the best of humanity will be told by their prison officials that if they are not successful at being selected by our

New Membership Panels, they will remain behind and forced into hard labor, extended sentences, or worse. If this threat materializes, how do we propose to handle it? First, how would any nation react to such threats of extortion? We would alert the world and inform the United Nations. Our first concern must be that we would continue with our screening process as our protocol allows, and select only the new members that match our criteria. People who earnestly and honestly come to our shores and are wanted for crimes in the nations of their birth will generally be returned. Exceptions will be made if The Society of Gays determines that sending them back will result in their being discriminated against because they are Gay. We cannot allow our nation-state to be perceived as a safe hideaway for all of the world's rejects and ne'er-do-wells.

From our very beginning, we will enforce our penal codes and will not tolerate those who operate to deter us from our mission of building our nation. If a crime is committed in our Gay state and our Council of Jurists determines a verdict of guilty, someone will receive and serve their sentence. Once that sentence is served and the guilty party atones for his or her actions, he will be released to participate as a member of the public to begin a new life.

The following is a story as told by Theodor Herzl, one of our inspirational leaders who lived more than 100 years ago and was an original founder of the concept of a Jewish state:

Here I should like briefly to relate a story I came across in an account of the gold mines of Witwatersrand. One day a man came to the Rand, settled there, tried his hand at various things, with the exception of gold mining, until he founded an ice factory, which did well. He soon won universal esteem by his respectability, but after some years he was suddenly arrested. He had committed some misappropriations as a banker in Frankfort, had fled from there, and had begun a new life under an assumed name. But when he was led away as prisoner, the most respected people in the place appeared at the station, bade him a cordial farewell and au revoir -- for he was certain to return.

How much this story reveals! A new life can regenerate even criminals, and we have a proportionately small number of these. We are probably disliked as much for our gifts as we are for our faults. But this strong arm of justice will be tempered with the hand of compassion.

We would expect that our Gay State would offer as much compassion to someone who has made a mistake and served the punishment for his crime. We will allow people a chance to be redeemed and start a new life.

BENEFITS OF THE EMIGRATION OF THE GAYS.

I imagine that governments will, either voluntarily or under pressure from those opposed to our Gay movement, pay certain attention to this plan. Some will be moved by our commitment and express their good will and encouragement to the Society of Gays. Most, I suspect, will be glad to see us go and not think twice over our departure.

Yet, many nations would benefit from our plan, particularly smaller nations where our exodus might be more felt. An era of prosperity will follow in these small countries when our Gay people leave a void for others to step in and fill a niche. It will bring great prosperity to some, or numerous business competitors may serve the void left behind. In the longer term, I believe these nations may experience a vacuum in the absence of their most creative citizens. Gay people are creative, known for their tenacity and perseverance, and their absence from the scene will be missed, although it won't be recognized for some time.

During and after a period of resettlement, there will begin to be a period of reverse trade. The settlers of our new Gay State may see and experience consumer items or services that were not available in the lands of their birth. Now as established and successful citizens of our land and dual passport holders, they may elect to do commerce between both nations and in doing so, every country on earth will learn of new products by way of our new Gay State.

"I long to tell them that it will be all right, that they are not an abomination, that they are gloriously made precisely as God wants them to be."

~ The Right Reverend Gene Robinson

"We will remember not the words of our enemies,
but the silence of our friends."

~ Rev. Martin Luther King, Jr.

Chapter Six.
International Laws and Discrimination Against Homosexuals After 3,000 Years of "Progress."

When one considers how the society of Man has changed since Biblical times, it is truly a historic shift that is difficult to fathom. The most senior of our readers have seen a lifetime of changes, from household luxuries to technological marvels—just since the 1930's or 1940's. With regard to the acceptance of Homosexuals and Gay Rights, there are large corners of the world that have witnessed tremendous advancements. If one is fortunate enough to live in one of these liberal pockets of the world, life can be vastly improved. Yet, one aspect of life that has changed very little is the reception Homosexuals receive over enormous stretches of the planet.

Over the last 2,000 to 3,000 years, Gays have been among the world's most persecuted people. In the time of Christ, Gays were put to death. This continues today. Men were subjected to public stonings, then as they are now. Gays continue to be killed by their parents to save the family "honor" and their "good name." Careers are lost, people are financially ruined, sometimes fined more than a full year's earnings for engaging in a Homosexual act; families are destroyed and lives are ruined, and I am not speaking of ancient Jerusalem. I am speaking of the 21ˢᵗ Century, as I write this in the year 2009 and it is published in 2010.

There are still five countries on Earth that imposes the death sentence for people discovered to commit Homosexual activity, even in the privacy of their own homes. A sixth nation is about to enact the Death Penalty as this goes to press. There are 80 countries that have made Gay Sex illegal and where punishment can range from five to ten to fifteen years in prison, and sometimes much more, and extreme hard labor. There is a seventh country, Gambia, that, as I write this, is rounding up all of the Gays they can entrap, and giving them 24 hours to leave the country or they will be beheaded. This is for Gay men and Lesbians. The list of atrocities against our people goes on and on, as you will see in the coming pages.

There will be readers, some of the most enlightened and the most modern of Gays, who reside in a handful of modern nations who will view these crimes against our people and will wish to downplay the reality of such extreme brutality. Let me write for a moment, directly to these Gay brothers and sisters. Yes, despite your comfortable lifestyle and your belief that the world has come to appreciate our contributions, outside of your liberal and progressive enclaves, this is not the case for tens of millions of our Gay brothers and sisters. To you, I ask you to imagine that you are the one lonely, uneducated, and impoverished Gay man or woman in a rural village that is frequently the subject of verbal abuse, physical violence, and repeated rapes; to know your family may count on your earnings but are embarrassed by you; to know you really have no way to improve your lot in life; or to know that suicide is the only way to end the misery. It may seem incredulous as you read this from your luxurious condo in Chelsea or The Castro, South Beach or Amsterdam, but make no mistake; there are millions who only dream of the life you lead. I have repeatedly referred to you Gay brothers and sisters who seek to downplay our suffering as the Assimilationist Gays.

Following are the laws that are on the books and oppose our people in all countries we could verify. Understand the reality is often worse than the words that appear on the page. The United States offers some glaring examples of a country that does not live up to its reputation for modernity. Vast regions of the US offer no protection for Gays. They are not protected from violence or discrimination. They can lose their jobs, their homes, and in some states they can lose their children because they are Gay. They cannot join the military and other basic duties of citizenship, and for Gay couples, they are denied more than 1,000 rights and privileges afforded to non-Gay couples. They are taxed without full representation and are equivalent to second class citizens with second class status. There is an American Gay Apartheid.

Gay bashings as well as all of the other forms of violence perpetrated against the Gay community have numbed us to the pain and brutality. Viewers see reports of such attacks on the nightly news and have grown immune to the emotions of guilt and outrage. In the States, even when a young Gay college student is savagely beaten, driven into the country, stripped, tied to a fence, and left to freeze to death, it will cause an outrage until the headlines disappear from the front page to be replaced with something else. Can you, gentle reader, imagine any other minority, African Americans, Jews, or Catholics that Americans, as a nation, would allow this sort of oppression to continue? In the 21st Century, what would be the uproar if African Americans were told they could not marry or keep their children? What would the reaction be if Catholics were arrested for observing their practices behind closed doors?

What should we as readers make of the killing of Gays as a form of entertainment in popular culture? There are, of course, the video games that young boys especially like to play. One very popular game has a hunter armed with a rifle hunting down and killing Gay men. Another example might lead a reader to conclude that I am speaking of atrocities in the Roman Coliseum, but in reality, of musical tours in the Autumn of 2009. Controversial Jamaican and Reggae artist Buju Banton is taking his "Kill Gays" tour throughout the United States. His music promotes the killing of Gay men by pouring acid on them to "burn him up bad like an old tire wheel." The lyrics of his songs go on to promote killing Gays by shooting them in the head with a submachine gun. Sold out concerts span the United States from Florida to New York, Ohio to California, and many venues in between. Influenced by his music in Jamaica, unyielding mobs of Heterosexuals chased down several Gay people, hacked at them with machetes, and lit them on fire. Being Gay, incidentally, is legal in the United States and illegal in Jamaica, yet the rule of law does very little to protect Gays.

In the 21st Century, Gay men have been savagely beheaded in both countries. In Haiti, another country where Homosexuality is technically "legal," it is reported that "these days," Homosexuals are "rarely" set on fire. It no longer happens "very often." One must wonder then, about the form of treatment in countries where Homosexuality remains illegal. And again, merely to offer perspective, would civilized nations stand by and tolerate a "Kill the Jews Tour?" Or "Kill the African Americans" Tour in 21st Century America? The thought of civilized societies tolerating this behavior should be reprehensible to us all. There would be an uproar of protestations for these tours, as there should be. As of this writing, no known groups other than LGBT groups have spoken out on the Buju Banton tours. Almost all of our friends have remained silent.

In the US, with its fast paced television news cycle, a story filled the air waves for several days over one Justice of the Peace in Louisiana who refused to marry one inter-racial couple. Such an uproar over one couple being denied marriage, and it is a tragedy for this couple to have been denied their right to marry. Where is the constant uproar over Gays, thousands every day, being denied their rights? Beyond the shock of the racism, this couple merely went to a different Justice of the Peace, and they were married all well and good! Gays, in this self-proclaimed "freest nation on Earth," have nowhere else to go for their marriage rights.

Finally, let me acknowledge Brazil, home to Rio de Janiero and Sao Paulo, often perceived as two of the world's most Gay-friendly cities. As more Gays, Lesbians, Bisexuals, and Transgender people reveal themselves and the number of Gay Pride parades increases, so too does the scourge of anti-Gayism. Catholicism is deeply rooted in the culture of this South American country, often viewed around the world for its modern and enlightened views of human rights. What then, explains that in one year the murders of Homosexuals soared by 55%? Of these, 64% of the victims were Gay and 32% were Transvestites. Transvestites in Brazil live their lives in a particular danger and are 259 times more likely to be murdered than Gay men. Lastly, given the history of oppression, I tend to believe the official numbers are usually under-reported. The point here is, although the Gay community achieves a level of visibility, it does not mean that the violence against us has dissipated. On the contrary, it is increasing as we begin to show ourselves.

The reader should not misinterpret my views on global opinions and its actions towards the global Gay community. I accept with knowledge that every minute of every day brings more discrimination against Gay brothers and sisters somewhere on our planet. Not all non-Gay Heterosexuals endorse our oppression. Some passively endorse the brutality by their silence, and we know throughout history that silence equals acceptance. Yet, there are non-Gay Heterosexuals who are our valued friends and supporters. The bravest among them stand by our sides and fight the global injustices that plague us. Many have had the courage to stand shoulder to shoulder with us when they could have easily avoided the issues. And there have been honorable religious men as well, who have understood the injustices done to the Gay, Lesbian, Bisexual, and Transgender community. They have acknowledged the long and twisted history that religious organizations have played a part in—their efforts to oppress and to exterminate us. Their honesty and acknowledgements are all appreciated and duly noted.

In contrast, there are surprisingly too many other minority groups who have endured their own struggles for human rights and who have proven to be our enemies in our fights for equality. As the majority of Gays are politically left of center in politics, Gays have usually been on the scene and often in the forefront, fighting for others human and civil rights. So, it is with surprise and disappointment to many in the Gay community that some of those we have most fought for, now remain seated and silent in our times of need. One such example is in the United States and the fight for the civil rights of African Americans. More than forty years have passed since they received their federal rights and equal protection under the law. Many of the religious leaders within their movement; individuals with significant influence over their African American flock, told their congregations to take a stand AGAINST OUR RIGHTS by voting in elections that were contrary to our freedom and equality. Thousand of years of history has taught us about the "religious," and the hypocrisy among religious leaders does not surprise me, except the wounds of a hard fought victory among the African Americans should be fresh enough for them to empathize and to understand our plight, and they should have endeavored to help end our suffering. They betrayed our trust, worked against our interests, and it is one more example of our friends being silent.

In 2009, there could be upwards of 600,000,000 Gay men and Lesbians throughout the globe. Here is a list of how the governments, most of which are members of the United Nations, regard their Gay citizens. More to the point, here are the nations that have outlawed who we are as people and the penalties imposed for our being, for our actions:

Note: In many nations, the use of the term Pederasty, does not imply sex with children, but instead sex between same-sex people. In other nations, Pederasty is a charge of committing sex with either children or Homosexual acts. Thirdly, some nations consider Pederasty to be sex with children, Homosexual sex, or sex between a human and animal.

Afghanistan

Male-Male: Illegal   Female-Female: Illegal

Penal Code, 1976 9 CHAPTER EIGHT: Adultery, Pederasty, and Violations of Honour

Article 427: —

(1) A person who commits adultery or pederasty shall be sentenced to long imprisonment.

(2) In one of the following cases commitment of the acts, specified above, is considered to be aggravating conditions:

a. In the case where the person against whom the crime has been committed is not yet eighteen years old.

b. ...

In Afghan legal terminology –pederasty appears to refer to intercourse between males regardless of age. The fact that pedophilia or sexual relations with persons under the age of consent falls under subsection 2(a) of article 427 indicates that this is the case. Terming sexual acts between adult men –pederasty has previously not been uncommon; this occurred for example in the translations of the Criminal Codes of Albania (1977) and Latvia (1933), and in the old Russian legal tradition a –pederast usually referred to a male who had anal intercourse with another male, regardless of age.

Islamic Sharia law, criminalizing homosexual acts with a maximum of death penalty, is applied together with the codified Penal law. However, no verifiable cases of death sentences have been handed out for homosexual acts after the end of Taliban rule but as they maintain their power outside the large cities, it is expected that this punishment continues.

Algeria

Male-Male: Illegal   Female-Female: Illegal

Penal Code (Ordinance 66-156 of June 8, 1966)

Art. 338 - —Any person guilty of a homosexual act shall be punished with a term of imprisonment of between two months and two years and a fine of between 500 and 2,000 Algerian dinars.

Angola

Male-Male: Illegal   Female-Female: Illegal

Penal Code of September 16, 1886, as amended in 1954 (Inherited from the Portuguese colonial era)

Articles 70 and 71 ad security measures on people who habitually practice acts against the order of nature, stating that such people shall be sent to labor camps.

Antigua and Barbuda

Male-Male: Illegal   Female-Female: Illegal

Sexual Offences Act of 1995 (Act No. 9) Buggery

Article 12. —

(1) A person who commits buggery is guilty of an offences and is liable on conviction to imprisonment –

(a) for life, if committed by an adult on a minor;

(b) for fifteen years, if committed by an adult on another adult;

(c) for five years, if committed by a minor.

(2) In this section "buggery" means sexual intercourse per anus by a male person with a male person or by a male person with a female person. Serious indecency Article 15. —(1) A person who commits an act of serious indecency on or towards another is guilty of an offences and is liable on conviction to imprisonment –

(a) for ten years, if committed on or towards a minor under sixteen years of age;

(b) for five years, if committed on or towards a person sixteen years of age or more,

(2) Subsection (1) does not apply to an act of serious indecency committed in private between –

(a) a husband and his wife; or

(b) a male person and a female person each of whom is sixteen years of age or more;

(3) An act of "serious indecency" is an act, other than sexual intercourse (whether natural or unnatural), by a person involving the use of genital organ for the purpose of arousing or gratifying sexual desire.

Bangladesh
Male-Male: Illegal   Female-Female: Legal
Penal Code, 1860 (Act XLV of 1860) Section 377 —
Unnatural Offences
"Whoever voluntary has carnal intercourse against the order of nature with man, woman, or animal, shall be punished with imprisonment of either description which may extend to life, or up to 10 years, and shall also be liable to fine. Explanation: Penetration is sufficient to constitute the offence as described in this section."

Barbados
Male-Male: Illegal   Female-Female: Illegal
Sexual Offences Act 1992, Chapter 154 Buggery Section 9. —Any person who commits buggery is guilty of an offence and is liable on conviction on indictment to imprisonment for life.
Serious indecency Section 12. —
(1) A person who commits an act of serious indecency on or towards another or incites another to commit that act with the person or with another person is guilty of an offence and, if committed on or towards a person 16 years of age or more or if the person incited is of 16 years of age or more, is liable on conviction to imprisonment for a term of 10 years.
(2) A person who commits an act of serious indecency with or towards a child under the age of 16 or incites the child under that age to such an act with him or another, is guilty of an offence and is liable on conviction to imprisonment for a term of 15 years.
(3) An act of —serious indecency is an act, whether natural or unnatural by a person involving the use of the genital organs for the purpose of arousing or gratifying sexual desire.

Belize

Male-Male: Illegal   Female-Female: Legal

Criminal Code [CAP. 101] (REVISED EDITION 2003) Unnatural Crime Section 53. —Every person who has carnal intercourse against the order of nature with any person or animal shall be liable to imprisonment for ten years.

Bhutan

Male-Male: Illegal   Female-Female: Illegal

Penal Code 2004 Unnatural sex Section 213. —

A defendant shall be guilty of the offence of unnatural sex, if the defendant engages in sodomy or any other sexual conduct that is against the order of nature.

Grading of unnatural sex Section 214. —The offence of unnatural sex shall be a petty misdemeanor.

Classes of crime Section 3. "For the purpose of this Penal Code, the classes of crimes shall be as follows:

(c) A crime shall be petty misdemeanor, if it is so designated in this Penal Code or other laws and provides for a maximum term of imprisonment of less than one year and a minimum term of one month for the convicted defendant."

Botswana

Male-Male: Illegal   Female-Female: Illegal

PENAL CODE [Chapter 08:01]

Section 164. Unnatural offences —Any person who;

(a) has carnal knowledge of any person against the order of nature;

(b) has carnal knowledge of any animal; or

(c) permits any other person to have carnal knowledge of him or her against the order of nature, is guilty of an offences and is liable to imprisonment for a term not exceeding seven years.

Section 165. Attempts to commit unnatural offences —Any person who attempts to commit any of the offences specified in section 164 is guilty of an offence and is liable to imprisonment for a term not exceeding five years.

Section 167. Indecent practices between persons —Any person who, whether in public or private, commits any act of gross indecency with another person, or procures another person to commit any act of gross indecency with him or her, or attempts to procure the commission of any such act by any person with himself or herself or with another person, whether in public or private, is guilty of an offence.

Brunei
Male-Male: Illegal   Female-Female: Legal
PENAL CODE, CHAPTER 22, revised edition 2001
Unnatural offences.
Section 377. —Whoever voluntarily has carnal intercourse against the order of nature with any man, woman, or animal, shall be punished with imprisonment for a term which may extend to 10 years, and shall also be liable to fine. [S 12/97] Explanation: Penetration is sufficient to constitute the carnal intercourse necessary to the offence described in this section.

Burundi
Male-Male: Illegal   Female-Female: Illegal
On 22 April 2009 the president of Burundi signed into law a revision of the Penal Code which for the first time in history includes a prohibition of same-sex relations. Article 567 now punishes such relations with up to two years imprisonment upon conviction.

Cameroon
Male-Male: Illegal   Female-Female: Illegal
Penal Code of 1965 and 1967, as amended in 1972
Section 347. Homosexuality– —
Any person who has sexual relations with a person of the same sex shall be punished with a term of imprisonment of five years and a fine of between 20,000 and 200,000 francs.

Comoros

Male-Male: Illegal   Female-Female: Illegal

Penal Code of the Federal Islamic Republic of Comoros

Article 318. – —

(3) Without prejudice to the more serious penalties provided for in the preceding paragraphs or by articles 320 and 321 of this Code, whoever will have committed an improper or unnatural act with a person of the same sex will be punished by imprisonment of between one and five years and by a fine of 50 000 to 1 000 000 francs. If the act was committed with a minor, the maximum penalty will always be applied.

Cook Islands (New Zealand Associate)

Male-Male: Illegal   Female-Female: Legal

Crimes Act 1969

Section 154. Indecency between males – —

(1) Every one is liable to imprisonment for a term not exceeding five years who, bring a male,-

(a) Indecently assaults any other male; or

(b) Does any indecent act with or upon any other male; or

(c) Induces or permits any other male to do any indecent act with or upon him.

(2) No boy under the age of fifteen years shall be charged with committing or being a party to an offence against paragraph

(b) or paragraph

(c) of subsection (1) of this section, unless the other male was under the age of twenty-one years.

(3) It is not defence to a charge under this section that the other party consented.

Section 155. Sodomy – —

(1) Every one who commits sodomy is liable-

(a) Where the act of sodomy is committed on a female, to imprisonment for a term not exceeding fourteen years;

(b) Where the act of sodomy is committed on a male, and at the time of the act that male is under the age of fifteen years and the offender is of over the age of twenty-one years, to imprisonment for a term not exceeding fourteen years;

(c) In any other case, to imprisonment for a term not exceeding seven years. (2) This offence is complete upon penetration.

(3) Where sodomy is committed on any person under the age of fifteen years he shall not be charged with being a party to that offence, but he may be charged with being a party to an offence against section 154 of this Act in say case to which that section is applicable.

(4) It is no defense to a charge under this section that the other party consented.

Note that Cook Islands is a New Zealand associate, and that the laws in Cook Islands are only applicable to the islands, and not to New Zealand proper.

Dominica
Male-Male: Illegal   Female-Female: Illegal
Sexual Offences Act 1998
Section 14. Gross Indecency —

(1) Any person who commits an act of gross indecency with another person is guilty of an offence and liable on conviction to imprisonment for five years. (2) Subsection (1) does not apply to an act of gross indecency committed in private between an adult male person and an adult female person, both of whom consent.

(3) For the purposes of subsection (2) –

(a) an act shall be deemed not to have been committed in private if it is committed in a public place; and

(b) a person shall be deemed not to consent to the commission of such an act if –

(i) the consent is extorted by force, threats or fear of bodily harm or is obtained by false and fraudulent representations as to the nature of the act;

(ii) the consent is induced by the application or administration of any drug, matter or thing with intent to intoxicate or stupefy the person; or

(iii) that person is, and the other party to the act knows or has good reason to believe that the person is suffering from a mental disorder.

(4) In this section —gross indecency is an act other than sexual intercourse (whether natural or unnatural) by a person involving the use of genital organs for the purpose of arousing or gratifying sexual desire.

Section 16 Buggery —

(1) A person who commits buggery is guilty of an offence and liable on conviction to imprisonment for –

(a) twenty-five years, if committed by an adult on a minor;

(b) ten years, if committed by an adult on another adult; or

(c) five years, if committed by a minor;

and, if the Court thinks it fit, the Court may order that the convicted person be admitted to a psychiatric hospital for treatment.

(2) Any person who attempts to commit the offence of buggery, or is guilty of an assault with the intent to commit the same is guilty of an offence and liable to imprisonment for four years and, if the Court thinks it fit, the Court may order that the convicted person be admitted to the psychiatric hospital for treatment.

(3) In this section —buggery means sexual intercourse per anum by a male person with a male person or by a male person with a female person.

Egypt

Male-Male: Illegal   Female-Female: Unclear

Sexual relations between consenting adult persons of the same sex in private are not prohibited as such. However,

Law 10/1961, aimed at combating prostitution, as well as for example Penal Code article 98w on —Contempt for Religion and article 278 on —Shameless public acts have been used to imprison gay men in the recent years. Law n° 10, 1961 on 'Combating of prostitution, incitement and its encouragement':

Article 9 (c) "Anyone who habitually engages in debauchery or prostitution is liable to a penalty of three months to three years imprisonment and/ or a fine of LE 25-300".

Eritrea

Male-Male: Illegal   Female-Female: Illegal

Penal Code of 1957 (Inherited from Ethiopian rule) Art. 600. —
Unnatural Carnal Offences. —

(1) Whosoever performs with another person of the same sex an act corresponding to the sexual act, or any other indecent act, is punishable with simple imprisonment.

(2) The provisions of Art. 597 are applicable where an infant or young person is involved.

Art.105.- Simple Imprisonment. —

(1) simple imprisonment is a sentence applicable to offences of a not very serious nature committed by persons who are not a serious danger to society. It is intended as a measure of safety to the general public and as a punishment to the offender. Subject to any special provision of law and without prejudice to conditional release, simple imprisonment may extend for a period of from ten days to three years; such period shall be fixed by the court.

(2) The sentence of simple imprisonment shall be served in such prison or in such section thereof as is appointed for the purpose.

Ethiopia

Male-Male: Illegal   Female-Female: Illegal

The Criminal Code of the Federal Democratic Republic of Ethiopia, Proclamation No. 414/2004

Article 629.- Homosexual and other Indecent Acts. —Whoever performs with another person of the same sex a homosexual act, or any other indecent act, is punishable with simple imprisonment.

Article 630.- General Aggravation to the Crime. —

(1) The punishment shall be simple imprisonment for not less than one year, or, in grave cases, rigorous imprisonment not exceeding ten years, where the criminal:

a) takes unfair advantage of the material or mental distress of another or of the authority he exercises over another by virtue of his position, office or capacity as guardian, tutor, protector, teacher, master or employer, or by virtue of any other like relationship, to cause such other person to perform or to submit to such an act; or

b) makes a profession of such activities within the meaning of the law (Art. 92).

(2) The punishment shall be rigorous imprisonment from three years to fifteen years, where:

a) the criminal uses violence, intimidation or coercion, trickery or fraud, or takes unfair advantage of the victim's inability to offer resistance or to defend himself or of his feeble-mindedness or unconsciousness; or

b) the criminal subjects his victim to acts of cruelty or sadism, or transmits to him a venereal disease with which he knows himself to be infected; or

c) the victim is driven to suicide by distress, shame or despair.

Article 106.- Simple Imprisonment. —

(1) Simple imprisonment is a sentence applicable to crimes of a not very serious nature committed by persons who are not a serious danger to society. Without prejudice to conditional release, simple imprisonment may extend for a period of from ten days to three years. However, simple imprisonment may extend up to five years where, owing to the gravity of the crime, it is prescribed in the Special Part of this Code, or where there are concurrent crimes punishable with simple imprisonment, or where the criminal has been punished repeatedly. The Court shall fix the period of simple imprisonment in its judgment.

(2) The sentence of simple imprisonment shall be served in such prison or in such section thereof as is appointed for the purpose.

Gambia

Male-Male: Illegal   Female-Female: Illegal

Criminal Code 1965, as amended in 2005

Article 144: Unnatural offences —

(1) Any person who—

(a) has carnal knowledge of any person against the order of nature; or

(b) has carnal knowledge of an animal; or

(c) permits any person to have carnal knowledge of him or her against the order of nature; is guilty of a felony, and is liable to imprisonment for a term of 14 years.

(2) In this section- —carnal knowledge of any person against the order of natural includes-

(a) carnal knowledge of the person through the anus or the mouth of the person;

(b) inserting any object or thing into the vulva or the anus of the person for the purpose of simulating sex; and

(c) committing any other homosexual act with the person.

Gaza Strip (Part of Palestinian Authority)

Male-Male: Illegal   Female-Female: Legal

Criminal Code Ordinance of 1936

Section 152 Unnatural offences —

(2) Anyone who:

(a) commits sexual intercourse with another person against the order of nature, or

(b) commits sexual intercourse with an animal, or

(c) permits or allows the above mentioned acts is considered to have committed a felony punishable by imprisonment for a term of ten years.

(Unofficial translation)

Ghana

Male-Male: Illegal   Female-Female: Legal

Criminal Code, 1960 (Act 29), as amended to 2003

Section 104—Unnatural Carnal Knowledge. —

(1) Whoever has unnatural carnal knowledge—

(a) of any person of the age of sixteen years or over without his consent shall be guilty of a first degree felony and shall be liable on conviction to imprisonment for a term of not less than five years and not more than twenty-five years; or

(b) of any person of sixteen years or over with his consent is guilty of a misdemeanour; or

(c) of any animal is guilty of a misdemeanour.

(2) Unnatural carnal knowledge is sexual intercourse with a person in an unnatural manner or with an animal.

Grenada

Male-Male: Illegal   Female-Female: Legal

Criminal Code as amended to 1990

Article 435. "If any two persons are guilty of unnatural connection, or if any person is guilty of an unnatural connection with an animal, every such person shall be liable to imprisonment for ten years".

Guinea

Male-Male: Illegal   Female-Female: Illegal

Penal Code of 1998

Article 325: —Any indecent act or act against nature committed with an individual of the same sex will be punished by six months to three years of imprisonment and a fine of 100,000 to 1,000,000 Guinean francs. If the act was committed with a minor under 21 years of age, the maximum penalty must be pronounced.

Guyana

Male-Male: Illegal   Female-Female: Legal

Criminal Law (Offences) Act

Section 352 - Committing acts of gross indecency with male person:
—Any male person, who in public or private, commits, or is a party to the
commission, or procures or attempts to procure the commission, by any
male person, of an act of gross indecency with any other male person shall
be guilty of misdemeanour and liable to imprisonment for two years.

Section 353 - Attempt to commit unnatural offences: —Everyone who –

(a) attempts to commit buggery; or

(b) assaults any person with the intention to commit buggery; or

(c) being a male, indecently assaults any other male person, shall be
guilty of felony and liable to imprisonment for ten years.

Section 354 – Buggery: —Everyone who commits buggery, either with a
human being or with any other living creature, shall be guilty of felony
and be liable to imprisonment for life.

India

Male-Male: Illegal   Female-Female: Legal

THE INDIAN PENAL CODE, 1860, ACT NO. 45

Section 377. —Unnatural offences.--Whoever voluntarily has carnal
intercourse against the order of nature with any man, woman or animal,
shall be punished with 1*[imprisonment for life], or with imprisonment
of either description for a term which may extend to ten years, and
shall also be liable to fine. Explanation.-Penetration is sufficient to
constitute the carnal intercourse necessary to the offence described in
this section.

1. Subs, by Act 26 of 1955, s. 117 and Sch., for "transportation for life."
A court ruling is expected to decriminalize Gay sex between consenting
adults but cannot be confirmed as of press time.

Indonesia
Male-Male: Legal*   Female-Female: Legal*
Same-sex relations are not prohibited according to the national Penal
Code. The only provision to deal with such relations is article 292 which
prohibits sexual acts between persons of the same sex, if committed with
a person under the legal age. However, in 2002 the national parliament
gave the Aceh province the right to adopt Islamic Sharia laws. Such laws
do apply to Muslims only. Moreover, for example the city of Palembang
in South Sumatra has introduced jail time and hefty fines for same-sex
relations.

Iran
Male-Male: Illegal   Female-Female: Illegal
Islamic Penal Code of Iran of 1991
Part 2: Punishment for Sodomy
Chapter 1: Definition of Sodomy
Article 108: Sodomy is sexual intercourse with a male.
Article 109: In case of sodomy both the active and the passive persons
will be condemned to its punishment.
Article 110: Punishment for sodomy is killing; the Sharia judge decides
on how to carry out the killing.
Article 111: Sodomy involves killing if both the active and passive
persons are mature, of sound mind and have free will.
Article 112: If a mature man of sound mind commits sexual intercourse
with an immature person, the doer will be killed and the passive one
will be subject to Ta'azir of 74 lashes if not under duress.
Article 113: If an immature person commits sexual intercourse with
another immature person, both of them will be subject to Ta'azir of 74
lashes unless one of them was under duress.
Chapter 2: Ways of proving sodomy in court —
Article 114: By confessing four lashes to having committed sodomy,
punishment is established against the one making the confession.

Article 115: A confession made less than four lashes (to having committed sodomy) does not involve punishment of —Had but the confessor will be subject to Ta'azir (lesser punishments).

Article 116: A confession is valid only if the confessor is mature, of sound mind, has will and intention.

Article 117: Sodomy is proved by the testimony of four righteous men who might have observed it.

Article 118: If less than four righteous men testify, sodomy is not proved and the witnesses shall be condemned to punishment for Qazf (malicious accusation).

Article 119: Testimony of women alone or together with a man does not prove sodomy.

Article 120: The Shariajudge may act according to his own knowledge which is derived through customary methods.

Article 121: Punishment for Tafhiz (the rubbing of the thighs or buttocks) and the like committed by two men without entry, shall be hundred lashes for each of them.

Article 122: If Tafhizand the like are repeated three lashes without entry and punishment is enforced after each time, the punishment for the fourth time would be death.

Article 123: If two men not related by blood stand naked under one cover without any necessity, both of them will be subject to Ta'azir of up to 99 lashes.

Article 124: If someone kisses another with lust, he will be subject to Ta'azir of 60 lashes.

Article 125: If the one committing Tafhiz and the like or a homosexual man, repents before the giving of testimony by the witnesses, his punishment will be quashed; if he repents after the giving of testimony, the punishment will not be quashed.

Article 126: If sodomy or Tafhizis proved by confession and thereafter he repents the Shariajudge may request the leader (Valie Amr) to pardon him.

Part 3: Lesbianism —

Article 127: Mosaheqeh (lesbianism) is homosexuality of women by genitals. Article 128: The ways of proving lesbianism in court are the same by which the homosexuality (of men) is proved.

Article 129: Punishment for lesbianism is hundred (100) lashes for each party. Article 130: Punishment for lesbianism will be established vis-a-vis someone who is mature, of sound mind, has free will and intention. Note: In the punishment for lesbianism there will be no distinction between the doer and the subject as well as a Muslim or non-Muslim. Article 131: If the act of lesbianism is repeated three lashes and punishment is enforced each time, death sentence will be issued the fourth time.

Article 132: If a lesbian repents before the giving of testimony by the witnesses, the punishment will be quashed; if she does so after the giving of testimony, the punishment will not be quashed.

Article 133: If the act of lesbianism is proved by the confession of the doer and she repents accordingly, the Sharia judge may request the leader (ValieAmr) to pardon her.

Article 134: If two women not related by consanguinity stand naked under one cover without necessity, they will be punished to less than hundred (100) lashes (Ta'azir). In case of its repetition as well as the repetition of punishment, hundred (100) lashes will be hit the third time.

Iraq

Male-Male: Unclear   Female-Female: Unclear

After the American invasion in 2003 the Penal Code of 1969 was reinstated in Iraq. This code does not prohibit same-sex relations.41 However, various reports have shown that self-proclaimed Sharia judges have sentenced people to death for committing homosexual acts, and that militias frequently have kidnapped, threatened and killed LGBT people. This has been confirmed by the UN-body UNAMI. The situation for LGBT people is quite dangerous in Iraq as of publication of this report.

Jamaica
Male-Male: Illegal   Female-Female: Legal
The Offences Against the Person Act
Article 76 (Unnatural Crime)
"Whosoever shall be convicted of the abominable crime of buggery [anal intercourse] committed either with mankind or with any animal, shall be liable to be imprisoned and kept to hard labour for a term not exceeding ten years."

Article 77 (Attempt) "Whosoever shall attempt to commit the said abominable crime, or shall be guilty of any assault with intent to commit the same, or of any indecent assault upon any male person, shall be guilty of a misdemeanour, and being convicted thereof shall be liable to be imprisoned for a term not exceeding seven years, with or without hard labour."

Article 78 (Proof of Carnal Knowledge) "Whenever upon the trial of any offence punishable under this Act, it may be necessary to prove carnal knowledge, it shall not be necessary to prove the actual emission of seed in order to constitute a carnal knowledge, but the carnal knowledge shall be deemed complete upon proof of penetration only."

Article 79 (Outrages on Decency) "Any male person who, in public or private, commits, or is a party to the commission of, or procures or attempts to procure the commission by any male person of, any act of gross indecency with another male person, shall be guilty of a misdemeanor, and being convicted thereof shall be liable at the discretion of the court to be imprisoned for a term not exceeding 2 years, with or without hard labour."

Kenya
Male-Male: Illegal   Female-Female: Legal
Cap.63 Penal Code
Section 162. Any person who—
(a) has carnal knowledge of any person against the order of nature; or

(b) has carnal knowledge of an animal; or is guilty of a felony and is liable to imprisonment for fourteen years: Provided that, in the case of an offence under paragraph (a), the offender shall be liable to imprisonment for twenty-one years if— (i) the offence was committed without the consent of the person who was carnally known; or (ii) the offence was committed with that person's consent but the consent was obtained by force or by means of threats or intimidation of some kind, or by fear of bodily harm, or by means of false representations as to the nature of the act.— —

Section 163. Any person who attempts to commit any of the offences specified in section 162 is guilty of a felony and is liable to imprisonment for seven years.

Section 165. Any male person who, whether in public or private, commits any act of gross indecency with another male person, or procures another male person to commit any act of gross indecency with him, or attempts to procure the commission of any such act by any male person with himself or with another male person, whether in public or private, is guilty of a felony and is liable to imprisonment for five years. (Sections amended by Act No. 5 of 2003.)

Kiribati

Male-Male: Illegal   Female-Female: Legal

Penal Code [Cap 67] Revised Edition 1977

Unnatural Offences Section 153. —Any person who-

(a) commits buggery with another person or with an animal; or

(b) permits a male person to commit buggery with him or her, shall be guilty of a felony, and shall be liable to imprisonment for 14 years.

Attempts to commit unnatural offences and indecent assaults

Section 154. —Any person who attempts to commit any of the offences it specified in the last preceding section, or who is guilty of any assault with intent to commit the same, or any indecent assault upon any male person shall be guilty of a felony, and shall be liable to imprisonment for 7 years.

Indecent practices between males

Section 155. —Any male person who, whether in public or private, commits any act of gross indecency with another male person, or procures another male person to commit any act of gross indecency with him, or attempts to procure the commission of any such act by any male person with himself or with another male person, whether in public or private, shall be guilty of a felony, and shall be liable to imprisonment for 5 years.

Kuwait
Male-Male: Illegal   Female-Female: Legal
Penal Code, Law No. 16 of June 2, 1960, as amended in 1976
Article 193. —Consensual intercourse between men of full age (from the age of 21) shall be punishable with a term of imprisonment of up to seven years.
Such relations with a man under 21 years of age are criminalised by article 192.

Lebanon
Male-Male: Illegal   Female-Female: Illegal
Penal Code of 1943 Article 534. —Any sexual intercourse against nature is punished with up to one year of imprisonment.

Lesotho
Male-Male: Illegal   Female-Female: Legal
Sodomy is prohibited as a common-law offence. It is defined as —unlawful and intentional sexual relationship per anum between two human males.

Liberia
Male-Male: Illegal   Female-Female: Illegal
Penal Law, Revised Liberian Statutes
Section 14.74 on —VOLUNTARY SODOMY‘ makes it an offence to engage in —deviate sexual intercourse under circumstances that is

not covered in Section 14.72 or 14.73. The offence is classified as a first degree misdemeanor.

Libya
Male-Male: Illegal   Female-Female: Illegal
Penal Code of 1953
Article 407: Sexual assault/rape —
(1) Any individual who has sexual intercourse with another person using violence, by means of threats or through deception shall be punished with a term of imprisonment of a maximum of ten years.
(2) This punishment shall also be imposed on any individual who has had sexual intercourse with the consent of a person who was not yet 14 years of age or with a person who did not resist on account of mental or physical disability. If the victim was not yet 14 years of age or was over 14 years of age but had not yet reached the age of 18, the maximum term of imprisonment shall be 15 years.
(3) If the offender is a relative of the victim, a guardian, a tutor or a custodian, or if the victim is his servant, or if the victim has a special dependant relationship to the offender, a term of imprisonment of between five and 15 years shall be imposed.
(4) If an individual has sexual intercourse with another person with their consent (outside marriage), the two persons involved shall be punished with a term of imprisonment of five years at most.
Article 408: Lewd acts —
(1) Any individual who commits lewd acts with a person in accordance with one of the methods specified in the preceding article shall be punished with a period of imprisonment of five years at most.
(2) This punishment shall also be imposed if the act has been committed in agreement with a person who was not yet 14 years of age or with a person who did not resist on account of a mental or physical disability. If the victim was between the ages of 14 and 18, the term of imprisonment shall be at least one year.

(3) If the offender belongs to one of the groups of offenders specified in paragraphs (2) and (3) of Article 407, a term of imprisonment of at least seven years shall be imposed. (4) If an individual commits a lewd act with another person with their agreement (outside marriage), both parties shall be punished with a term of imprisonment.

Malawi
Male-Male: Illegal   Female-Female: Legal
Penal Code Cap. 7:01 Laws of Malawi
Section 153 —Unnatural offences —Carnal knowledge of any person against the order of nature or "permitting a male person to have carnal knowledge of [a male or female person] against the order of nature - up to fourteen years imprisonment, with or without corporal punishment.
Section 156 —Indecent practices between males Gross indecency with another male person in public or private – up to five years imprisonment.

Malaysia
Male-Male: Illegal   Female-Female: Illegal
Penal Code (Consolidated version 1998)
Unnatural Offences
Section 377A.Carnal intercourse against the order of nature. —Any person who has sexual connection with another person by the introduction of the penis into the anus or mouth of the other person is said to commit carnal intercourse against the order of nature. *Explanation:* Penetration is sufficient to constitute the sexual connection necessary to the offence described in this section.
Section 377B.Punishment for committing carnal intercourse against the order of nature. —Whoever voluntarily commits carnal intercourse against the order of nature shall be punished with imprisonment for a term which may extend to twenty years, and shall also be liable to whipping. Section 377C. Committing carnal intercourse against the order of nature without consent, etc. —Whoever voluntarily commits

carnal intercourse against the order of nature on another person without the consent, or against the will, of the other person, or by putting other person in fear of death or hurt to the person or any other person, shall be punished with imprisonment for a term of not less than five years and not more than twenty years, and shall also be liable to whipping.
Section 377D. Outrages on decency.
—Any person who, in public or private, commits, or abets the commission of, or procures or attempts to procure the commission by any person of, any act of gross indecency with another person, shall be punished with imprisonment for a term which may extend to two years.

Moreover, several states in Malaysia have instated Islamic Sharia laws, applying to male and female muslims, criminalizing homosexual and lesbian acts with up to three years imprisonment and whipping.56 The Sharia Penal law in the Malaysian state of Syriah prescribes penalties for sodomy (Liwat) and lesbian relations (Musahaqat) with fines of RM5,000.00, three years imprisonment and 6 lashes of the whip. All these penalties can be combined.

Maldives
Male-Male: Illegal   Female-Female: Illegal
The Penal Code of Maldives does not regulate sexual conduct. It is instead regulated by uncodified Muslim Sharia law, which criminalises homosexual acts between both men and between women. For men the punishment is banishment for nine months to one year or a whipping of 10 to 30 strokes, while the punishment for women is house arrest for nine months to one year. There have been reports of women being sentenced to a whipping as well for lesbian acts.

Mauritania
Male-Male: Illegal   Female-Female: Illegal
Penal Code of 1984
ART. 308. - Any adult Muslim man who commits an impudent act against nature with an individual of his sex will face the penalty of

death by public stoning. If it is a question of two women, they will be punished as prescribed in article 306, first paragraph.

ART. 306(1). - Any person who commits an outrage on public decency and Islamic morals or violates the sacred places or assists in the breach, will be punished by a sentence of between three months to two years imprisonment and a fine of 5,000 to 60,000 UM, if such action is not covered by the crimes of Ghissass or Diya.

(Unofficial translations)

Mauritius

Male-Male: Illegal   Female-Female: Legal

Criminal Code of 1838 Section 250 Sodomy and bestiality —(1) Any person who is guilty of the crime of sodomy or bestiality shall be liable to penal servitude for a term not exceeding 5 years.

Morocco

Male-Male: Illegal   Female-Female: Illegal

Penal Code of November 26, 1962 63 Article 489. —Any person who commits lewd or unnatural acts with an individual of the same sex shall be punished with a term of imprisonment of between six months and three years and a fine of 120 to 1,000 dirham's, unless the facts of the case constitute aggravating circumstances.

Mozambique

Male-Male: Illegal   Female-Female: Illegal

Penal Code of September 16, 1886, as amended in 1954 (Inherited from the Portuguese colonial era) Articles 70 and 71 ad security measures on people who habitually practice acts against the order of nature, stating that such people shall be sent to labor camps.

Myanmar/Burma

Male-Male: Illegal   Female-Female: Legal

Penal Code, Act 45/1860, Revised Edition Section 377 —Whoever voluntarily has carnal intercourse against the order of nature with any man, woman or animals shall be punished with transportation for life, or with imprisonment of either description for a term which may extend to 10 years, and shall be liable to fine.

Namibia

Male-Male: Illegal   Female-Female: Legal

Sodomy remains a crime in Nambia according to the Roman-Dutch common-law, which was imposed by the South Africans. Common-law is a legal tradition based mainly on precedent court verdicts, why there is no codified sodomy provision in Nambia.

Nauru

Male-Male: Illegal   Female-Female: Legal

Criminal Code of Queensland in its application to Nauru on 1 July 1921 Section 208. Unnatural Offences —

Any person who:

(1) Has carnal knowledge of any person against the order of nature; or

(2) Has carnal knowledge of an animal; or

(3) Permits a male person to have carnal knowledge of him or her against the order of nature; is guilty of a crime, and is liable to imprisonment with hard labour for fourteen years"

Section 209. Attempt to commit Unnatural Offences —Any person who attempts to commit any of the crimes defined in the last preceding section is guilty of a crime, and is liable to imprisonment with hard labour for seven years. The offender cannot be arrested without warrant.

Section 211. Indecent Practices between Males —Any male person who, whether in public or private, commits any act of gross indecency with another male person, or procures another male person to commit any act of gross indecency with him, or attempts to procure the commission of any such act by any male person with himself or with another male person, whether in public or private, is guilty of a misdemeanor, and is liable to imprisonment with hard labour for three years.

Nigeria
Male-Male: Illegal   Female-Female: Legal*
Criminal Code Act, Chapter 77, Laws of the Federation of Nigeria 1990
Section 214. —Any person who-
(1) has carnal knowledge of any person against the order of nature; or
(2) has carnal knowledge of an animal; or
(3) permits a male person to have carnal knowledge of him or her against the order of nature; is guilty of a felony, and is liable to imprisonment for fourteen years.
Section 215. —Any person who attempts to commit any of the offences defined in the last preceding section is guilty of a felony, and is liable to imprisonment for seven years. The offender cannot be arrested without warrant.
Section 217. —Any male person who, whether in public or private, commits any act of gross indecency with another male person, or procures another male person to commit any act of gross indecency with him, or attempts to procure the commission of any such act by any male person with himself or with another male person, whether in public or private, is guilty of a felony, and is liable to imprisonment for three years. The offender cannot be arrested without warrant.
Note that several Northern Nigerian states have adopted Islamic Sharia laws, criminalizing sexual activities between persons of the same sex. The maximum penalty for such acts between men is death penalty, while the maximum penalty for such acts between women is a whipping and/or imprisonment.
These laws differ from the federal law, as most of these prohibit also sexual relations between women. The states which have adopted such laws are: Bauchi (the year 2001), Borno (2000), Gombe (2001), Jigawa

(2000), Kaduna (2001), Kano (2000), Katsina (2000), Kebbi (2000), Niger (2000), Sokoto (2000), Yobe (2001) and Zamfara (2000).

Oman
Male-Male: Illegal   Female-Female: Illegal
Penal Code, 1974
Article 223. —Any individual who commits sexual acts with a person of the same sex shall be prosecuted, even if no complaint is made, for committing homosexual or lesbian acts if the act causes a public nuisance and shall be punished with a term of imprisonment of between six months and three years.

Pakistan
Male-Male: Illegal   Female-Female: Legal
Penal Code (Act XLV of 1860)
Section 377 —Unnatural offences' "Whoever voluntarily has carnal intercourse against the order of nature with any man, woman or animal, shall be punished with imprisonment for life, or with imprisonment of either description for a term which shall not be less than two years nor more than ten years, and shall also be liable to a fine."

Palau
Male-Male: Illegal   Female-Female: Legal
Palau National Code; Penal Code § 2803. Sodomy. —Every person who shall unlawfully and voluntarily have any sexual relations of an unnatural manner with a member of the same or the other sex, or shall have any carnal connection in any manner with a beast, shall be guilty of sodomy, and upon conviction thereof be imprisoned for a period of not more than 10 years; provided, that the term —sodomy shall embrace any and all parts of the sometimes written —abominable and detestable crime against nature.

Papua New Guinea
Male-Male: Illegal   Female-Female: Legal
Criminal Code 1974, as amended in 2002
Section 210. UNNATURAL OFFENCES. —
(1) A person who–
(*a*) sexually penetrates any person against the order of nature; or
(*b*) sexually penetrates an animal; or
(*c*) permits a male person to sexually penetrate him or her against the order of nature, is guilty of a crime. Penalty: Imprisonment for a term not exceeding 14 years.
(2) A person who attempts to commit an offence against Subsection (1) is guilty of a crime. Penalty: imprisonment for a term not exceeding seven years.
Section 212. INDECENT PRACTICES BETWEEN MALES. —
(1) A male person who, whether in public or private–
(*a*) commits an act of gross indecency with another male person; or
(*b*) procures another male person to commit an act of gross indecency with him; or
(*c*) attempts to procure the commission of any such act by a male person with himself or with another male person, is guilty of a misdemeanour. Penalty: Imprisonment for a term not exceeding three years.

Qatar
Male-Male: Illegal   Female-Female: Illegal
The Penal Code (Act No. 11 of 2004)
Sexual acts with a female over the age of 16 are prohibited by article 281, while sexual acts with a male are prohibited by article 284. The penalty is up to seven years imprisonment for both female and male acts.
Along with the civil Penal Code also Islamic Sharia law is in force in Qatar, although only applicable to Muslims.
The offence of —Zina makes any sexual act by a married person outside of marriage punishable by death, while sexual acts by non-married

persons are punish by flogging – both offences no matter if they were heterosexual or homosexual.

Saint Kitts and Nevis
Male-Male: Illegal   Female-Female: Legal
Offences against the Person Act
Section 56 —The abominable crime of buggery - up to 10 years imprisonment, with or without hard labor.
Section 57 —Whosoever attempts to commit the said abominable crime, or is guilty of any assault with intent to commit the same, or of any indecent assault upon any male person, is guilty of misdemeanor, and being convicted thereof shall be liable to be imprisoned for any term not exceeding four (4) years with or without hard labour.

Saint Lucia
Male-male: Illegal   Female-Female: Illegal
Criminal Code, No. 9 of 2004 (Effective January 1, 2005)
Gross Indecency
Section 132.— —
(1) Any person who commits an act of gross indecency with another person commits an offence and is liable on conviction on indictment to imprisonment for ten years or on summary conviction to five years.
(2) Subsection (1) does not apply to an act of gross indecency committed in private between an adult male person and an adult female person, both of whom consent.
(3) For the purposes of subsection (2) —
(*a*) an act shall be deemed not to have been committed in private if it is committed in a public place; and
(*b*) a person shall be deemed not to consent to the commission of such an act if —
(i) the consent is extorted by force, threats or fear of bodily harm or is obtained by false and fraudulent representations as to the nature of the act; (ii) the consent is induced by the application or administration

of any drug, matter or thing with intent to intoxicate or stupefy the person; or

(iii) that person is, and the other party to the act knows or has good reason to believe that the person is suffering from a mental disorder.

(4) In this section —gross indecency is an act other than sexual intercourse (whether natural or unnatural) by a person involving the use of the genital organs for the purpose of arousing or gratifying sexual desire. Buggery

Section 133.— —

(1) A person who commits buggery commits an offence and is liable on conviction on indictment to imprisonment for —

(*a*) life, if committed with force and without the consent of the other person; (*b*) ten years, in any other case.

(2) Any person who attempts to commit buggery, or commits an assault with intent to commit buggery, commits an offence and is liable to imprisonment for five years.

(3) In this section —buggery means sexual intercourse per anus by a male person with another male person.

Saint Vincent and the Grenadines

Male-Male: Illegal   Female-Female: Illegal

Criminal Code, 1990 Edition

Section 146 —Any person who —

(a) commits buggery with any other person;

(b) commits buggery with an animal; or

(c) permits any person to commit buggery with him or her; is guilty of an offence and liable to imprisonment for ten years.

Section 148 "Any person, who in public or private, commits an act of gross indecency with another person of the same sex, or procures or attempts to procure another person of the same sex to commit an act of gross indecency with him or her, is guilty of an offence and liable to imprisonment for five years."

Somoa

Male-Male: Illegal   Female-Female: Legal

Crimes Ordinance 1961, Consolidated Acts of Samoa 2007-2008

Section 58D. Indecency between males – —

(1) Everyone is liable to imprisonment for a term not exceeding 5 years who, being a male:

(a) Indecently assaults any other male; or

(b) Does any indecent act with or upon any other male; or

(c) Induces or permits any other male to do any indecent act with or upon him.

(2) No boy under the age of 16 years shall be charged with committing or being a party to an offence against paragraph

(b) or paragraph

(c) of subsection (1), unless the other male was under the age of 21 years.

(3) It is no defense to a charge under this section that the other party consented.

Section 58E. Sodomy – —

(1) Everyone who commits sodomy is liable:

(a) Where the act of sodomy is committed on a female, to imprisonment for a term not exceeding 7 years.

(b) Where the act of sodomy is committed on a male, and at the time of the act that male is under the age of 16 years and the offender is of or over the age of 21 years, to imprisonment for a term not exceeding 7 years.

(c) In any other case, to imprisonment for a term not exceeding 5 years.

(2) This offence is complete upon penetration.

(3) Where sodomy is committed on any person under the age of 16 years he shall not be charged with being a party to that offence, but he may be charged with being a party to an offence against section 58D of this Act in any case to which that section is applicable.

(4) It is no defense to a charge under this section that the other party consented.

Sao Tome and Principe
Male-Male: Illegal   Female-Female: Illegal
Penal Code of September 16, 1886, as amended in 1954 (Inherited from the Portuguese colonial era) Articles 70 and 71 ad security measures on people who habitually practice acts against the order of nature, stating such people shall be sent to labor camps. For text of the law in Portuguese – see Mozambique section!

Saudi Arabia
Male-Male: Illegal   Female-Female: Illegal
There is no codified Penal Law in Saudi-Arabia. Instead, the country applies strict Islamic Sharia law. According to the interpretation sodomy is criminalized.

For a married man the penalty is death by stoning, while the penalty for an unmarried man is 100 blows of the whip as well as banishment for a year.

For a non-Muslim, who commits sodomy with a Muslim, the penalty is death by stoning. For conviction of sodomy, it must be proved either by confession of the culprit four times, or —testimony of four trustworthy Muslim men. Moreover are all sexual relations outside of marriage illegal in Saudi-Arabia according to the Sharia law, including sexual relations between women.

Senegal
Male-Male: Illegal   Female-Female: Illegal
Penal Code of 1965 Article 319:3. —Without prejudice to the more serious penalties provided for in the preceding paragraphs or by articles 320 and 321 of this Code, whoever will have committed an improper or unnatural act with a person of the same sex will be punished by imprisonment of between one and five years and by a fine of 100,000 to 1,500,000 francs. If the act was committed with a person below the age of 21, the maximum penalty will always be applied.

Seychelles
Male-Male: Illegal   Female-Female: Legal
Criminal Code of 1955 Section 151. —Any person who – a. has carnal knowledge of any person against the order of nature; or b. has carnal knowledge of an animal; or c. permits a male person to have carnal knowledge of him or her against the order of nature, is guilty of a felony, and is liable to imprisonment for fourteen years.

Sierra Leone
Male-Male: Illegal   Female-Female: Legal
Offences against the Person Act 1861
Section 61 of the above named act, criminalizes buggery and bestiality, with a penalty of life imprisonment.

Singapore
Male-Male: Illegal   Female-Female: Legal
Penal Code (Chapter 22), Revised Edition 2007 Outrages on decency. Section 377A. —Any male person who, in public or private, commits, or abets the commission of, or procures or attempts to procure the commission by any male person of, any act of gross indecency with another male person, shall be punished with imprisonment for a term which may extend to 2 years.
Section 377 criminalizing —carnal knowledge against the order of nature has been repealed by the Penal Code (Amendment) Act 2007, No. 51, which came into force on 1 February 2008.

Solomon Islands
Male-Male: Illegal   Female-Female: Illegal
Penal Code (Revised Edition 1996)
Section 160. Unnatural offences —Any person who-
(a) commits buggery with another person or with an animal; or
(b) permits a male person to commit buggery with him or her, shall be guilty of a felony, and shall be liable to imprisonment for fourteen years.

Section 161. Attempts to commit unnatural offences —Any person who attempts to commit any of the offences specified in the last preceding section, or who is guilty of any assault with intent to commit the same, or any indecent assault indecent assaults upon any male person shall be guilty of a felony, and shall be liable to imprisonment for seven years.

Section 162. Indecent practices between persons of the same sex (Inserted by Act 9 of 1990, s. 2) —Any person who, whether in public or private –

(a) commits any act of gross indecency with another of the same sex;

(b) procures another of the same sex to commit any act of gross indecency; or

(c) attempts to procure the commission of any act of gross indecency by persons of the same sex, shall be guilty of a felony and be liable to imprisonment for five years.

Somalia

Male-Male: Illegal   Female-Female: Illegal

Penal Code, Decree No. 5/1962 (Effective April 3, 1964)

Article 409 Homosexuality —Whoever

(a) has carnal intercourse

(b) with a person of the same sex shall be punished, where the act does not constitute a more serious crime, with imprisonment from three months to three years.

Where a) the act committed b) is an act of lust different from carnal intercourse, the punishment imposed shall be reduced by one-third.

Article 410 Security Measures —A security measure may be added to a sentence for crimes referred to in Articles 407, 408, and 409.Somalia has not had a functioning central government since the fall of the dictator Mohamed Siad Barre in 1991, and the enforcement of the national Penal Code can be questioned.

In the southern parts Islamic courts rule, having imposed Islamic Sharia law punishing homosexual acts with death penalty or flogging. However, Somaliland in the north has declared itself independent, and it still applies the Penal Code.

Sri Lanka

Male-Male: Illegal   Female-Female: Illegal

Penal Code of 1883 No 2 (Cap. 19)

Article 365 – —Volontarily carnal intercourse with man, woman or animal against the order of nature - imprisonment for a term which may extend ten years.

Article 365A (as introduced by the —Penal Code (Amendment) Act, No. 22 of 1995 Any person who, in public or private, commits, or is a party to the commission of, or procures or attempts to procure the commission by any person of any act of gross indecency with another person, shall be guilty of an offence and shall be punished with imprisonment of either description for a term which may extend to two years or with a fine, or with both and where the offence is committed by a person over eighteen (18) years of age in respect of any person under sixteen (16) years of age shall be punished worth rigorous imprisonment for a term not less than 10 years and not exceeding 20 years and with a fine and shall also be ordered to pay compensation of amount determined by court to the person in respect of whom the offence was committed for the injuries caused to such a person.

Sudan

Male-Male: Illegal   Female-Female: Illegal

The Penal Code 1991 (Act No. 8 1991)

Section 148 Sodomy. —

(1) Any man who inserts his penis or its equivalent into a woman's or a man's anus or permitted another man to insert his penis or its equivalent in his anus is said to have committed Sodomy.

(2) (a) Whoever commits Sodomy shall be punished with flogging one hundred lashes and he shall also be liable to five years imprisonment.

(b) If the offender is convicted for the second time he shall be punished with flogging one hundred lashes and imprisonment for a term which may not exceed five years.

(c) If the offender is convicted for the third time he shall be punished with death or life imprisonment.

Section 151. Indecent Acts —Whoever commits an act of gross indecency upon the person of another person or any sexual act which does not amount to Zina or Sodomy shall be punished with not more than forty lashes and shall also be liable for imprisonment for a term which may not exceed one year or fine. In 2003 the south parts of Sudan (also known as New Sudan) gained some autonomy, and adopted its own Penal Code the same year. As the federal Penal Code, this Penal Code criminalizes sodomy, however with a milder punishment, according to the following section:

Section 318. Unnatural Offences: —Whoever has carnal intercourse against the order of nature with any person and whoever allows any person to have such intercourse with him commits an offence and shall on conviction, be punished with imprisonment for a term not exceeding ten years and may also be liable to fine; and if such intercourse is done without consent he shall be punished with imprisonment for a term not exceeding fourteen years and may also be liable to fine; provided that a consent given by a person below the age of eighteen years to such intercourse shall not be deemed to be a consent within the meaning of this section. Explanation: Penetration is sufficient to constitute the carnal knowledge necessary to the offence described in this section.

Swaziland
Male-Male: Illegal   Female-Female: Legal
Sodomy - it is sexual intercourse per anus between two human males - is prohibited as a common law offence. The Government has plans to include prohibitions of all male homosexual acts and lesbian acts in it's' revision of the Sexual Offences laws. The proposed penalties are imprisonment for a minimum period of two years, or a minimum fine of E5 000. It has, however, not been adopted as of publication of this report.

Syria
Male-Male: Illegal   Female-Female: Illegal
Penal Code of 1949
Article 520. —Any unnatural sexual intercourse shall be punished with a term of imprisonment of up to three years.

Tanzania
Male-Male: Illegal   Female-Female: Illegal
Penal Code of 1945 (As amended by the Sexual Offences Special Provisions Act, 1998) Section 154.
Unnatural of offences —
(1) Any person who-
(a) has carnal knowledge of any person against the order of nature; or
(b) has carnal knowledge of an animal; or
(c) permits a male person to have carnal knowledge of him or her against the order of nature commits an offence, and is liable to imprisonment for life and in any case to imprisonment for a term of not less than thirty years.
(2) where the offence under subsection (1) of this section is committed to a child under the age of ten years the offender shall be sentenced to life imprisonment.
Section 155. Attempt to commit unnatural offences —Any person who attempts to commit any of the offences specified under section 154 commits an offences and shall on conviction be sentenced to imprisonment for a term not less than twenty years.
Section 138A. Gross indecency —Any person who, in public or private commits, or is a party to the commission of, or procures or attempts to procure the commission by any person of, any act of gross indecency with another person, is guilty of an offence and liable on conviction to imprisonment for a term not less than one year and not exceeding five years or to a fine not less than one hundred thousand and not exceeding three hundred thousand shillings; save that where the offence is committed by a person of eighteen years of age or more in respect of

any person under eighteen years of age, a pupil of a primary school or a student of secondary school the offender shall be liable on conviction to imprisonment for a term not less than ten years, with corporal punishment, and shall also be ordered to pay compensation. Of all amount determined by the court to the person in respect of whom the offence was committed or any injuries caused to that person.

Togo
Male-Male: Illegal   Female-Female: Illegal
Penal Code of 13 August 1980
Article 88 – —Impudent acts or crimes against the nature with an individual of the same sex are punished with three (03) years imprisonment and 100,000-500,000 franc in fine.
(Unofficial translation)

Tonga
Male-Male: Illegal   Female-Female: Legal
Laws of Tonga, Criminal Offences [Cap 18] 1988 Edition Sodomy and bestiality.
Section 136. —Whoever shall be convicted of the crime of sodomy with another person or bestiality with any animal shall be liable at the discretion of the Court to be imprisoned for any period not exceeding ten years and such animal shall be killed by a public officer. Substituted by Act 9 of 1987.) Attempted sodomy, indecent assault upon a male.
Section 139. —Whoever shall attempt to commit the said abominable crime of sodomy or shall be guilty of an assault with intent to commit the same or of any indecent assault upon any male person shall be liable at the direction of the Court to imprisonment for any term not exceeding 10 years. Evidence. Section 140. —On the trial of any person upon a charge of sodomy or carnal knowledge it shall not be necessary to prove the actual emission of seed but the offence shall be deemed complete on proof of penetration only. Whipping for certain offences.

Section 142. —Whenever any male person shall be convicted of any offence against sections 106, 107, 115, 118, 121, 122, 125, 132, 136 and 139 of this Act the Court may, in its discretion in lieu of or in addition to any sentence of imprisonment authorised under this Act order the person so convicted to be whipped in accordance with the provisions of section 31 of this Act. (Substituted by Act 9 of 1987.)

Trinidad and Tobago
Male-Male: Illegal   Female-Female: Illegal
Sexual Offences Act 1986, Consolidated Version 2000
Section 13. —(1) A person who commits buggery is guilty of an offence and is liable on conviction to imprisonment—
(a) if committed by an adult on a minor, for life;
(b) if committed by an adult on another adult, for twenty-five years;
(c) if committed by a minor, for five years.
(2) In this section —buggery means sexual intercourse per anus by a male person with a male person or by a male person with a female person.
Section 16. —(1) A person who commits an act of serious indecency on or towards another is guilty of an offence and is liable on conviction to imprisonment—
(a) if committed on or towards a minor under sixteen years of age for ten years for a first offence and to imprisonment for fifteen years for a subsequent offence;
(b) if committed on or towards a person sixteen years of age or more for five years. (2) Subsection (1) does not apply to an act of serious indecency committed in private between—
(a) a husband and his wife; or
(b) a male person and a female person each of whom is sixteen years of age or more, both of whom consent to the commission of the act.
(3) An act of —serious indecency is an act, other than sexual intercourse (whether natural or unnatural), by a person involving the use of the genital organ for the purpose of arousing or gratifying sexual desire.

Tunisia
Male-Male: Illegal   Female-Female: Illegal
Penal Code of 1913 (as modified)
Article 230. —The sodomy, that is not covered by any of the other previous articles, is punished with imprisonment for three years.
(Unofficial translation)

Turkish Republic of Northern Cyprus (Unrecognized State)
Male-Male: Illegal   Female-Female: Legal
Criminal Code, Chapter 154
Article 171. Whoever –
(a) has sexual intercourse against the order of nature with any person, or
(b) allows sexual intercourse against the order of nature with a male, commits a heavy crime and is punished with up to five years imprisonment.
Article 173. —Whoever attempts to commit one of the crimes mentioned above in art. 171, commits a heavy crime and is punished with up to three years imprisonment. There are plans to repeal these articles, but such a reform has not occurred as of publication of this report.

Turkmenistan
Male-Male: Illegal   Female-Female: Legal
Criminal Code of 1997 (Effective January 1, 1998)
Article 135. Sodomy —
(1) Sodomy, that is the sexual relations of the man with the man, is punished by imprisonment for the term of up to two years.
(Unofficial translation.)

Tuvalu
Male-Male: Illegal   Female-Female: Legal
Laws of Tuvalu, Penal Code [Cap 8] Revised Edition 1978 Unnatural offences.

Section 153. —Any person who-

(a) commits buggery with another person or with an animal; or

(b) permits a male person to commit buggery with him or her, shall be guilty of a felony, and shall be liable to imprisonment for 14 years. Attempts to commit unnatural offences and indecent assault.

Section 154. —Any person who attempts to commit any of the offences specified in the last proceeding section, or who is guilty of any assault with intent to commit the same, or any indecent assault upon any male person shall be guilty of a felony, and shall be liable to imprisonment for 7 years. Indecent practices between males.

Section 155. —Any male person who, whether in public or private, commits any act of gross indecency with another male person, or procures another male person to commit any act of gross indecency with him, or attempts to procure the commission of any such act by any male person with himself or with another male person, whether in public or private, shall be guilty of a felony, and shall be liable to imprisonment for 5 years.

Uganda

Male-Male: Illegal   Female-Female: Illegal

The Penal Code Act of 1950 (Chapter 120) (as amended)

Section 145. Unnatural offences. —Any person who—

(a) has carnal knowledge of any person against the order of nature;

(b) has carnal knowledge of an animal; or

(c) permits a male person to have carnal knowledge of him or her against the order of nature, commits an offence and is liable to imprisonment for life.

Section 146. Attempt to commit unnatural offences. —Any person who attempts to commit any of the offences specified in section145 commits a felony and is liable to imprisonment for seven years.

Section 148. Indecent practices.

—Any person who, whether in public or in private, commits any act of gross indecency with another person or procures another person

to commit any act of gross indecency with him or her or attempts to procure the commission of any such act by any person with himself or herself or with another person, whether in public or in private, commits an offence and is liable to imprisonment for seven years.

United Arab Emirates
Male-Male: Illegal   Female-Female: Illegal
All sexual acts outside of heterosexual marriage are banned in the United Arab Emirates. However, whether sodomy is punished with death penalty remains in dispute. The Arabic text of article 354 is ambiguously phrased and can be translated in different ways. Some sources indicate that the article punishes rape of a woman or forced sodomy with a man, while others indicate that it punishes rape on women and sodomy between men.

The semi-official translation used by attorneys in the Emirates states that —any individual who forcibly compels a woman to carnal copulation or a man to sodomy is punished by death. In a German parliamentary report the article has been translated as follows: —Irrespective of the provisions of the Act on Delinquent and Vagrant Juveniles, any person who forcibly engages in sexual intercourse with a woman, or a homosexual act with a homosexual, shall be punished with the death penalty. Coercion shall be recognised if the condemned person was fourteen years of age at the time of the commission of the offence. Sofer, on the other hand, means that the article can be translated differently; —Whoever commits rape on a female or sodomy with a male.

Amnesty International, finally, considers article 354 to apply to rape only, and not to consensual same-sex acts. However, the organization states that the —Zina provision according to Sharia law, punishing sexual acts by married persons outside of marriage by death, could possible apply in the UAE, although it is not aware of any such death sentences for consensual same-sex conduct. Apart from federal law, consensual sodomy is criminalized in the emirates of Dubai and Abu Dhabi.

Article 80 of the Dubai Penal Code punishes sodomy with a penalty of up to 14 years imprisonment, while article 177 of the Abu Dhabi Penal Code punishes such acts with a penalty of up to ten years imprisonment.

Uzbekistan
Male-Male: Illegal   Female-Female: Legal
Criminal Code of 1994
Article 120. Besoqolbozlik* (Homosexual Intercourse) —Besoqolbozlik, that is, voluntary sexual intercourse of two male individuals – shall be punished with imprisonment up to three years.

Yemen
Male-Male: Illegal   Female-Female: Illegal
Penal Code 1994
Article 264. —Homosexuality between men is defined as penetration into the anus.
Unmarried men shall be punished with 100 lashes of the whip or a maximum of one year of imprisonment, married men with death by stoning.
Article 268. —Homosexuality between women is defined as sexual stimulation by rubbing. The penalty for premeditated commission shall be up to three years of imprisonment; where the offence has been committed under duress, the perpetrator shall be punishable with up to seven years detention.

Zambia
Male-Male: Illegal   Female-Female: Legal
The Penal Code Act, 1995 Edition
Section 155. —Any person who-
(a) has carnal knowledge of any person against the order of nature; or
(b) has carnal knowledge of an animal; or
(c) permits a male person to have carnal knowledge of him or her against the order of nature; is guilty of a felony and is liable to imprisonment for fourteen years. (As amended by No. 26 of 1933) Unnatural offences.

Section 156. —Any person who attempts to commit any of the offences specified in the last preceding section is guilty of a felony and is liable to imprisonment for seven years. (As amended by No. 26 of 1933) Attempt to commit unnatural offences.

Section 158. —Any male person who, whether in public or private, commits any act of gross indecency with another male person, or procures another male person to commit any act of gross indecency with him, or attempts to procure the commission of any such act by any male person with himself or with another male person, whether in public or private, is guilty of a felony and is liable to imprisonment for five years. (As amended by No. 26 of 1933) Indecent practices between males.

Zimbabwe
Male-Male: Illegal   Female-Female: Legal
CRIMINAL LAW (CODIFICATION AND REFORM) ACT (Effective July 8, 2006) Section 73. Sodomy
—(1) Any male person who, with the consent of another male person, knowingly performs with that other person anal sexual intercourse, or any act involving physical contact other than anal sexual intercourse that would be regarded by a reasonable person to be an indecent act, shall be guilty of sodomy and liable to a fine up to or exceeding level fourteen or imprisonment for a period not exceeding one year or both.
(2) Subject to subsection (3), both parties to the performance of an act referred to in subsection (1) may be charged with and convicted of sodomy. (3) For the avoidance of doubt it is declared that the competent charge against a male person who performs anal sexual intercourse with or commits an indecent act upon a young male person—
(a) who is below the age of twelve years, shall be aggravated indecent assault or indecent assault, as the case may be; or
(b) who is of or above the age of twelve years but below the age of sixteen years and without the consent of such young male person, shall be aggravated indecent assault or indecent assault, as the case may be; or

(c) who is of or above the age of twelve years but below the age of sixteen years and with the consent of such young male person, shall be performing an indecent act with a young person.

LGBT RIGHTS GLOBAL REVIEW.

The year in brackets refers to the year when the reform came into force. If no year is stated, either there has never been any regulation in the relevant area, or the information is unknown.

HOMOSEXUAL ACTS ARE LEGAL (115 COUNTRIES)

Under no circumstances should the reader presume that Homosexual conduct is safe from violence and discrimination merely because it is legal. In many of the countries below, people remain fearful to be themselves as societal values, and local law enforcement have not followed the laws.

Africa:
Benin, Burkina Faso, Cape Verde (2004), Central African Republic, Chad, Congo-Brazzaville, Côte d'Ivoire, Democratic Republic of Congo, Equatorial Guinea (1931), Gabon, Guinea-Bissau (1993), Madagascar, Mali, Niger, Rwanda, South Africa (1998)

Asia:
Bahrain (1976), Cambodia, China (1997),118 East Timor (1975), Indonesia, Israel (1988), Japan (1882), Jordan (1951), Kazakhstan (1998), Kyrgyzstan (1998), Laos, Mongolia, Nepal (2007), 119 North Korea, Philippines (1823), South Korea, Taiwan, Tajikistan (1998), Thailand (1957), Turkey (1858), Vietnam, as well as the West Bank (1951) in the Palestinian Authority

Europe:
Albania (1995), Andorra, Armenia (2003), Austria (1971), Azerbaijan (2000), Belgium (1795), Bosnia and Herzegovina (1998), Bulgaria

(1968), Croatia (1977), Cyprus (1998), Czech Republic (1962), Denmark (1933), Estonia (1992), Finland (1971), France (1791), Georgia (2000), Germany (1968/69), Greece (1951), Hungary (1962), Iceland (1940), Ireland (1993), Italy (1890), Kosovo (1994), Latvia (1992), Liechtenstein (1989), Lithuania (1993), Luxembourg (1795), Macedonia (1996), Malta (1973), Moldova (1995), Monaco (1793), Montenegro (1977), Netherlands (1811), Norway (1972), Poland (1932), Portugal (1983), Romania (1996), Russia (1993), San Marino (1865), Serbia (1994), Slovakia (1962), Slovenia (1977), Spain (1979), Sweden (1944), Switzerland (1942), Ukraine (1991), United Kingdom (see foot note for the UK and associates), Vatican City

North America:
Bahamas (1991), Canada (1969), Costa Rica (1971), Cuba (1979), Dominican Republic, El Salvador, Guatemala, Haiti, Honduras, Mexico (1872), Nicaragua (01-feb-2008), Panama (31-jul-2008), United States (2003,) as well as the Dutch associates Aruba and the Netherlands Antilles

Oceania:
Australia, Fiji (2005), Marshall Islands (2005), Micronesia, New Zealand (1986), Vanuatu and the New Zealand associates of Niue (2007) and Tokelau (2007)

South America:
Argentina (1887), Bolivia, Brazil (1831), Chile (1999), Colombia (1981), Ecuador (1997), Paraguay (1880), Peru (1924), Suriname, Uruguay (1934), Venezuela

***Same-sex activities have never been criminalized in: Benin, Burkina Faso, Central African Republic, Chad, Congo-Brazzaville, Côte d'Ivoire, Democratic Republic of Congo, Gabon, Madagascar, Mali, Niger and Rwanda.

HOMOSEXUAL ACTS ARE ILLEGAL (80 COUNTRIES)

Africa:
Algeria, Angola, Botswana, Burundi, Cameroon, Comoros, Egypt,128 Eritrea, Ethiopia, Gambia, Ghana, Guinea, Kenya, Lesotho, Liberia, Libya, Malawi, Mauritania (death penalty), Mauritius, Morocco, Mozambique, Namibia, Nigeria (death penalty in some states), São Tomé and Principe, Senegal, Seychelles, Sierra Leone, Somalia, Sudan (death penalty), Swaziland, Tanzania, Togo, Tunisia, Uganda, Zambia, Zimbabwe

Asia:
Afghanistan, Bangladesh, Bhutan, Brunei, Burma, India, Iran (death penalty), Kuwait, Lebanon, Malaysia, Maldives, Oman, Pakistan, Qatar, Saudi Arabia (death penalty), Singapore, Sri Lanka, Syria, Turkmenistan, United Arab Emirates, Uzbekistan, Yemen (death penalty), as well as the Gaza Strip in the Palestinian Authority

Europe:
Turkish Republic of Northern Cyprus (internationally unrecognized.)

North America:
Antigua and Barbuda, Barbados, Belize, Dominica, Grenada, Jamaica, St Kitts & Nevis, St Lucia, St Vincent & the Grenadines, Trinidad and Tobago.

Oceania:
Kiribati, Nauru, Palau, Papua New Guinea, Samoa, Solomon Islands, Tonga, Tuvalu; as well as the New Zealand associate of Cook Islands.

South America:
Guyana

LEGAL STATUS OF HOMOSEXUAL ACTS UNCLEAR (2 COUNTRIES)

Africa:
Djibouti

Asia:
Iraq (See Iraq section above.)

Europe:
None

North America:
None

Oceania:
None

South America:
None

HOMOSEXUAL ACTS ARE PUNISHABLE BY DEATH PENALTY (5 COUNTRIES AND SOME PARTS OF NIGERIA AND SOMALIA)

Africa:
Mauritania, Sudan as well as 12 northern states in Nigeria and the southern parts of Somalia. Legislation pending to enforce the death penalty in Uganda and Beheadings in Gambia for Homosexuals who do not leave the country.

Asia:
Iran, Saudi Arabia, Yemen

Europe:
None

North America:

None

Oceania:

None

South America:

None

EQUAL AGE OF CONSENT FOR HOMOSEXUAL AND HETEROSEXUAL ACTS (97 COUNTRIES.)

Africa:

Burkina Faso (1996), Cape Verde (2004), Democratic Republic of Congo, Equatorial Guinea (1931), Mali (1961), Guinea-Bissau (1993), South Africa (2007)

Asia:

Cambodia, China,129 Israel (2000), Japan (1882), Jordan (1951), Kazakhstan (1998), Kyrgyzstan (1998), Laos, Mongolia, Nepal (2007), North Korea, Philippines (1822), South Korea, Taiwan, Tajikistan (1998), Thailand (1957), Turkey (1858), Vietnam, as well as the West Bank (1951) in the Palestinian Authority

Europe:

Albania (2001), Andorra, Armenia (2003), Austria (2002), Azerbaijan (2000), Belgium (1985), Bosnia & Herzegovina (1998), Bulgaria (2002), Croatia (1998), Cyprus (2002), Czech Republic (1990), Denmark (1976),130 Estonia (2002), Finland (1999), France (1982, for associates see foot note),131 Georgia (2000), Germany (1994/89),132 Hungary (2002), Iceland (1992), Ireland (1993), Italy (1890), Kosovo (2004), Latvia (1999), Liechtenstein (2001), Lithuania (2003), Luxembourg (1992), Macedonia (1996), Malta (1973), Moldova (2003), Monaco (1793), Montenegro (1977), Netherlands (1971),133 Norway (1972),

Poland (1932), Portugal (2007), Romania (2002), Russia (1997), San Marino (1865), Serbia (2006), Slovakia (1990), Slovenia (1977), Spain (1979), Sweden (1978), Switzerland (1992), Ukraine (1991), United Kingdom (2001, for associates see foot note),134 Vatican City

North America:
Costa Rica (1999), Cuba (1997), Dominican Republic, El Salvador, Guatemala, Haiti, Honduras, Mexico (1872), Nicaragua (2008), Panama (31-jul-2008), United States, as well as the Dutch associates Aruba and the Netherlands Antilles

Oceania:
Australia,135 Fiji (2005), Marshall Islands, Micronesia, New Zealand (1986), Vanuatu (2007) and the New Zealand associates of Niue (2007) and Tokelau (2007)

South America:
Argentina (1887), Bolivia, Brazil (1831), Colombia (1981), Ecuador (1997), Peru (1924), Uruguay (1934), Venezuela

UNEQUAL AGE OF CONSENT FOR HOMOSEXUAL AND HETEROSEXUAL ACTS (16 COUNTRIES)

Africa:
Benin, Chad, Congo-Brazzaville, Côte d'Ivoire, Gabon, Madagascar, Niger, Rwanda

Asia:
East Timor, Indonesia

Europe:
Greece (only in seduction cases), as well as some United Kingdom associates136

North America:

Bahamas, Canada, as well as some United Kingdom associates,137 and Nevada in the United States

Oceania:

The Australian state of Queensland

South America:

Chile, Paraguay, Suriname

PROHIBITION OF DISCRIMINATION IN EMPLOYMENT BASED ON SEXUAL ORIENTATION (48 COUNTRIES.)

Africa:

Mauritius (2008), Mozambique (2007), South Africa (1996) (Namibia repealed such a law in 2004)

Asia:

Israel (1992), Taiwan (2007), as well as a few cities in Japan.

Europe:

Andorra (2005), Austria (2004), Belgium (2003), Bosnia and Herzegovina (2003),138 Bulgaria (2004), Croatia (2003), Cyprus (2004), Czech Republic (1999), Denmark (1996),139 Estonia (2004), Finland (1995), France (2001), Georgia (2006), Germany (2006), Greece (2005), Hungary (2004), Ireland (1999), Italy (2003), Kosovo (2004), Latvia (2006), Lithuania (2003), Luxembourg (1997), Malta (2004), Netherlands (1992), Norway (1998), Poland (2004), Portugal (2003), Romania (2000), Serbia (2005), Slovakia (2004), Slovenia (1998), Spain (1996), Sweden (1999), United Kingdom (2003, for associates see foot note)140

North America:

Canada (1996), Costa Rica (1998), Mexico (2003), Nicaragua (2008), as well as some parts of the United States141

Oceania:
Australia,142 Fiji (2007), New Zealand (1994)

South America:
Colombia (2007), Venezuela (1999), as well as Rosario (1996) in Argentina, and some parts of Brazil143

PROHIBITION OF DISCRIMINATION IN EMPLOYMENT BASED ON **GENDER IDENTIFICATION** (16 COUNTRIES.)

Africa:
None

Asia:
None

Europe:
Hungary (2004), Sweden (1-jan-2009). Moreover discrimination of transgender people is covered by the gender discrimination prohibitions in Austria, Belgium, Denmark, Finland, France, Germany, Ireland, Italy, Latvia, Netherlands, Poland, Slovakia and United Kingdom.

North America:
Northwest Territories (2004) in Canada, as well as some parts of the United States144

Oceania:
Australia145

South America:
The Argentinean city of Rosario (2006)

CONSTITUTIONAL PROHIBITION OF DISCRIMINATION BASED ON SEXUAL ORIENTATION (10 COUNTRIES.)

Africa:
South Africa (1994 and 1997)

Asia:
None

Europe:
Kosovo (15-jun-2008), Portugal (2004), Sweden (2003), Switzerland (2000), as well as some parts of Germany

North America:
Canada (1998) and the United Kingdom associate of British Virgin Islands (200

Oceania:
Fiji (1997)

South America:
Bolivia (7-jan-2009), Colombia (2000), Ecuador (1998), as well as some parts of Argentina and Brazil

HATE CRIMES BASED ON SEXUAL ORIENTATION CONSIDERED AN AGGRAVATING CIRCUMSTANCE (16 COUNTRIES.)

Africa:
None

Asia:
None

Europe:
Andorra (2005), Belgium (2003), Croatia (2006), Denmark (2004), France (2003), Netherlands (1992), Portugal (2007), Romania (2006), Spain (1996), Sweden (2003), United Kingdom (2004/05)

North America:
Canada (1996), Nicaragua (2008), as well as several parts of the United States

Oceania:
New Zealand (2002)

South America:
Colombia (2001), Uruguay (2003)

HATE CRIMES BASED ON **GENDER IDENTITY** CONSIDERED AN AGGRAVATING CIRCUMSTANCE (1 COUNTRY.)

Africa:
None

Asia:
None

Europe:
None

North America:
Some parts of the United States

Oceania:
None

South America:
Uruguay (2003)

WHERE INCITEMENT OF HATRED BASED ON SEXUAL ORIENTATION IS PROHIBITED (17 COUNTRIES.)

Africa:
None

Asia:
None

Europe:
Belgium (2003), Croatia (2003), Denmark (1987),155 Estonia (2006), France (2005),156 Iceland (1996), Ireland (1989), Lithuania (2003), Luxembourg (1997), Netherlands (1992), Norway (1981), Portugal (2007), Romania (2000), Spain (1996), Sweden (2003), as well as Northern Ireland (2004) in the United Kingdom

North America:
Canada (2004)

Oceania:
Some parts of Australia

South America:
Uruguay (2003)

MARRIAGE OPEN FOR SAME SEX COUPLES (7 COUNTRIES.)

Africa:
South Africa (2006)

Asia:
None

Europe:
Belgium (2003), Netherlands (2001), Norway (1-jan-2009), Spain (2005), Sweden (1-may-2009)

North America:
Canada (2005), as well as Connecticut (2008), Iowa (27-apr-2009), Maine (14-sep-2009), Massachusetts (2004) and Vermont (1-sep-2009) in the United States

Oceania:
None

South America:
None

WHERE SAME SEX COUPLES ARE OFFERED MOST OR ALL RIGHTS OF MARRIAGE BUT UNDER A DIFFERENT NAME (Civil Partnerships, Registered Partnerships, Civil Unions, Etc.) (8 Countries.)

Africa:
None

Asia:
None

Europe:
Denmark (1989), Finland (2002), Germany (2001), Iceland (1996), Switzerland (2007), United Kingdom (2005)

North America:
Some states in the United States

Oceania:
New Zealand (2005), as well as some parts of Australia

South America:

Colombia (2007-2009)

WHERE SAME SEX COUPLES ARE OFFERED SOME RIGHTS OF MARRIAGE (12 COUNTRIES)

Africa:

None

Asia:

Israel (1994-)

Europe:

Andorra (2005), Austria (2003), Croatia (2003), Czech Republic (2006), France (1999), Hungary (1996), Luxembourg (2004), Portugal (2001), Slovenia (2006)

North America:

The Mexican states of Coahuila (2007) and Federal District (2007), as well as a few states and a number cities and towns in the United States

Oceania:

Australia (2008-2009)

South America:

Uruguay (10-jan-2008) as well as Buenos Aires (2003), Rio Negro (2003) and Villa Carlos Paz (2007) in Argentina, and Rio Grande do Sul (2004) in Brazil

WHERE JOINT ADOPTION BY SAME SEX COUPLES IS LEGAL (10 COUNTRIES.)

Africa:

South Africa (2002)

Asia:
Israel (2008)

Europe:
Andorra (2005), Belgium (2006), Iceland (2006), Netherlands (2001), Norway (1-jan-2009), Spain (2005), Sweden (2003), United Kingdom (2005)

North America:
Most of the Canadian provinces, and some parts of the United States

Oceania:
Capital Territory (2004) and Western Australia (2002) in Australia

South America:
The Brazilian city of São Paulo (2005)

Moreover, Second parent adoption by same-sex couples is also legal in Denmark (1999) and Germany (2005), as well as Tasmania (2004) in Australia, and Alberta (1999) in Canada.

COUNTRIES THAT PROHIBIT ENTRY BY LGB PEOPLE (4 COUNTRIES.)

Africa:
Lesotho, Swaziland

Asia:
None

Europe:
None

North America:
Belize, Trinidad and Tobago

Oceania:
None

South America:
None

LAW ON GENDER RECOGNITION AFTER GENDER REASSIGNMENT TREATMENT (15 COUNTRIES.)

Africa:
South Africa (2004)

Asia:
Japan (2004), Turkey (1988)

Europe:
Belgium (2007), Finland (2003), Germany (1981), Italy (1982), Netherlands (1985), Romania (1996), Spain (2007), Sweden (1972), United Kingdom (2005)

North America:
Panama (1975), as well as most parts of Canada and the United States

Oceania:
Australia, New Zealand (1995)

South America:
None

*Moreover, a number of other countries recognize the new gender as well as the right to marry after Gender Reassignment treatment through general statutes or case-law.

VIEWS OF UNITED NATIONS MEMBERS.

It might be too optimistic to say that a full five percent of nations on this Earth give us full and equal rights, equivalent to the majorities within their borders. Even if this statistic bears itself out, another full 95 percent of the nations on Earth discriminate against their Gay citizens and treat them as less than equal. The United Nations is comprised of these nations, so it should be no surprise that the very international organizations that we look to for support in our quest for independence would have people in powerful positions who support their national laws and practices that deny us full citizenship and our march for human rights.

The question becomes how do we continue forward when we are marginalized on all fronts?

The shining rays of hope can be found in many dark pockets of despair. We do have some friends in the United Nations who speak on our behalf. They encourage the body to recognize our rights to exist and our rights to equality.

The voices that speak on our behalf include **Mrs. Navanethem Pillay**, the High Commissioner for Human Rights to the United Nations. In a speech to the UN, she said that we are "full and equal members of the human family and deserve to be treated as such." But there are many others as well who speak for us, including **Michael O'Flaherty**, a member of the UN Human Rights Committee; **Maxime Verhagen**, the Minister of Foreign Affairs, The Netherlands, as well as several prominent global organizations that have received Consultative Status to the United Nations and such organizations include **ABGLT (the Brazilian Association of Gay, Lesbian and Transgendered.)** We wish to thank several organizations for organizing, compiling or providing the national data and legal codes; particularly ilga.org, the United Nations and globalgayz.com

We, as a people, are coalescing around our shared culture and are beginning to organize as such on every continent on Earth. The work to morph the thinking within the United Nations will continue.

"I'd rather light a candle than curse the darkness."

~ Eleanor Roosevelt

"God doesn't require us to succeed; He only requires that you try."
                                              ~ Mother Teresa

Chapter Seven.
The Conclusion of *The Gay State* And How We Move Forward.

I have reached the point in my plan that, should I continue, I risk mentioning so many particulars that the naysayers will be encircling, ready to pounce and exterminate any hope of survival before the concept has any chance whatsoever of flying on its own. I do not idealize the plan as building a Utopia; such nonsense would end in utter failure and set us back generations. Not to say I have not already thought those aspects through countless times. More details and minutia have been laid out to establish crucial and fundamental building blocks across the board than could be contained in this booklet. But, of course, there is a right way, a wrong way, and then there is the best way. I want our Gay State to serve up to the world, that the possibilities are astonishing when we are allowed to pursue our freedom and sovereignty. With all of the pent-up passion that our community possesses, we will make remarkable strides to right thirty centuries of oppression.

This booklet leaves so many questions unanswered. The work in multiple think tanks covers every topic one might imagine, and they will be shared in upcoming literature. And yet there are an infinite number of details that are fluid for which we are unable to foresee at this time.

Critics will observe more than several useless repetitions throughout this pamphlet. I have thought over some of the finer points and revised others and still felt some issues were crucial enough to deserve to be driven home more than once. Other points, a reader may decide, were superficial and not worthy of the time we spent on a particular topic. While other topics, we barely touched upon that deserved more attention.

I can only hope most of you, the readers most impassioned with the prospect of joining us in the creation of the world's first Gay State, will overlook all of the stylistic errors to this pamphlet. If I have managed to create a drive to participate and offer up your intellect, your muscle, and multitude of talents toward our pursuit, then we will have sufficiently succeeded. If one of you feels that I have spoken to you at your deepest core, I will be honored and deeply grateful for your willingness to accept the words on these pages.

I know, as do you, that we will have multiple roadblocks along our path. If this were such a carefree and simple exercise, someone would have succeeded in establishing a nation for us generations ago. How sweet it would have been, the countless lives that could have been saved and countless others immeasurably improved! To think we could all be dual passport holders and could have experienced a life as an equal, not as someone who gets by on the margins of a life. But creating this land is our task for our age, and it is a participatory process. No one of us can do it alone.

I have often thought before, during, and after every Congress we hold, that if only all potential 600 million Gay citizens each gave $50.00 USD, then we would have $30 billion to launch our Gay Nation-State, create a first rate power that stresses the arts, culture, science, citizenry, and in essence show the world how it is all done. Of course, such monetary thoughts are wishful thinking. But none of us can do it alone. We must all row in the same direction if we are to make any progress. But the process, this unity, will help us become a better, more perfect democracy.

One of the biggest hurdles we face is from those that believe that every group has issues. "So what if the Gays feel persecuted. Get over it!," they say. We are not the only people who have had issues to overcome, they will say. Here, I would say that healing the psyche that has hindered us for centuries allows us to mend as a people and that that makes for a good start. We don't need excuses; we don't want a false parallel reality. We just wish to be free from the never-ending cycle of oppression that has hindered our development as one people.

As Theodor Herzl had said, *"It might further be said that we ought not to create new distinctions between people; we ought not to raise fresh barriers, we should rather make the old disappear. But men who think in this way are amiable visionaries; and the idea of a native land will still flourish when the dust of their bones will have vanished tracelessly in the winds. Universal brotherhood is not even a beautiful dream. Antagonism is essential to man's greatest efforts."*

We cannot request to be free, and we cannot wait to be granted permission to be free, as that is not freedom. We must proclaim our independence, take a sturdy possession of it, and we must proclaim it to the world. We have seen that half-measures under the jurisdiction of other, majority people, will never be equal to independence.

Some believe that once our new Gay State is free and independent, we will have no more problems with outside countries. They overlook the power of hate. Our people, Gay people everywhere, have endured 3,000 years of being the societal scapegoat. Nations, leaders, and the average man on the street feel a need to persecute someone. Once we are together in our new land, we will refuse to be that people. And after 3000 years and they no longer have us to blame for their nation's internal woes, who, I wonder, will they decide to blame for their inadequacies, their failures and shortcomings?

For us, the privilege to fail on our own is a beautiful music. To be given the latitude to fail or succeed on our merits is an opportunity so many other nations have squandered. We pray that we reap all that we sow, and as a good and virtuous people, may the rewards be bountiful.

The enthusiasm many of us have for the prospects of establishing an independent Gay State has been met with some surprising reactions even within the Gay family. First there are Gays in the developed world, living in the lap of relative comfort and luxury, going about their lives, and they could not be bothered with the enormous undertaking of creating a new world. Many of these Gay elites do not want the world to change. A sub-group of this segment are the professionals that work to advance GLBT issues in their individual cities, states, and countries. An organization such as this is, of course, their ally, but may be seen as a threat or as a competitor to their fundraising efforts. We only pose a threat to some of them who do not wish to see any attention taken away from their causes that might detract from their donor base. In this respect, every group is competition in the non-profit world.

Some believe that initiating our movement gives our enemies ammunition. Why are we promoting our displeasure with the status quo to the world, they ask? The poorest and most desperate among us will be singled out for even more terror, making their lives more miserable than before. I believe our idea must make its way into the most distant, miserable holes where our people dwell. They will awaken from their depression and resignation that their lives will be only fractionally lived, but for into their lives will come a new significance. Every man need think only of himself, and the movement will assume vast proportions. As word spreads to every dark corner of the world, a light will shine, offering hope where before there was none. And make no mistake; the word will span the globe in astonishing speed. The internet will blaze the means of communication which will convey the details to all.

Men and womyn in our churches will rally around our efforts. Our friends and supporters will offer prayers for our success. They will join in the efforts to afford relief for those in the most despair. And the light of hope will ease the burdens of those who suffer most. To them we say

"We are coming!" We are working quickly. And most of us could very well live to see this miracle come to pass.

Curiously enough, there are groups from the other end of the political spectrum who loathe seeing us succeed and prosper. These are a segment of the religious fundamentalists and political conservatives who detest all that we are and are compelled to be against anything we might be for. Then there are, just to be fair, people who consider us an abomination in the eyes of God. These religious leaders and their religious flock express constipation at the prospects of our prosperity. Without these groups sabotaging and opposing our every move, we just might succeed on our own. Savor the irony that our Gay State surpasses theirs both in terms of our modernity as well as our humanity. An interesting sub-group, whose numbers we cannot accurately predict, is in favor of our attempts. This group of religious fundamentalists and the pious as well as the Conservatives would prefer we just leave. They do not seem to wish our utter demise, like many of their peers; they just simply want us gone. They wish to live their lives peacefully and contentedly, without our chaffing their ideological incantations. We would agree that a parting of ways would be beneficial for all concerned. This struggle that has claimed so many lives on our side need not go on another 3,000 years.

The timing is another matter that should be considered, not that I would advocate for more, longer, and increased suffering. Unlike my political friends in Washington, I do not favor the patience of waiting. In the Gay movement, particularly in America, many leaders stress incremental advancements in our equality, and I have had enough of the "incrementalism." In the state-by-state struggle for equality, as one state grants us rights, another state repeals the rights they had previously granted. The time for such small thinking is over. I wouldn't favor extending the detention of the Jews for a go-slow approach, and I wouldn't favor waiting to grant civil rights to African Americans. And I wouldn't wait any longer to secure Gay rights in the United States, nor should we delay any longer on the global stage. No. Three thousand years or two thousand years, all the same, we have waited long enough. The most desperate around the world are screaming "Wake up America!" "Wake up Europe!" "They are killing us and there is no more time to wait!"

To that extent I would not give a wit about timing but our people continue to endure wretched suffering and for what? There is a shift happening in the global paradigm. Events are occurring in fits and starts as they tend to do, but an acceleration of change is afoot. The movement to the creation of a Gay State should be a part of that mix. Americans are a people who are predisposed to "blowing up and starting over," in terms of reinventing themselves and not being afraid of taking risks. It is a national characteristic, and it is a good one. To not be anchored to the past enhances the possibilities of a brighter future. And sometimes, we must let go of the past to become who we are meant to be. Many proponents of a monarchal government would be opposed to this thinking, I am sure. But for the American Question is now at this moment in time; how can such a great and abundant nation find itself utterly broken and in such dire circumstances? Well beyond America's shores, the paradigm shift of global leadership may result in a conclusion that even enemies of America will be displeased with. So, in the midst of such global upheaval, our time is also now. As the might of the U.S. declines relative to other powers, our movement will not find advantages. Therefore, I can not foresee world developments being any more advantageous to our cause in ten or twenty or fifty years than they are now.

Some will say that if our quest was possible, it would have happened long ago. To them, I say we live in a unique time. The marvels, the machinery, and the money can all be found within our global Gay community. We can do things and push through achievements that were never before possible. Our moneyed citizens, those who know how to earn it, understand how much money can do.

Let me repeat my opening words again: The Gays who wish to live with freedom and liberty in their own democratic and prosperous state will have their state.

We shall live at last as free men and womyn on our own soil, and as old Gay men and womyn, will die peacefully in our own homes in our own Gay state.

The world will be freed by our liberty, enriched by our wealth, inspired by our fortitude, and magnified by our greatness.

And whatever we attempt to accomplish in our new land for our own betterment will have a powerful and beneficial impact for all people. We currently reside in every nation on Earth. Our global Gay community spans the world. And now, we are coming home.

"There are those who look at things the way they are, and ask why... I dream of things that never were, and ask why not?"

Robert Kennedy

"A lie gets halfway around the world before
the truth has a chance to get its pants on."

~ Winston Churchill

Chapter Eight.
Suggested Sources, Furthering The Gay State Movement.

This is a booklet intended to create further discussion on the essential realities of the formation of an independent Gay State. It was written not for an Academic, but for everyman and everywomyn. It is meant to be understood by the masses. In the process, I have come to conclude there is an enormous body of information and data that could be collected and presented in an extremely thorough Encyclopedia with multiple volumes. It would be a brilliant undertaking filled with a richness and excitement that I will leave for someone else to discover. For that, for now, I will content myself with the thoughts that we will some day have a National Library that will house the world's largest collection of Gay, Lesbian, Bisexual, and Transgender Studies in the world.

Until that time arrives, here is a small compilation of suggested references that I have used in recent years that have molded my thinking and played a role in the writing of this pamphlet. While all data found on the internet must be greeted with some degree of scrutiny, it has been a phenomenal resource, especially in regard to contacting fellow authors and researchers.

As for the published sources, you will find that these various and eclectic works cover a wide range of Gay related topics, and these particular works have been used throughout my life, and I recommend them, at least in part.

As for websites that are useful, more appear on the internet every day. I have followed these particular sites for my information, pleasure and to whatever extent, a certain entertainment value, for quite some time. Many of the websites are operated in conjunction with an association or society and their mission statements are apropos to our quest of developing a Gay State.

If you as a reader are so inclined to join our movement as a Patriot and know of a resource that would assist in any of our ongoing research, you may contact me at: **GarrettGrahamAndTheGayState@GMail.com.**

New perspectives are always welcome, although I must apologize now, though I make a concerted effort to set aside a block of time every day to respond to the public, I am not always able to personally respond to *every* note or suggestion that I receive, and my limited staff can be overwhelmed on occasion. I hope if this subject appeals to you and sufficiently holds your interest and I encourage you to visit our website and enroll in F.I.G.S. If you believe we should be free, to live in peace and liberty, become a "Figgie" and play your part in changing our world for the better.

My sincere best wishes,
Garrett Graham.

If the topic continues to interest you, take the time to review the following suggested references. Thank you.

Anderson, Eric. *Inclusive Masculinity: The Changing Nature of Masculinity.* New York, Routledge, 2009.

Anderson, Eric. *In The Game: Gay Athletes and the Cult of Masculinity.* Albany, NY; State University of New York Press, 2005.

Aldrich, Robert. *Gay Life and Culture: A World History*. New York, Universe, 2006.

Ayres, Ian. *Straightforward: How to Mobilize Heterosexual Support for the Gay Rights*. Princeton, NJ. Princeton University Press, 2005.

Badgett, M. V. Lee, *When Gay People Get Married: What Happens When Societies Legalize Same Sex Marriage*. New York, New York University Press, 2009.

Badgett, M. V. Lee and Frank, Jefferson. *Sexual Orientation Discrimination: An International Perspective*. London, Routledge, 2007.

Barker, Paul. *Hello Sailor! The Hidden History of Gay Life at Sea*. London, Longman, 2003.

Baumgardner, Jennifer. *Look Both Ways: Bisexual Politics*. New York, Farrar, Straus and Giroux, 2007.

Beger, Nicole J. *Tensions in the Struggle for Sexual Minority Rights in Europe: Que(e)rying Political Practices*. Manchester, Manchester University Press, 2004.

Berco, Cristian. *Sexual Hierarchies, Public Status: Men, Sodomy and Society in Spain's Golden Age*. Toronto, University of Toronto Press, 2006.

Bergman, David. *Gay American Autobiography: Writings from Whitman to Sedaris*. Madison, University of Wisconsin Press, 2009.

Bishop, Ryan. *Post Colonial Urbanism: Southeast Asian Cities and Global Processes*. New York, Routledge, 2003.

Boellstorff, Tom. *The Gay Archipelago: Sexuality and Nation in Indonesia*. Princeton, NJ. Princeton University Press, 2005.

Cammermeyer, Margarethe. *Serving In Silence*. New York. Viking, 1994.

Cook, Matt; Mills, Robert; Trumbach, Randolph; Cocks, Harry. *A Gay History of Britain: Love and Sex Between Men Since the Middle Ages.* Oxford, Greenwood World Pub., 2007.

Crimmins, Cathy. *How the Homosexuals Saved Civilization: The True and Heroic Story of How Gay Men Shaped the Modern World.* New York, Penguin, 2005.

Crompton, Louis. *Homosexuality and Civilization.* London, Harvard University Press, 2003.

David, Steven; Kimmel, Douglas C.; Rose, Tara. *Lesbian, Gay, Bisexual and Transgender Aging: Research and Clinical Perspectives.* New York, Columbia University Press, 2006.

Djupe, Paul A.; Olson, Laura R. *Religious Interests in Community Conflict: Beyond The Culture Wars.* Waco, Baylor University Press, 2007.

Drescher, Jack; Zucker, Kenneth J. *Ex-Gay Research: Analyzing the Spitzer Study and It's Relation to Science, Religion, Politics and Culture.* New York, Harrington Park Press, 2006

Duralde, Alonso. *101 Must-See Movies for Gay Men.* New York, Alyson Books, 2005.

Eskridge, Jr., William N. *Dishonorable Passions: Sodomy Laws in America, 1861-2003. New York, Viking Press, 2008.*

Fejes, Fred. *Gay Rights and Moral Panic: The Origin of America's Debate on Homosexuality.* New York, Palgrave MacMillan, 2008.

Friedman, Jonathan C. *Rainbow Jews: Jewish and Gay Identity in the Performing Arts.* Lanham, MD, Lexington Books, 2007.

Garcia, J. Neil C. *Philippine Gay Culture: Binabie to Bakla, Silahis to MSM.* Diliman, Quezon City, University of The Philippines Press, 2008.

Garreau, Joel. *The Nine Nations of North America*. Boston, Houghton Mifflin. 1981

Gilley, Brian J. *Becoming Two-Spirit: Gay Identity and Social Acceptance in Indian Country*. Lincoln. University of Nebraska Press. 2006.

Glave, Thomas. *Our Caribbean: A Gathering of Lesbian and Gay Writing from the Antilles*. Durham, Duke University Press, 2008.

Griffiths, Robin. *Queer Cinema in Europe*. Bristol, UK, Intellect Books, 2008.

Guzman, Manolo. *Gay Hegemony/Latino Homosexualities* New York, Routledge, 2006.

Halperin, David. *What Do Gay Men Want? An Essay on Sex, Risk and Subjectivity*. Ann Arbor, University of Michigan Press, 2007.

Hoad, Neville Wallace. *African Intimacies: Race, Homosexuality and Globalization*. Minneapolis, University of Minnesota Press, 2007.

Holleran, Andrew. *Dancer From The Dance*. New York. Penguin Group, 1986.

Houlbrook, Matt. *Queer London: Perils and Pleasures in the Sexual Metropolis, 1918-1957*. Chicago, University of Chicago Press, 2005.

Hunter, Ski. *Midlife and Older LGBT Adults: Knowledge and Affirmative Pracitice for the Social Services*. New York, Haworth Press, 2005.

Isay, Richard. *Becoming Gay: The Journey To Self Acceptance*. New York, Vintage Books, 2009

Jennings, Kevin. *One Teacher in 10: LGBT Educators Share Their Stories*. Los Angeles, Alyson Books, 2005.

Johnson, E. Patrick. *Sweet Tea: Black Gay Men in the South*. Chapel Hill, University of North Carolina Press, 2007.

Johnston, Lydia. *Queering Tourism: Paradoxical Performances of Gay Pride Parades*. London, New York, Routledge Studies in Human Geography, Routledge, 2005.

Jung, Richard M.; Minter, Shannon Price. *Transgender Rights*. Minneapolis, University of Minnesota Press, 2007.

Kirkman, Allison. *Sexuality Down Under: Social and Historical Perspectives*. Dunedin, NZ, Otago, 2005.

Koshy, Susan and Radhakrishnan, R. *Transnational South Asians: The Makings of a Neo-Diaspora*. Delhi, Oxford University Press, 2008.

Krahulik, Karen Cristel. *Provincetown: From Pilgrim Lnding to Gay Resort*. New York, New York University Press, 2005.

Kramer, Larry. *The Tragedy of Today's Gays*. New York, Penguin, 2005.

Leavitt, David. *The Man Who Knew Too Much: Alan Turing and the Invention of the Computer*. New York, WW Norton, 2006.

Manalansan, Martin F. *Global Divas: Filipino Gay Men in the Diaspora*. Durham, Duke University Press, 2003.

McLelland, Mark J. *Queer Japan: From the Pacific War to the Internet Age*. Landham, MD; Rowman & Littlefield Publishers, 2005.

Mixner, David; Bailey, Dennis. *Brave Journeys: Profiles in Gay and Lesbian Courage*.

Mixner, David B. *Stranger Among Friends*. New York. Bantam Books, 1996.

Morris, Charles E.; Morris III, Charles E. *Queering Public Address: Sexualities in American Historical Discourse*. Columbia, SC, University of South Carolina Press, 2007.

Myers, David G. *What God Has Joined Together: The Christian Case For Gay Marriage.* San Francisco, Harper San Francisco, 2005.

Nathaniel, Frank. *Unfriendly Fire: How the Gay Ban Undermines the Military and Weakens America.* New York, Thomas Dunne Books, 2009.

Niven, William John. *Politics and Culture in Twentieth Century Germany.* Rochester, NY; Camden House, 2003.

Oster, Emily. *HIV and Sexual Behavior Change: Why Not Africa?* Cambridge, MA., National Bureau of Economic Research, 2007.

Padilla, Mark. *Caribbean Pleasure Industry: Tourism, Sexuality and AIDS in the Dominican Republic.* Chicago, University of Chicago Press, 2007.

Provencher, Denis M. *Queer French: Globalization, Language and Sexual Citizenship in France.* Aldershot, England, Ashgate, 2007

Reddy, Gayatri. *With Respect to Sex: Negotiation Hijra Identity in South India.* Chicago, University of Chicago Press, 2005.

Robertson, Jennifer. *Same-Sex Cultures and Sexualities: An Anthropological Reader.* Malden, MA; Blackwell Publishing, 2005.

Rofel, Lisa. *Desiring China: Experiments in Neo-Liberalism, Sexuality and Public Culture.* Durham, Duke University Press, 2007.

Saval, Malina. *The Secret Lives of Boys: Inside the Raw Emotional World of Male Teens.* New York, Basic Books, 2009.

Savin-Williams, Ritch C. *The New Gay Teenager.* London. Harvard University Press, 2005.

Schehr, Lawrence. *French Gay Modernism.* Urbana, University of Illinois Press, 2004.

Schulman, Sarah. *Ties That Bind: Familial Homophobia and Its Consequences.* New York, New Press, 2009.

Sender, Katherine. *Business, Not Politics: The Making of the Gay Market.* New York, Columbia University Press, 2004.

Shepard, Judy. *The Meaning Of Matthew.* New York. Hudson St. Press, 2009.

Shilts, Randy. *And The Band Played On.* New York. St. Martin's Griffin, 1988.

Shilts, Randy. *Conduct Unbecoming: Lesbians and Gays in the U.S. Military, Vietnam to the Persian Gulf.* New York. St. Martin's Press, 1993.

Snyder, Jane McIntosh. *Sappho.* Philadelphia, Chelsea House Publishers, 2005.

Stern, Keith. *Queers In History.* Dallas. Banbella Books, 2009.

Streitmatter, Rodger. *From "Perverts" to "Fab Five:" The Media's Changing Depiction of Gay Men and Lesbians.* New York, Routledge, 2009.

Sullivan, Andrew. *Love Undetectable: Notes on Friendship, Sex and Survival.* New York. Alfred A. Knopf, 1998.

Sullivan, Andrew. *Virtually Normal: An Argument About Homosexuality.* New York. Alfred A. Knopf, 1995.

Thumma, Scott. *Gay Religion.* Walnut Creek, CA; AltaMira Press, 2005.

Tin, Louis-Georges. *The Dictionary of Homophobia: A Global History of Gay And Lesbian Experience.* Vancouver, Arsenal Pulp Press, 2008.

Vidal, Gore. *Inventing a Nation: Washington, Adams, Jefferson.* New Haven, Yale University Press, 2003.

Vidal, Gore. *Perpetual War for Perpetual Peace: How We Got To Be So Hated.* New York, Thunder's Mouth Press, 2002.

Vidal, Gore. *Point to Point Navigation: A Memoir, 1964-2006.* New York, Doubleday, 2006.

Vidal, Gore. *The Decline and Fall of the American Empire.* Berkeley, Odonian Press, 1992.

Wolf, Sherry. *Sexuality and Socialism.* Chicago, Haymarket, 2009.

Yoshino, Kenji. *Covering: The Hidden Assault on our Civil Rights.* New York, Random House, 2006.

Zizek, Slavoj. *First As Tragedy, Then As Farce.* Brooklyn. Verso, 2009.

Zizek, Slavoj. *The Monstrosity of Christ.* Cambridge. MIT Press, 2009.

Zizek, Slavoj. *Violence.* New York. Picador, 2008.

Internet-based Websites, Blogs and Periodicals:

365 Gay, News Website
http://www.365Gay.com

The Advocate Magazine
http://Advocate.com

After Elton
http://www.AfterElton.com

Andrew Sullivan's The Daily Dish
http://AndrewSullivan.TheAtlantic.com

Andy Towle's Weblog
http://www.Towleroad.com

Commercial Closet / Research on media images
http://CommercialCloset.org

Daily Kos / Markos Moulitsas Zuniga's Political Weblog
http://www.DailyKos.com

Dan Savage, Advice Columnist
http://www.TheStranger.com/Savage

David Mixner's Website and Blog
http://DavidMixner.com

Diversity Village
http://www.DiversityVillage.com

Dutch/Gay News
http://coc.nl
&
http://GK.nl

Empire State Pride Agenda
http://www.PrideAgenda.org

European Union Gay News
http://EUGayNews.com

Faith In America, To End Religious Bigotry
http://www.FaithInAmerica.Info

GAY – Good As You
http://GoodAsYou.org

Gay and Lesbian Tourism Australia
http://GALTA.com.au

Gay Africa News, based in South Africa
http://www.MambaOnline.com

Gay Australia – Sydney Star Observer; Australia's leading G&L news
   Source.
http://StarObserver.com.au

Gay India
http://www.thegully.com

Gay New Zealand
http://www.GayNZ.com

GLBT Historical Society
http://GLBTHistory.org

The Gay Agenda
http://GayAgenda.com

Gay and Lesbian Alliance Against Defamation.
http://glaad.org

The Gay and Lesbian Review, Bimonthly Literary Journal
http://GLReview.com

Gay Lesbian Straight Education Network
http://www.GLSEN.org

Gay Middle East
http://www.GayMiddleEast.com

The Gay and Lesbian Victory Fund
http://www.VictoryFund.org

Gay Chicago Magazine
http://GayChicagoMagazine.com

Gay Diving Website
http://Gay-Dive.com

Gay Men's Health Crisis Center
http://www.GMHC.org

The Gay State Blog
http://TheGayStateBlog.gs

GNN, The Gay News Network
http://GNN.gs

GGNN, The Global Gay Night News Blogcast, an International News
    Hour.
http://GGNN.TV

GlobalGayz
http://GlobalGayz.com

God's Love We Deliver
http://www.GodsLoveWeDeliver.org

Huffington Post
http://www.HuffingtonPost.com

The Human Rights Campaign, Washington, DC.
http://www.HRC.org

Iain Dale's Weblog
http://www.IainDale.Blogspot.com

International Conference of the Gay and Lesbian Leadership Institute.
http://www.GLLI.org

International Gay and Lesbian Travel Association.
http://iglta.org

International Lesbian, Gay, Bisexual, Trans and Intersex Association.
http://ilga.org

International Gay News
http://GayNewsBits.com

Joe.My.God.
http://www.JoeMyGod.Blogspot.com

Jonathan Calder
http://www.LiberalEngland.Blogspot.com

Lambda Legal
http://LambdaLegal.org

Michael Musto and La Dolce Musto
http://www.blogs.VillageVoice.com/DailyMusto/

Michaelangelo Signorile
http://www.Signorile.com

The Monthly Review, Is Holland The Best Hope?
http://MonthlyReview.org

National Gay and Lesbian Task Force
http://www.TheTaskForce.org

New England's Largest GLBT Newspaper
http://BayWindows.com

New York City, Gay City News
http://GayCityNews.com

New York City, LGBT Community Center
http://GayCenter.org

New York City, Museum of Sex
http://MuseumOfSex.com

On Top Magazine.
http://ontopmag.com

Out Magazine
http://Out.com

Out Professionals / Networking Association for Gay and Lesbian Professionals
http://OutProfessionals.org

Outlooks, Canada's GLBT Magazine
http://Outlooks.ca

Parents, Families and Friends of Lesbians and Gays, USA
http://www.PFLAG.org

Perez Hilton's Celebrity Blog
http://www.PerezHilton.com

The Pew Forum on Religious and Public Life
http://PewForum.org

Pink News.
http://pinknews.co.uk

Pink Paper, European Gay News Source
http://www.PinkPaper.com

Religious Blog.
http://www.EndTheHarm.com

Robert Reich
http://www.RobertReich.Blogspot.com
&
http://www.RobetReich.org

San Francisco, Edge Newspaper
http://EdgeSanFrancisco.com

Services and Advocacy for Gay-Lesbian-Bisexual-Transgender Elders
http://www.SageUSA.org

Sodomy Laws Around the World.
http://glapn.org

South Florida Blade Newspaper
http://FloridaBlade.com

The Tides Center, San Francisco
http://TidesCenter.org

This Gay Christian's Blog
http://GayChristianBlog.com

UK and the EU Political Culture
http://www.EUReferendum.Blogspot.com

United Nations Commission on Human Rights
http://www.ohchr.org/EN/Pages/WelcomePage.aspx

United Nations World Conference on Racism, April, 2009
http://www.un.org/durbanreview2009/

United Nations Committee on Economic, Social and Cultural Rights
http://www2.ohchr.org/english/bodies/cescr/index.htm

United Nations Human Rights Council
http://www2.ohchr.org/english/bodies/hrcouncil

Violations of the Rights of Lesbian, Gay, Bisexual and Transgender
   Persons in Georgia.
http://www2.ohchr.org/english/bodies/hrc/docs/ngos/GRPJ_Georgia.pdf

Washington Blade Newspaper
http://WashBlade.com

West Point Academy, LGBT Alumni
http://www.KnightsOut.org

"All oppression creates a state of war."

~ *Simone De Beauvior*

"Our lives begin to end the day we become silent about things that matter."
~ Martin Luther King, Jr.

Say YES to the Establishment of new Gay Nation-State, and express your support to all international Political leaders and UN Members.

Published by The Coalition Members of the Second Congress of Fire Island, 2009

<u>Categories:</u> Political Science, International Relations, Human Rights
<u>Region:</u> Global
<u>Target:</u> Global Gay Citizens, Human Rights Activists, Politicians, UN Members
<u>Website:</u> www.TheGayState.EU

Background (Preamble): We, Citizens of the World, representing every nation on Earth, Gay citizens and non-Gay citizens alike, recognize that, Gays, Lesbians, Bisexuals, and Transgender People have endured thousands of years of persecution in the lands of their birth. We acknowledge that in 80 nations on Earth, expressing ones Homosexuality is a crime, punishable by death, extreme prison sentences, public lashings, or hard labor. We also acknowledge that Gay people are discriminated against in virtually every nation on Earth; that in nearly all countries they are treated as second class citizens at best and as a people that should be exterminated at worst. We recognize that Gay people everywhere deserve liberty, equality, freedom, and democracy. In as much that nations cannot or will not accommodate the rights of this oppressed minority, we support the establishment of a Gay Nation-State where they may pursue life, liberty, freedom, and happiness, without oppression from an alternate majority, without infringing on the rights of the majorities in every other nation on Earth that has a majority Heterosexual population.
To sign the petition, please go to the bottom of the petition.

"The biggest disease today is not leprosy or tuberculosis, but rather the feeling of being unwanted."

~ Mother Teresa

PETITION:

We, Citizens of the World, representing every nation on Earth, Gay citizens and non-Gay citizens alike, recognize that, Gays, Lesbians, Bisexuals, and Transgender People have endured thousands of years of persecution in the lands of their birth. We acknowledge that in 80 nations on Earth, expressing ones Homosexuality is a crime, punishable by death, extreme prison sentences, public lashings, or hard labor. We also acknowledge that Gay people are discriminated against in virtually every nation on Earth; that in nearly all countries they are treated as second class citizens at best and as a people that should be exterminated at worst. We recognize that Gay people everywhere deserve liberty, equality, freedom, and democracy. In as much that nations cannot or will not accommodate the rights of this oppressed minority, and extend to them equal rights, we support the establishment of a Gay Nation-State where they may pursue life, liberty, freedom, and happiness, without oppression from an alternate majority, without infringing on the rights of the majorities in every other nation on Earth that has a majority Heterosexual population.

We recognize that Gay citizens everywhere are a people – one people, one tribe, and they share a unique status as a minority population that no other minority group inherently owns and should, therefore, be afforded the territorial rights of a recognized minority.

We acknowledge that their oppression at the hands of the majority non-Gay Heterosexual governments is so massive and widespread as to exist in a full 95 percent of all nations on Earth. While advancements in their human rights have occurred, they have done so at a very slow pace, extending over many centuries. We also must admit that Gay people have been marginalized, and their advances have often been repealed by governments unfriendly to their plight and political administrations in need of a political and cultural scapegoat, as government often are.

Furthermore, we wish to acknowledge that Gay citizens are oppressed in ways beyond the oppression witnessed in most other minorities. The physical violence, psychological terrorism, and financial hardships imposed on Gay people worldwide goes so far as to prevent them from gathering in sizable numbers as other minorities have done, resulting in their oppression being largely invisible to the outside world.

Toward a resolution that would refrain from the continued oppression and violence afflicted on Gay citizens, but without sacrificing the rights, cultural, and religious beliefs of the vast majority of nations on Earth, we submit that a territory be transferred to Gay people to create their own Gay Nation-State where they can flourish and prosper or struggle and despair, according to their own abilities and innate talents and quest for democracy.

Therefore, as Citizens of the World, representing every nation on planet Earth, we endorse the establishment of a Gay Nation-State and support the actions to create a peaceful transfer of a territory where they can create their own culture and live to the best of their ability.

_____

Signature in support of Petition.

_____

Printed Name in Support of Petition.

_____

City and Country of Residence (optional.)

_____

Date Petition is Submitted.

_____

E-mail of Signator (optional)

"Your silence will not protect you."

~ *Audre Lorde*

<u>Request for Asylum and Citizenship in the world's first independent</u>
<u>Gay State.</u>

<u>Date:</u> _____

<u>Name:</u> _____

<u>Address:</u> _____

<u>City:</u> _____

<u>State/Province:</u> _____

<u>Country:</u> _____

<u>Country/Postal/Zip Code:</u> _____

<u>E-Mail:</u> _____

<u>Month/Year of Birth:</u> _____

I, _____

(print name clearly)

being of sound mind and under no duress by another individual who is forcing me to make this request for citizenship against my will, hereby request a new membership that will lead to eventual citizenship into the worlds first independent Gay State. At the time of this application, I am: _____under 18 years _____18-23 years. _____24-29 years. _____30-38 years. _____39-47 years. _____48-58 years. ___59-67 years. _____68-77 years. _____78-82 years. _____83 years and older.

Please check any that apply to your personal circumstances:

_____ Insofar as having been subjected to discrimination in my life due to my sexual orientation, have been subjected to verbal abuse, physical violence, threats upon my person by my government or by the ruling majority, I am requesting emergency refugee relocation status.

_____ Insofar as the discrimination against me as a Gay, Lesbian or Transgender person, has evolved beyond harassment and suppression of my human rights and into a daily violence that leaves me in a state of fear for my life; violence or physical attacks that may, if carried out, would result in my death, I request to be accepted as a new member in the worlds first independent Gay State.

_____ Insofar as my or my family being under emotional and financial duress due to my sexual orientation; their/our ability to earn a living due to the discrimination and persecution imposed on us due to my sexual orientation, I am requesting to be resettled into our independent Gay State.

_____ Insofar as I have been threatened with imprisonment by my government because I am a Homosexual, or have served prison time due to my sexual orientation, I am requesting to be relocated to the worlds first Gay State.

_____ Insofar as remaining in the nation of my birth, I believe I will continue to live a life that is marginalized and minimized by oppression, discrimination and violence against people of Gay, Lesbian and Transgender orientation; and because I am being persecuted, I request citizenship into the new Gay State.

_____

Signature   Name Printed.

Scan, Download and Email this form to:
CitizenshipInTheNewGayState@GMail.com and your name will be added to our Pre-State Independence Registry. Initially, applicants will be contacted in accordance with the date application received. Fill out one petition per person requesting asylum and citizenship.

"Never look down on anybody unless you are helping him up."
~ Rev. Jesse Jackson

Virtues, Sins and the Philosophical Steps to Good Citizenship in Homotannia.

Eleven Virtues of Homotannia
1. Appreciation – gratefulness, gratitude, thankfulness.
2. Bravery – strength, courage, endurance, resoluteness.
3. Devotion – loyalty, allegiance, hopefulness, fidelity, worship.
4. Forgiveness – empathy, pardon, clemency, absolution, grace, amnesty.
5. Justice – honesty, impartiality, fairness, equity, rightness, dispassion.
6. Kindness – thoughtfulness, sweetness, compassion, generosity.
7. Loving – physical, emotional, spiritual affections; passion, lust.
8. Perseverance – fortitude, backbone, grit, resolution, tenacity.
9. Prudence – wisdom, vigilance, carefulness, thoughtfulness, discretion.
10. Service – charity, generosity, helpfulness, mercy, benevolence.
11. Trust – faith, belief, loyalty, conviction, fidelity.

Eleven Sins of Homotannia
1. Anger – rage, violence, indignation, fury, resentment.
2. Betrayal – deception, deceit, lying, faithlessness.
3. Boastfulness – narcissism, egoism, arrogance, self-worship, superiority.
4. Criming – committing crimes against people, property and community.
5. Greed – covetousness, excess, gluttony, selfishness.
6. Discrimination – bigotry, hatred, injustice, intolerance, unfairness.
7. Indifference – alienation, callousness, negligence, carelessness.
8. Sloth – slacker, shiftlessness, sluggishness, dormancy.
9. Squalor – filthy, dirty, miserable, wretched.
10. Theft – cheating, extortions, fraud, swindle.
11. Violence, Verbal and Physical.

The Twelve Philosophical Steps to Good Citizenship in Homotannia.
as assembled by the Initial Founders of the Pre-Gay State during the Fire
Island Congress of 2009. These Philosophical Steps are more commonly
referred to as "The Twelve GayMandments:"

1. Feed the hungry
2. Give drink to the thirsty.
3. Give shelter to those in need.
4. Visit the infirmed.
5. Show grace and humanism to the downtrodden.
6. Honor the dead and departed.
7. Leave our world cleaner than you found it.
8. Humility to those less fortunate.
9. Offer a kindness to others.
10. Pay someone a compliment.
11. Volunteer to make your world a better place.
12. Teach a man to fish.

To my readers;
With this third revised and expanded edition, it will be my final
edition of The Gay State.
In time I will be returning to my retirement and I will gladly live out
my years in service to our Gay community. Much work needs to be
done and all service to mankind is an honorable deed. I will eagerly
await meeting the man or womyn who will assume the mantle and
may that person bring all of the vitality one can muster.
So in closing,
I ask you to remember as we all march forward in life,
we are one human family rising together
against anti-Gayism, crusading against hatred and intolerance,
to reach our destiny of freedom and liberty.
For each of you, I want that you will live a life, filled with love, peace,
prosperity, strong health and moral fiber;
celebrations of who you are and who you were made to be
and that you will share it openly, unashamedly and fulfilled.
Go forward one and all and may we one day meet in our own
Gay State.

"Straight (people) need…
an education of the heart and soul. They must understand – to begin
with – how it can feel to spend years denying your own deepest truths, to
sit silently through classes, meals and church services while people you love
toss off remarks that brutalize your soul."

~ Bruce Bawer

Notes:

_____

_____

_____

_____

_____

_____

_____

_____

_____

_____

_____

_____

_____

_____

_____

Remember to check in frequently with our website www.TheGayState.EU for ongoing and recent developments. There will be frequent webinars and free telephone updates from our Consuls and representatives from various regions around the world. Events are occurring at such a rapid pace, potential members won't want to miss out.

Also remember that no matter where you currently live in the world, you can reserve a place with a membership application and receive certification direct from F.IG.S. headquarters in New York City.

If you want to order the book in bulk for your friends, family or members of any of the other LGBT or social organizations, contact us for considerable discounts. We don't want someone to miss out on life changing opportunities because of the cost. Purchasing the book as an E-Book and as a book on CD-Rom are other very affordable options!

Just e-mail us at TheGayState@GMail.com.

Lastly, remember that the Gay State Gift Shop offers so many products for you to show off your loyalty and patriotism. They make perfect gifts for birthdays, holidays and are great "pick-me-ups" for people who need to remember that life is full of beautiful possibilities! All monies will go to further the cause of creating a Gay state where we will all be assured democracy, equality, peace, liberty, security and freedom.